THE CRIMINAL,
THE JUDGE, AND
THE PUBLIC

A Psychological Analysis

by FRANZ ALEXANDER, M.D.,
and HUGO STAUB

Revised Edition, With New Chapters by
FRANZ ALEXANDER, M.D.

Original Edition Translated by
GREGORY ZILBOORG, M.D.

THE FREE PRESS
GLENCOE, ILLINOIS

&

THE FALCON'S WING PRESS

TRANSLATOR'S NOTE*

THE APPEARANCE OF *The Criminal* IN German at once attracted the attention not only of the general press but particularly of a number of judges and criminal lawyers of the German-speaking countries. Berlin, the seat of the first Psychoanalytical Institute which recently celebrated its tenth anniversary, proved to be very progressive, and the Psychoanalytical Institute soon found it necessary to organize a seminar for members of the legal profession under the leadership of the authors, Franz Alexander and Hugo Staub.

The German judge, being an appointee of the State, faces greater moral responsibility in many respects than a judge dependent on the electorate, and therefore frequently less free from political entanglements and pressure. Moreover, the political and social reconstruction of present-day Germany overthrew a number of old traditions and created an atmosphere of greater curiosity, if not responsiveness, in regard to newer ideas in the field of sociological problems. Hence—the response to *The Criminal*.

On the other hand, the Psychoanalytical Institute of Berlin, under the direction of Freud's very loyal and gifted disciple, Dr. Max Eitingon, has been for ten years broadening

---

* *Publisher's Note:* The Translator's Note which Dr. Zilboorg wrote for the original American edition of 1931 is here reprinted unaltered, providing a valuable signpost as regards the changes in the public attitude toward psychoanalysis during the past twenty-five years as well as the development of psychoanalysis itself.

and deepening its scientific activity so that it succeeded in demonstrating that psychoanalysis is more than a system of therapy and that it is a scientific discipline dealing with the psychological dynamic forces within the human being, whatever the manifestations of these forces might be: mental disease, artistic endeavor, religious thought, literary expression, or social psychology and behavior. The Institute did a great deal in calling attention to the deeper psychological problems of education, anthropology and sociology, since these subjects are taught in regular courses and in seminars within the walls of the Institute. It was therefore quite natural that Berlin should respond with a great deal of interest to the book the English rendition of which the translator has now the pleasure of submitting to the American reader.

The translator is all too well aware of the difficulties of rendering a foreign treatise into another tongue. He has no apologies to offer, but would plead for the reader's tolerance, since the English terminology of the subject has not yet become quite definitely established and since many of the terms with which the professional analyst is easily conversant had to be rendered in English in a more simple and more descriptive form than are their rather condensed and, at times, too specialized German equivalents. The translator is confident that the reader will find no great difficulty in following the thesis of the book. As a matter of fact, the American reader, although we have not yet a Psychoanalytical Institute of our own and although Americans still find it necessary to go abroad for their psychoanalytical training, is more conversant with some fundamentals of psychoanalysis than is the European reader; for the medical profession in this country proved much less refractory to newer psychological ideas than their European colleagues. As a result, a quarter of a century of psychoanalysis culminated in America in the invitation of one of the authors of this book, Dr. Franz Alexander, to become visiting professor of psychoanalysis in one of our leading universities, the University of Chicago—a scientific experiment upon which none of the European universities would as yet venture. Due to this greater responsiveness of the medical profession, psychoanalysis has become a rather familiar subject to a cultivated American reader; he will find it easier to follow these pages for yet another reason. They start with a very concise and lucid recapitulation of the fundamental principles of psychoanalysis, taking very little for granted, and thus introduce the reader to the complex problems of crime and punishment gradually and with an enviable clarity. The translator hopes that he has succeeded to some extent in preserving the simple clearness which is characteristic of the authors' text.

Aside from being a vital book, because of the importance of the problem and because of the bold treatment of the latter, this book presents to the American reader an interesting phenomenon from a historical point of view, for it is the first authoritative, scientific, psychoanalytical study of criminal psychology and of the psychology of punishment to be offered in this country to the general reader. Until recently the psychoanalytical literature in this country could be roughly divided into two classes: (1) the medical professional literature which became available primarily, thanks to the endeavors of Dr. A. A. Brill, and (2) a host of popular exposés of greater or lesser specific gravity dealing mostly with the supposed-to-be-ever-alluring features of sex and love in the narrowest and shallowest sense of these words. Hence, with very rare exceptions, the general reader has been steadily regaled with a mass of popularized catchwords surrounded by a questionable halo of erotic inferences under the guise of psychoanalysis. *The Criminal,* while it will be read by professional men, is yet a book for the general reader who is interested in social problems, and it offers him a concise but comprehensive exposé of what scientific psychoanalysis has to say about some very vital problems of today; it does it without sacrificing scientific earnestness to popularity, or clarity, or common sense to terminological intricacies.

The fact that one of the authors and the translator are physicians is not an accidental feature. It is through medicine that psychoanalysis was born as a scientific discipline, and the greatest majority of scientific psychoanalysts still consist of medical men. The particular field of criminology could not be studied with sufficient depth without medical men any more than public health could be properly administered without them. It is true that many activities like those of public and individual hygiene can and are now easily directed by lay chemists, serologists, physiologists, etc., but no public or individual health measure could ever be approached rationally without a thorough preliminary study of the morbid, the abnormal, the unhealthy, the perverted—and such a study lies primarily within the province of medicine. Moreover, in the field of social sciences, particularly that of criminology, an enormous degree of detachment is required; as a matter of fact, a greater measure of scientific tolerance is required in matters sociological than in any other. Our political, social, moral, racial, and religious prejudices play too great a part in the formation of our judgments and make it difficult for us to investigate our own everyday social reactions without emotional resistances. The combination of medical and psychoanalytical attitudes is the most favorable for a tolerant and unemotional study of human behavior, particularly social behavior. For the medical man, by virtue of his calling, treats without sitting in moral judgment; a fractured skull in a thug will always absorb more of his attention than a minor cut on the face of an officer of the law. It is the relative importance and danger of a skull fracture as compared with that of a skin cut that he is envisaging, rather than the respective moral values of the thug and the policeman. Psychoanalysis not only does not alter this fundamental attitude, but reënforces it and makes it possible to the fullest extent in so far as it enables the individual to understand before he is blinded by feeling, and thus creates the only possible psychological attitude which permits us to study facts of social behavior before passing judgment on them. Such a psychological attitude, which is ideal for scientific work, usually obtains only in the study of things which do not concern man's social or instinctual life, such as physics or mathematics, but in matters of human behavior, the whole mass of emotional reactions, conscious or unconscious, that are characteristic of our psychic apparatus is set into play, and without that attitude which I should call medico-analytical, proper evaluation of such material as is considered in this book would be impossible. Therefore, it is not accidental that it was conceived by a medical psychoanalyst and a psychoanalyzed criminal lawyer.

In conclusion, I wish to thank Dr. S. W. Hamilton, Assistant Director of Bloomingdale Hospital, for reading the manuscript of the English text and for his suggestions.

GREGORY ZILBOORG, M.D.

PREFACE TO THE REVISED EDITION

THIS BOOK WAS ORIGINALLY PUBLISHED IN Germany twenty-seven years ago. An English translation by Gregory Zilboorg followed in 1931. The German publication aroused the interest of William Healy, an American pioneer in the application of psychoanalytic principles to the problem of delinquency. He visited me in Berlin in 1929 and told me some of his reactions to our publication. He agreed with many of our conclusions, but thought that the type of neurotic criminal which we described was relatively rare in the United States. This type was first described by Freud: a man who violates the law not because he lacks a conscience, but—paradoxical as this may sound—because he has a severe and rigid conscience, which produces in him an unconscious sense of guilt. He feels guilty because of unconscious tendencies, never carried out in reality, which go back into his early experiences in the family and which mostly emanate from his Œdipus complex, his early relationship to his mother and father. He commits crimes not so much for rational motives of material gain or from resentment against the social order, but in order to relieve his unconscious guilt feelings. With a concrete, relatively harmless transgression of the law for which he is punished, he ties his unconscious guilt for patricidal or fratricidal tendencies to a much smaller offense. He is punished for this lesser crime, and the punishment relieves his guilt. He atones for a greater unconscious crime by a relatively slight punishment for some banal transgression. Such a person is clearly neurotic; his delinquency is a direct outcome of his emotional disturbance.

In 1932, in collaboration with Healy, we had opportunity in Boston to test the validity of his contention. We studied a number of neurotic delinquents as well as some of those who belonged to the category which in this book is called normal, non-neurotic criminals—professional delinquents whose Superegos have criminal tendencies.[1]

This group, common in the United States, was largely neglected in our German studies, chiefly because our interest was primarily psychological. These professional offenders against the law have more sociological than psychological interest. They belong to a special community which has its moral code different from that of the rest of society. Their antisocial acts are acceptable to them because their value systems correspond to that of their group and form a small community within the larger community.

The American reader may feel that this book covers only a small although puzzling group of criminals, of no great social significance in comparison with a large group of professional criminals, such as pickpockets, burglars, receivers of stolen goods, and the great variety of gangsters. Since these people are primarily products of a special social environment, their criminal behavior is not necessarily the outcome of unconscious, neurotic trends reaching back into early childhood.

The prevalence of the latter group in the United States is beyond question. The motivational studies in this book, however, apply also to this category of offenders, because both conscious and unconscious motivations operate in all human beings. It is only a difference in degree in which unconscious motivations contribute to normal and neurotic behavior.

Since the original publication of this book, interest among

---

[1] These studies were published in Franz Alexander, M.D., and William Healy, M.D. *Roots of Crime* (New York: Alfred A. Knopf, 1935).

psychiatrists in the motivations of criminal behavior has steadily increased. Ben Karpman's *Case Studies in the Psychopathology of Crime*,[2] Winfred Overholser's *The Psychiatrist and the Law*,[3] and Gregory Zilboorg's *The Psychology of the Criminal Act and Punishment*,[4] are only a few examples of comprehensive studies.

In spite of this advancement in the theoretical understanding of criminal behavior, the existing penal codes all over the world are still based on pre-Freudian psychology, which does not recognize the existence of unconscious forces. In the United States, the McNaughton Act restricts the plea of insanity to persons who cannot distinguish between right and wrong. A large group of neurotic criminals cannot be evaluated on the basis of this ruling. Unconscious neurotic motivations over which the conscious mind has no control may determine the delinquent act of a person who is fully capable of distinguishing between right and wrong.

The corresponding Paragraph 51 of the German penal code is based on the same primitive psychiatric concepts as the McNaughton Act. This law was conceived in ignorance of the influence of unconscious psychological processes on human behavior. It restricts responsibility only if a person acts in a state of unconsciousness or complete psychological disorganization. It is applicable to the comparatively rare cases of advanced psychoses, epileptics, hysterical twilight cases, and cases of extreme intoxication.

In this book we have pleaded for a modification of Paragraph 51, that it be replaced by a new interpretation of mental illness, based on a broader consideration of the relative significance of the conscious Ego and of unconscious tendencies in a given criminal act. We propose a more consistent application of the principle that not the deed but the doer should be punished, a principle first promulgated by Liszt, the great German criminologist of the nineteenth cen-

---

[2] Washington, Medical Science Press, 1933-1948. 4 vols.
[3] New York, Harcourt, Brace and Co., Inc., 1953.
[4] New York, Harcourt, Brace and Co., Inc., 1954.

tury. The implementation of this principle requires expert diagnostic judgment which can be expected only from specially trained, psychiatric experts. Before any sentence is imposed, a medical-legal diagnosis should be required. This would amount to an official recognition of unconscious motivations in all human behavior. The neurotic criminal obviously has a limited sense of responsibility. Primarily he is a sick person, and his delinquency is the outcome of his emotional disturbances. This fact, however, should not exempt him from the consequences of his action. If he is curable, he should be incarcerated for the duration of psychiatric treatment so long as he still represents a menace to society. If he is incurable, he belongs in a hospital for incurables for life.

It is of interest that twenty-three years after the publication of this book in the United States, the McNaughton Act was replaced by the Durham ruling. In 1954 Judge Bazelon of the United States Court of Appeals of the District of Columbia, in the "Durham versus United States" case[5] ruled that the McNaughton Act is obsolete, and he applied the ruling of New Hampshire, first applied by Judge Ray as early as 1870. It states that if the defendant's act is a product of a mental disease, he is not guilty.

It should be emphasized that even though the criminal is not guilty but sick, he must face the consequences of his disease, which has such drastic social consequences. Guilty or not in the legal sense, he still constitutes a menace to society.

On the basis of the Durham ruling, Manfred S. Guttmacher defines the role of the psychiatric expert in court procedures:[6]

1. A statement should be made as to whether the defendant is suffering from definite and generally recognized mental disease and why and how this conclusion was reached.
2. If it had been asserted that the defendant suffered from

---

[5] Durham v. United States, No. 11859, United States Court of Appeals, District of Columbia Circuit, Federal Reporter Second Series, Vol. 214, page 862, (St. Paul, Minn., West Publishing Co., 1954).
[6] Guttmacher, Manfred S., M.D., "Why Psychiatrists Do Not Like to Testify in Court," *The Practical Lawyer,* Vol. 1, No. 5, May 1955.

a mental disease, its name and its chief characteristics and symptoms, with particular emphasis on its effect on an individual's judgment, social behavior and self-control, should be given.

3. There should then follow a statement of the way and degree in which the malady has affected the particular defendant's behavior, especially in regard to his judgment, social behavior, and self-control.

4. The psychiatrist should then be asked whether the alleged criminal act was, in his opinion, the result of, or was committed under the influence of, his disease.

If this book can claim even a small part in bringing about this new interpretation of individual responsibility and this new recognition of the function of the court psychiatrist, its republication may be of interest to the American reader.

Four chapters have been added to the original text: An expert opinion given to a German court (jury) about the case of a nineteen-year-old double murderer, published in *The Psychoanalytic Review,* April, 1937; an expert opinion given on the case of a delinquent waiter under the title "A Possessed Automobilist," published in the *Imago* in 1931; a chapter on psychic determinism and responsibility, based on an address delivered May 12, 1952 before the Guild of Catholic Psychiatrists in Atlantic City; and a final chapter on psychiatric contributions to crime prevention, which was published in the *Federal Probation Quarterly,* May, 1940. The latter is an attempt to draw some practical conclusions from our original views which appear timely in the United States.

I wish to thank Dr. Nolan D. C. Lewis, Editor of the *Psychoanalytic Review,* Mr. Victor H. Evjen, Editor of the *Federal Probation Quarterly,* and Mr. Paul A. Wolkin, Editor of the *Practical Lawyer,* for permission to reprint articles which appeared in their journals.

FRANZ ALEXANDER, M.D.

Institute for Psychoanalysis
Chicago, Illinois
February, 1956

FOREWORD

A PHYSICIAN AND A JURIST ENDEAVOR IN this book to utilize our psychoanalytical knowledge in an attempt to gain an understanding of the criminal personality. The authors are convinced that the criminal is as legitimate an object for psychological investigation as is the neurotic or the normal individual.

Contrary to common presumption, psychoanalysis is not merely a method of treatment of mental disorders; it is hoped that the pages which follow will bring proof that in addition to being a method of treatment psychoanalysis is a scientific discipline which studies the workings of the human psychic apparatus as such; hence, any field of human knowledge that deals with psychic processes of man lies *eo ipso* within the scope of psychoanalytical investigation.

The authors hope that their venture will serve at least as a stimulus toward the future development of a psychoanalytic criminology; thus, along with the newly developed psychoanalytic ethnology and pedagogy the teaching of Freud might be utilized for the understanding of yet another aspect of our civilization.

These pages, therefore, do not solicit primarily the attention of the medical psychoanalyst but rather that of the medico-legal expert and the jurist. Too, since justice is usually dispensed under the valuable control of public opinion, this book is also addressed to the general public. The professional analyst will, therefore, find in this book little which is not of purely elementary nature. However, in dealing with such subjects as dream interpretation, slips of the tongue or action, symptom formation, etc., we view them from the particular angle of criminology. May we express the hope that those who devote themselves to psycho-analytical therapy only will find in this new angle of approach a stimulus for the development of a newer point of view.

We collaborated for four years endeavoring to work out both the theoretical and practical aspects of the problem, our work consisting of the psychoanalytical study of criminal cases which were of medico-legal interest. Our first case was studied in 1925. This special study gave us, we believe, sufficient insight into the problem to warrant our theoretical constructions. We illustrated these by some especially striking criminal histories.

In conclusion we consider briefly those psychosociological factors which throw some light on the emotional difficulties with which the practical application of our views would be beset.

THE AUTHORS

Berlin

INTRODUCTION

IT IS NO LONGER NECESSARY TO TRY TO justify the claims psychoanalysis makes in understanding the mentally sick and in extending to them therapeutic help.

Yet, not so many centuries ago, hysteria still belonged to a domain other than medicine; it was a phenomenon on which only the law courts were supposed to be competent to pass judgment. The woman suffering from hysteria was called a witch and she was punished as such; the punishment was severe, severer than the one meted out today to a murderer. It is not improbable that our treatment of the criminal will undergo a similar change in the future. The very fact that in "doubtful" cases today a medical expert, i.e., a psychiatrist, is usually asked by the court for an opinion, is the first step in this direction. A deeper knowledge of the psychology of the criminal would increase considerably the number of such "doubtful" cases. Yet our plea for a better understanding of the criminal seems to require some justification. Is not the criminal a public menace? Should not the interest we have in him be limited to an endeavor to make him harmless and to make the punishment imposed upon him serve as an example to others? Thus, a deeper study of the criminal personality might at first appear as nothing but a luxury, a manner of squandering one's scientific zeal. Is it not true that *Tout comprendre c'est tout pardonner?* Is it not true that the psychologist who strives to understand the criminal must at first put himself in the criminal's place, or as we say in psychoanalysis, he must identify himself with the criminal? One might even become suspicious that such a psychologist seeks to help the criminal rather than society; thus, the psychologist becomes open to suspicion of disloyalty to society.

The authors hope that in the course of this study they will succeed in clearing themselves of any such suspicion; they wish, however, to try to prove in the beginning that a psychological understanding of the criminal does not primarily help the criminal but, on the contrary, serves the interests of society. In order to do this we will have to deviate from our main line of thought, but this deviation will furnish us incidentally with some basic ideas which will prove the need for a psychoanalytical criminology.

We are justified, we believe, in assuming that sentence on a criminal, which is generally perceived as just presupposes the psychological understanding of the person responsible for the act judged; in other words, it presupposes a knowledge of motives underlying the given act. One and the same act may be approved or condemned, depending upon the motives underlying it. We praise the killing of the enemy in war; we condone a murder committed in self-defense; we sometimes forgive the killing of a person when it is done in a state of understandable affect, but the murderer who kills to rob is unanimously condemned. As far as the act itself is concerned, it is identical in all cases cited; our judgment on it seems to depend merely upon the various conscious aims it has and its various emotional motivations. Without the knowledge of these motivations one is unable to form any attitude toward a given act. The main question whether or no a given act is to be considered criminal depends entirely upon the psychological diagnosis we make. This paramount importance of psychology by which the judge is guided will be considered in detail later. It is mentioned here only in order to establish definitely that the feeling that a given court sentence is just is closely bound with the proper evaluation of the motives which lead to a given act.

Yet this reason alone does not appear to justify sufficiently a too zealous seeking for the psychological understanding of the criminal from whom society seeks to protect itself. We may say, of course, that our intention to study the psychic life of the criminal in detail is justified because we want to assure for the criminal a just judgment of the law. But why this intense need of a theoretical justice in cases of frankly antisocial individuals? It might almost seem that we try to find a way to protect the criminal from society and not society from the criminal. Thus, our previous assertion that we seek to serve the interests of society appears unwarranted. This apparent contradiction might disappear only if it could be definitely proved that the judgment pronounced upon the criminal, which we perceive as just really serves the interests of society. Hence, for the purpose of clarity we are ready to submit to cross-examination by the Solicitor General of Society, who might want to bring the authors of these pages to account and say:

"Why this wish to understand the criminal at any cost? It is much more important to seize him and free society of his presence. Why not turn your psychological ardor toward the understanding of more worthy objects? Your great ardor despite all you say does appear to me nothing but an attempt to help the criminal."

No, our chief aim is not this. We want to understand the criminal in order to be able to judge him correctly, so that our judgment may be just beyond question. Our assertion that our clear understanding of the criminal serves the interests of society is based on the fact that the sense of justice belongs to the most fundamental factors of human social organization; any disturbance of the common sense of justice has a destructive effect upon society. When the sense of justice is disturbed, then that part of our Ego which was called by Freud the Superego and which is yet in a rather weak state of organization, loses its power over the asocial impulses of the average individual.

We thus try to justify our interest in the criminal by means of an assertion, the correctness of which is admittedly not yet proved. Our problem resolves itself into an attempt to prove that our assertion is correct. In order to do this we shall have to discuss the following three problems which have not as yet been solved:

(1) What is that feeling of being right which the jurist calls "sense of justice"? Justice as an abstraction does not interest us. What social significance has this sense of justice?

(2) What is criminality and who is criminal?

After these two questions are answered, a third question inevitably imposes itself:

(3) What shall we do with the criminal?

The first question presupposes and also justifies our intention to occupy ourselves with the personality of the criminal in greater detail than has been done heretofore. Thus, our intention, which appeared at first almost superfluous, acquires a definite value; like any attempt to gain a deeper understanding of a phenomenon, it requires a deeper sympathetic inquiry into the personality of the criminal.

The chief part of this book consists of the study of the criminal personality and of the search for an understanding of it. The authors are mindful of the fact that the reader will be able to follow them without resistance only if and when they succeed in proving the social value of that judgment of the criminal which they perceive as just.

The problem of what should be done with the criminal is barely touched upon in these pages. We left out the detailed considerations of practical measures reluctantly, for we realize that the solution of the problem depends not only upon the scientific understanding acquired, but also upon many practical considerations.

These pages merely try to make clear that our present-day manner of dealing with the criminal, i.e., the imposing of punishment is in need of critical revision.

CONTENTS

CONTENTS

Part II

SOME CRIMINAL CASES IN THE LIGHT OF PSYCHOANALYSIS

Part I

THE PROBLEM OF CRIME IN THE LIGHT OF PSYCHOANALYTICAL THEORY

THE BATTLE FOR JUSTICE

A NUMBER OF HISTORICAL FACTS COULD serve as illustrations of how demoralizing an effect miscarriage of justice has upon every type of social organization. Sentences may be passed upon suspects who actually did not commit the crime imputed, or sentences may prove unjust because the penalty may appear too severe for the given crimes; both types of miscarried justice have a disturbing effect upon the psychology of popular masses, who, as a result, become unwilling to accept the established order and its laws. They *rise in protest;* a social adjustment heretofore stable becomes unstable.

Out of consideration for his fellow-men, man imposed a number of restrictions upon his instinctual impulses; it matters little whether these restrictions are adhered to with or without insight, i.e., whether they are a result of voluntary subjection or of social suppression. Once, however, the common sense of justice is injured by a miscarriage of justice, the stability of these restrictions is shaken.

Before every great social revolution one usually observes an increasing number of miscarriages of justice which, while in no way being the cause, yet play the role of precipitating moments of these social changes. One might say that there always exists a *chronic* feeling of injustice because the individual always feels the restrictions imposed upon him by society; however, this feeling does not possess the dynamic force which is necessary to transform the revolutionary tendency into revolutionary action; but in cases of acute offense of the citizen's sense of justice like miscarriage of justice, the chronic feeling referred to arouses a protest and this protest serves as a stimulus for revolutionary action; i.e., for the breaking through of instinctual impulses which heretofore were held in check. Miscarriages of justice thus transform the chronic, yet static, state of embitterment into an acute dynamic state of rebellion. Thus, the French Revolution began with an accumulation of miscarriages of justice. Any mutiny breaks out as a result of severely unjust treatment of the people; the Reformation had as its basis the indulgences which the Catholic Church dispensed to the rich only. In the history of every revolution we find that the first march of the revolutionaries is toward the prisons; the prisoners of justice must be set free.

One might thus postulate that whenever the common sense of justice is sufficiently offended the following two psychological consequences generally take place:

(1) Acts of injustice become more and more the center of interest of the popular masses. Every individual of a given class perceives as his own the wrong which falls upon another of the same social stratum. Apparently this psychological effect of injustice is based on the mechanism of identification; as if the individual says: "This might happen to any one of us."

(2) The equilibrium heretofore stable between the social restrictions and the tension of one's antisocial instinctual impulses becomes disturbed; and every member of the same social group becomes aware of the fact that this equilibrium is disturbed; this disturbance favors the impulses which hitherto had remained inhibited. A regression from instinctual restriction to the breaking through of the instinctual drives ensues.

While the effect the injury of the sense of justice has upon the psychology of masses is quite clear, the regressive process just mentioned requires a more detailed consideration. We shall draw upon the psychoanalytical theory of Ego development in order to gain an understanding of this process.

In general, any restriction of an impulse is undertaken or accepted as a result of two factors: fear of pain and expectation of pleasure. Such restrictions are expressions of the adjustment which our subjective instinctive drives make to the objective demands of reality. One renounces the satisfaction of certain impulses either because such gratification is impossible, or because such gratification would cause more pain than the renunciation. In order to avoid the pain of immediate gratification of an impulse, it is not infrequently sufficient to defer such a gratification to the future and in the meantime bear a certain amount of tension; such a postponement may also serve as an insurance of gratification with which external circumstances might otherwise interfere for the present. Freud called this process the evolution of the individual from the pleasure principle to the reality principle. The reality principle thus represents nothing else but the pleasure principle which adjusted itself to the demands of reality.

Human instinctual drives demand expression, gratification. Reality puts obstacles in the way of expression; the reality principle consists of a purposive adjustment of the instinctual demands to the available possibilities of gratification. It is quite natural that renunciation goes just as far as it is possible, not further. Thus an equilibrium is established between renunciation and gratification of the demands of one's impulses. If an added renunciation is demanded, the equilibrium becomes disturbed.

The whole process of education is based on this principle. Education presents a systematic guidance in the direction of adjustment of the instinctual, originally asocial, impulses of the child to the demands of the educator. The adjustment to society, like the adjustment to reality, is based on the evolutionary transition from the pleasure principle to the reality principle. The unpleasant or painful sensations, which we experience when our actions do not honor the demands of nature, correspond in the field of education and in the domain of social life in general to *punishment*.

To the joy of gratified desires corresponds in the field of education, the compensation for our renunciation, which is the love or approval of those who demanded from us the renunciation. Fear of punishment and hope of being loved thus represent the two social regulators of human instinctive life. Freud came to these simple formulations in his last two works on instinctual life. ("The Ego and the Id," and "Inhibition, Symptom and Anxiety.")

Freud and his pupils described in detail the psychological meaning of punishment. Punishment is a copy, as it were, of the relationship of impersonal Nature to the instinctive life of man. That part of our instinctual behavior which is not adjusted to the environment results in painful discomfort. The punishing educator takes over the role of impersonal Nature as the causative agent of pain.[1] When a child in high spirits runs uncontrollably about a room until it runs into the edge of the table, the painful bump on its head is interpreted to him by his preceptor as a punishment for his bad behavior; later on, bodily punishment imposed on children for transgressions represents but an imitation of the simple situation just described.

The second factor, the hope of being loved, or what amounts to the same thing, the fear of losing love, needs to be gone into more deeply here than has been done heretofore in the psychoanalytic literature. The self-imposed restrictions of instinctual impulses which are caused by fear of punishment are undertaken as a result of an authoritative decision, while the limitation of instinctual expression which is self-imposed in expectation of love is undertaken by virtue of a silent contract, a sort of a love agreement. This agreement would read approximately as follows: "I shall refrain from gratifying some of my desires, to which you object. I renounce the pleasure for your sake in order to keep your love. The value of this love I recognize first of all by the

---

[1] Cf. Franz Alexander, *Psychoanalysis of the Total Personality* (Nervous and Mental Diseases. Monographs, 1930).

security it guarantees for me." Thus, being loved provides us not only with the pleasure which results from being loved, but also with a feeling that some of the instinctual strivings may be gratified with security; that is why the feeling of being loved is intimately connected with the feeling of security. The love contract therefore represents an exchange of gratification for being loved which latter has a pleasure value in itself.

This bargaining for love in exchange for a renunciation begins in earliest childhood. Love is a gift which the child receives first from his mother: milk, warmth, care, belong to the first perceptible expressions of mother's love; the mother guided by her instinct knows how to distribute these gifts of love, how to wean the child of them, and then to exert a definite influence on the instinctual life of the child. Because of this capacity to give and to refuse love, the mother finds herself in possession of a great weapon; she can force the child into the renunciation of a part of his instinctual life. On the other hand the element of punishment, i.e., infliction of pain, coming from the father as an educative agent, appears much later in the life of the child. Thus, the mother stands out more as a source of pleasure while the father arises as the first representative of the harsh reality principle. Only later, after the child has gradually lost the complete dependence upon the mother and has become an increasingly independent being, the educational principle, based upon giving and refusing love, loses its efficacy and punishment, i.e., direct inflicting of pain, takes its place. The more independent of the mother the child becomes, the less important for him the state of being loved; for once independent, the child can gratify his wishes by means of his own efforts instead of depending on the love of the mother. It is at this point that the force of punishment as an inhibitory factor becomes necessary.

Thus, fear of punishment and of not being loved (this, too, is a special form of punishment) are the two factors of education; later, throughout the life of the adult, these two factors remain the chief regulators of the instinctual life of man. Our analytical experience shows us that the conscious self-restraint of one's instinctual life plays but a very modest role as compared with the above-mentioned emotional factors. The fundamental principle of all adjustment is that of obtaining pleasure and of avoiding pain.

These considerations contain a silent recognition of the following fact: in the case of each restriction of our instinctual life, we deal with an outer world whose power to restrict this instinctual life happens to be stronger than our instinctual demands; it does not matter particularly who or what happens to be the representative of this restricting outer world; it may be Nature, educator, public leader, or the stronger social class. This process of restriction of our instinctual expressions, i.e., the adjustment to a stronger, restricting force brings about a state of equilibrium; in this state our psychic apparatus renounces just the minimal necessary amount of its wishes in order to obtain the greatest possible security in the matter of gratifying the remaining instinctual demands. What is called social order means just the equilibrium between the renunciation of instinctual demands and the assured gratification; it is a sort of a contract between the powers which restrict our instinctual expression and the instinctual demands of the individual. The very sensitive, emotional regulator of this equilibrium is the *sense of justice*. This is not developed as a result of the knowledge of the demands of the law. As Ihering in his *The Battle for Justice* well recognized, it is an indicator that functions purely instinctively, it is something comparable to anxiety (fear) or, according to Ihering, pain. Fear is the signal of a coming danger. The sense of justice acts in a similar way; whenever the accepted instinctual gratifications, which were acquired through such bitter restrictions of one's instinctual life, are threatened the sense of justice feels injured. Man senses with astounding precision when his acquired right (and each right was once acquired) is in some way threatened or diminished; to each violation of his right,

he reacts with strong notice that the contract has been violated; this he does by means of freeing himself from some
of the restrictions of his instinctual life which he heretofore
accepted. Thus a regression takes place; man regresses from
instinctual inhibition to instinctual expression.

The great sensitivity of the sense of justice, the violation
of which is capable of setting afire the emotions of masses of
people, is explained particularly by the fact that the contract
on which the above-mentioned equilibrium is based is con-
cluded between two parties, one of which is much weaker
than the other.

The Ego accomplishes the self-restriction of its instinctual
demands with great difficulty; it makes this sacrifice in favor
of the stronger party (society) only because it expects a compensation, the nature of which we described as being loved.
The social manifestations of this being loved is public recognition, respect, the whole scale of social recognition, from
individual liberty granted to every citizen to the highest public distinctions. These compensations make it easier to bear
the limitations of individual sovereignty. If, however, these
compensations are not forthcoming, if an individual is
treated unjustly, his fellow members of the same community,
to whom the same might happen, perceive it as a betrayal,
for it appears then that one gained nothing by renunciation.
Thus, one rebels; there appears a spiteful determination to
live out fully and unrestrainedly all those instinctual drives
which one held heretofore in check.

This is the reason why one feels so stirred and provoked
when a miscarriage of justice occurs and either an innocent
man is convicted by mistake and thus treated like a criminal,
or when it comes to light that too harsh a sentence has been
imposed as a result of arbitrary judgment of those in power.
Literary masters of all ages had a predilection for this stirring
theme; it is particularly true of the situation in which the
honest man, who has faith in the ultimate victory of justice,
yet remains silent too patiently and too long, until sooner or
later he himself falls victim to injustice. The spiteful patience

of a Michael Kohlass, for instance, is like a weird silence before a storm; for behind his silence gather storm clouds of growing instinctual drives.

The hero of Kleist is but a tragic victim of this natural process of instinctual regression, which takes place when one's sense of justice is injured. The corruption of those in power breaks down the power of their inner representative, the inhibiting forces of morality, and man is thus transformed into a plaything in the hands of his unchained instincts. After all hope for redress for the great injustice he suffered has disappeared, Michael Kohlass, the righteous and honest man, became a thief, a robber, a murderer. In other words, as soon as his confidence in worldly authority was shattered, the power of his Superego (his conscience) also dwindled. Only Luther acknowledges that there is a secret hatred behind the screen of fanaticism of justice and that its actions are fundamentally determined by hate.

It must be borne in mind that it is not a mere willfulness of phantasy, it is not a literary trick used for the purpose of arousing emotion, nor is it a mere accident that it is the righteous man who most frequently suffers from injustice; the righteous man is the champion of the abstract idea of justice and fair play; his courageous devotion to this idea, his tenacious observance of his moral obligations presents the strongest obstacles for the willfulness of the powers that be; thus, the latter are compelled to observe their obligation to dispense justice justly. However, if justice is to be betrayed, then it is necessary that the most violent defender of it be got out of the way. He then becomes the heroic defender of that invisible contract between the individual and society, the nature of which is but faintly reflected in the written laws, no matter in how exhaustive and detailed terms these laws may be expressed. This heroic defender reminds us that the individual retained a part of his liberty as a compensation for the abandoned instinctual demands, and that therefore the contract must insure this individual liberty. Thus, at first he perseveres in following the law in order to demonstrate the injustice of the party of the second part, and then to have a right to set aside the inhibitions imposed by the law.

In the deepest layers of our personality, in our primordial yearning for the unrestricted expression of our instinctual drives, we all feel with him. The unfair treatment to which he is subjected appears to justify us also in our wish to break down the chain of restrictions.

The fact that this phantasy always makes a profound impression on man proves quite clearly that in the deepest part of his personality the individual, while an integral part of society, watches carefully and as soon as the party of the second part violates the *contrat social* he is ready to snatch his opportunity and to return to his primordial and actually never abandoned individualism.

Thus, it is not difficult to see that the sense of justice is but a form of the pleasure principle, which became quite modest under the harsh pressure of reality; it wears the mask of defender of the absolute right; the individual by means of his sense of justice keeps a constant and desperate watch over the remnants of his personal liberty, which is so badly curtailed.

THE CRISIS OF PRESENT-DAY JUSTICE

THE SENSE OF JUSTICE MUST BE RECOGnized as one of the foundations of social life. It may be considered as a sort of an inner psychic regulator, which automatically guarantees certain self-imposed restrictions in the interest of the community. As we pointed out, any injury to this sense of justice brings about an embitterment and rebellion, and the individual finds himself, as a result, unwilling to continue the renunciation which he observed heretofore. Under the latter circumstances, the continuation of law and order becomes possible only through the increase of the external power of the law. We must remember that within every law-abiding citizen there must live a police officer, for it is practically impossible to keep law and order only by means of external compulsion; the psycho-economic significance of the citizens' voluntary readiness to support the law becomes self-evident; this readiness, as we have seen, is based upon the common sense of justice remaining uninjured. When the public shows undisturbed confidence in the legal institutions and their official representatives, then we may say that the common sense of justice is in harmony with the demands of the powers that be.

The judgment as to what is to be considered a crime and what should be done with the criminal is left in the hands of specially trained jurists; however, the actual dispensing of justice remains under the constant control and is carried out with the strict participation of the public. There is hardly any other part of public life which is watched with so much

suspicion and zeal as the work of the machine of justice.
So long as the State remains powerful and the law authoritative, the faith in the infallibility of the judge remains undisturbed; certain modes of thinking and certain forms of judgment, under the circumstances, may well be even excessively taxing, both from the actual and the scientific point of view, yet the common sense of justice does not become appreciably damaged. However, there are times such as war, economic stress, unemployment, in which the individual faces an exceptional increase in the demands made upon him by society; such times bring about an especially jealous watchfulness on the part of the individual over the remnants of his personal liberty. This is the situation in the world today; it is true at least of present-day Europe; the formal authorities and ideologies of yesterday have been shattered; only through dictatorship, i.e., through bare might, is law and order upheld and not through inner moral forces like religion and loyalty as in days gone by. Under these circumstances, we find that justice also is robbed of the confidence it enjoyed in the past.

The present system of justice is not supported by any moral affective forces; it stands stripped before the critical public judgment with nothing to offer but a mere matter-of-fact structure, poor in content and with outlived institutions. The result is a general crisis of matters concerning justice. Only the great external power exercised by the State and the general indolence of the popular masses make this crisis less conspicuous.

Under such circumstances it is timely to undertake a fundamental revision of the whole system of administration of justice.

We have already pointed out that a given act can be passed upon only when, in addition to our knowledge of the facts, we also understand the motives which have led the individual to commit the given act. As long as psychology was not an exact scientific discipline, the judge faced an unsolvable problem when he attempted to evaluate a given situation from the individual psychological point of view. The opinion of the judge would, at best, be nothing more than a personal opinion based upon his personal or social bias and his intuitive understanding of human nature. In order to correct as much as possible this deficiency which created an extraordinary insecurity in the administration of justice, the following three elements were introduced into the modern penal practice:

(1) An orderly casuistic arrangement of facts; this has as its aim the elimination, as much as possible, of the individual psychological viewpoint on the case. We shall designate this procedure as the *pseudo-exact* tendency of jurisprudence.

(2) The introduction of trial by jury; this presents a confession of ineptitude on the part of the pseudo-exact objective justice; psychology is thus again introduced into the court room in the form of *lay judgment* based upon common-sense understanding of human nature.

(3) The introduction of the medical expert; this is an attempt to obtain help from the *so-called scientific psychology* which appears under the well-known guise of *Psychiatry*.

Present-day administration of justice is robbed of its authority; it is exposed to sharp public criticism; it finds itself in a critical situation. In the pages that follow, we shall attempt to show why the three above-mentioned factors failed to remedy the situation.

The present-day statute books are based on the principle of classification of certain acts which are considered criminal; these are classified on the basis of abstract conceptions. The task of the judge consists in placing a given act, which he has under consideration, in a definite category which is prescribed by the statute book. Such a method is supposed to eliminate the possible uncertainty and inexactness coming from the purely personal opinion of the judge; it is supposed to lead automatically to a just opinion by means of a happy fitting of the case to one of the paragraphs of the law book.

The makers of the law evidently wanted to arrange matters so that the judge should not be guided by personal opinion as to whether or no a given act is to be considered a crime; this is supposedly achieved by the purely objective investigation of the mere fact; one must bear in mind, however, that no system of justice is ever able to evaluate the fact of the crime as a cold fact without taking into consideration the person who committed the crime; one cannot abstract a deed from the doer. Any opinion rendered by a judge must be based fundamentally, not only on the establishment of the fact that a crime was committed, but also on the psychological evaluation of the crime. It is impossible to administer justice without the utilization of psychology.

And yet, in order to make the psychological evaluation of the crime independent of the judge's bias, psychology itself is shrouded in abstract formulæ.

Very coarse psychological concepts serve at times as decisive factors in the official differentiation between two crimes which are objectively alike. (Murder and manslaughter, premeditation and accident, the presence or absence of the idea of gain, etc.) To what absurd conclusions such pseudo-exact classifications may lead can be seen in the Portuguese law which considers murder as premeditated when it is established that the intention to kill existed at least twenty-four hours before the crime was committed.[1] The lawmakers wanted to exclude the arbitrariness of personal psychological bias and therefore substituted for it a series of pseudo-exact dead figures!

However, all present-day systems of criminal law succeeded only to a small degree in substituting even a psychology clad in abstract formulæ for the living psychological understanding of a given criminal case; on the other hand, as a result of this tendency the interest in the real psychological understanding of the criminal was gradually weakened; for if one goes deeper into human psychology, one finds it impossible to fulfill the task of fitting a human being into preconceived pigeonholes. Hence, real psychology presents a certain inconvenience to the modern judge. Yet even

[1] Article 325 of the Portuguese *Code Penal.*

the little psychology that is used for the purpose of evaluating a given crime makes it almost impossible to carry out the pigeonholing successfully; hence, a system full of sophistry is evolved, a system which does not go beyond the narrow confines of existing schemata, unless it is by means of creating ever newer, purely abstract psychological criteria and of purely deductive scholastic juggling—all of which is used to prove that a given crime fits well into this or that dead category. Thus, the present-day system of justice becomes a sort of a secret technique of the learned judge; this technique is not based on the understanding of the average man; nor is it founded on common sense.

The flight of the judge into the world of pseudo-exact paragraphs of the law, this puzzling horror with which the learned jurist tries to avoid the understanding of the human motive of the crime, signifies but a flight from personal responsibility. When, with the help of the written law, one succeeds in fitting a given crime into a given legal paragraph, then one's own sense of justice is satisfied, for the responsibility for a possible injustice is then shouldered by the impersonal written law. One can explain this flight away from psychology also by the fact that until lately there existed no scientific psychology of the total personality of a given individual; the understanding of human acts was, until recently, left to the intuitive insight of single individuals, and perforce remained the privilege of the literary man and the artist. It becomes thus conceivable why the judge is compelled to turn away with a shudder from the Scylla of the mysteries of human motives and flee into the Charybdis of the law paragraphs; the latter stand ready at least to relieve him from the responsibility for the solution of a seemingly insoluble problem.

It was generally felt that scholastic jurisprudence is devoid of life; the need of instilling some life into it became evident; the learned judge had to be relieved from the pressure of mere paragraphs; the demands of the inner sense of justice had to be met, at least in part the element of human intui-

tion and instinctive psychological judgment had to be introduced into the court; as a result deeper psychological
evaluation of the motives of the single individual was
brought into the court through various back doors. Thus,
for instance, the judge was given a certain latitude when
imposing sentence: he may impose a severe sentence, he may
suspend it; this made it possible to take into consideration, at
least to some extent, special psychological circumstances of
specific cases. Next to this the trial by jury was introduced,
a method which apparently was intended to soften to some
extent the unbending power of the paragraphs. In this way,
the written law recognized its own ineptitude. It is a paradoxical situation which exists in no other branch of scientific
endeavor: a situation in which the specialist asks the layman
to correct him. At any rate, the introduction of trial by jury
marked a definite step forward, for the layman is unable to
flee from his responsibility before the world into the world
of paragraphs, because luckily he has little knowledge of
those paragraphs.

The layman finds himself face to face with his responsibility; he must needs sit in judgment and he can render this
judgment only by way of a psychological understanding of
the offender. However, the heavy burden of responsibility
which such a layman must carry, i.e., the responsibility of
taking the consequences of a judgment based on his individual insecure intuition, is made easier in the following two
ways: First, the judgment rendered is not an individual but
a collective one, that of the whole jury; and second, the
majorities of penal codes leave it to the learned judge who,
under the protection of the paragraphs of the law, limits
their influence on the sentence and thus relieves the jury
from a part of their responsibility. One can hardly be surprised to find that the attempt to protect the blindness of
the world of paragraphs by means of the lame intuition of
the average layman is not a real way out of the crisis of our
judicial systems.

It thus becomes clear that if we care at all to have an opinion about a given criminal act, an opinion which would be based on some sociological foundation, we can do so only by way of individual psychological evaluation of each individual case. This remains true whatever the given system of penal law and whatever the measures taken against the individual offender.

We are rather critical of the various forms of punishment as they exist today; and we question the value of the whole concept of punishment, yet we would wish to consider the problem of criminological diagnosis. The latter can be considered independently of the various punitive measures. Such diagnosis offers the only reliable basis for the choice of corresponding punitive measures. We must do something with the criminal; what we shall do with him depends entirely upon the psychological evaluation of the individual case, which means the diagnosis.

THE ROLE OF PSYCHOLOGY IN THE UNDER-

STANDING OF THE CRIMINAL

THE COMPLEX PROCESSES OF ADMINISTRA-tion of justice are generally based on the following sociological and psychological trend. Society asks the offender: "What have you done?" This question, however, is asked only in order to establish the following: "Why did you do this?"

"Did you wish to act for or against us?"

"Are you dangerous or useful to us?"

"Are you dangerous because you are incapable of evaluating the consequences of your own action?"

"Are you sick?" (psychiatric diagnosis) or

"Do you consider yourself not a member of our community?" And finally:

"Did you, perhaps, act with good intentions, but met with misfortune?"

We believe that the fundamentals of any given system of criminal law are covered by these few questions. Any penal system, even the one which is based on purely objective criteria, has as its aim the establishment of the motives of the crime; in other words, one depends upon psychology in order to administer justice.

As we had already pointed out, all systems of justice recognize to a greater or lesser degree this need; as a matter of fact as they progress the importance of psychology comes to the foreground and through its influence the purely objective norms become increasingly less important. Liszt was the first who stated that not the deed, but the doer, should be punished; this principle he made the basis of his theory of criminal law. Despite this principle, the public and criminal justice grow more and more apart; despite this principle we face a definite and general break in the confidence which people once had in their criminal laws. We shall attempt to show in these pages that the crisis is mainly due to the fact that the principle promulgated by Liszt cannot be fulfilled; that the kind of psychology used by our systems of justice is not the psychology of the living human individual. The psychological methods which have been in use till now do not occupy themselves with the individual personality; at their best they occupy themselves with generalities of psychological experience, they devote themselves mostly and mainly to abstract construction.

They are conversant with the psychology of will, emotions, memory, reaction to stimuli, etc.; as to real human motives, actual feelings, in brief, as to the living personality, of this they have no knowledge.

All these methods suffer from the same defect as the methods of the objective evaluation of the objective data of a given crime. Objective criteria of circumstances, even if they are combined with abstract psychological theses, are hardly able to furnish direct, pictorial knowledge of a given individual or the motivations for his actions.

Psychoanalysis was the first branch of human knowledge which undertook to investigate the psychology of the real individual, i.e., of the deeper motive powers of human actions. Psychoanalysis, therefore, claims a right to speak when the matter of the judging of the criminal is considered; it believes that it could, by means of its special methods, lead to a complete understanding of the criminal and his acts.

Psychology before Freud was unable to formulate a clear concept of the individual personality because it remained an abstract, rather philosophical, speculative system of thought; moreover, the fundamental fact that a given human personality does not represent a homogeneous unit, remained unknown to the older psychologist. Real psychology must be founded on the recognition of this fact. It was uncovered by Freud. The conscious Ego, which was the exclusive object of investigation of the psychologists before Freud, represents but a minor part of the human psychic apparatus. This conscious self is built over the great reservoir of unconscious drives, motives, and presentations; it depends upon these in the greatest variety of ways.

The significance for criminology of this basic fact which was discovered by psychoanalysis can be formulated as follows: The central question to be answered in the course of a trial is the question: "Why did you do this or that?" Any direct question of this kind can be answered only partially; only those motives could be brought to light which appear in the conscious portion of the individual's psychic apparatus. The unconscious motives which not infrequently exert a greater dynamic influence on our actions remain unknown. That is why it is even impossible for the offender to give a really valid, causal explanation of his acts.[1]

The whole technique of the examination of the criminal or of the court hearing, the constant search for the definite, conscious motivations, the snatching at contradictions, the endeavor to consider these contradictions as a proof of the untruthfulness of the offender, and thus to put the moral integrity of the criminal under serious question—all this is quite inadmissible because it is a false procedure.

Not the judge is right who during the trial succeeds in establishing certain contradictions, but the criminal who becomes involved in contradictions, because the majority of human acts are performed as a result of many self-contradictory motives. In our psychic life it is not the "either this or that" that makes us act, but "this as well as that." If the criminal on trial were able to tell the whole truth, i.e., if he himself knew all his motivations, then he would inevitably fall into contradictions.

---

[1] Cf. also Reik, *Geständniszwang und Strafbedürfins* (Wien: 1930).

Human activity is always overdetermined, and the various determinants (motives) frequently contradict each other.

Psychoanalysis has shown us that one may consciously love, and unconsciously hate, one and the same person or the reverse. One may then commit murder because of both love and hate combined. One steals because of the desire to acquire and, at the same time, because of unconscious compulsive pleasure strivings which have nothing to do with the material advantage gained. This overdetermination is characteristic not only of the criminal act, but also of the socially accepted behavior. The sadistic impulses of a colonizer are a transparent cover for his cruelty; but he rationalizes the latter by saying that he has the task of making a civilized person out of the primitive man, and, he asserts, he can achieve this by means of strict discipline.

The same self-contradictory tendencies are found operating under a somewhat different guise in people who are actively engaged in educational work; first there is a conscious socialized will to rear properly a new member of the community; and, second, there is an unconscious, cruel drive to dominate another being. The two tendencies are equally active factors in the psychology of the severe prison guard, or sergeant, or the strict teacher; yet only the social component of this psychology is accessible to our consciousness; the other component, the unsocial, remains repressed into the unconscious, and its expression remains unnoticed. People, who appear righteous to themselves and whose conscious motivations appear to explain their actions sufficiently clearly, do not see why it is necessary to recognize also the existence of rather disconcerting unconscious motivations. However, when one's behavior cannot be explained entirely by conscious motivations, and when the unconscious trends begin to come to expression too poignantly, only then one begins to suspect that there might exist something heretofore unknown and hidden behind our conscious motivations.

Thus a paradoxical situation may arise wherein a criminal act may be committed out of unconscious non-criminal mo-

tives and a socially acceptable act might be dictated by unconscious, unsocial motives. The psychoanalyst, for instance,
knows only too well that certain highly honored callings of
great social importance, like those of the surgeon or state
attorney, are activated by a set of unconscious sadistic trends
which not only play an important role in the given professional activities but are not infrequently the decisive factors
in the matter of choosing a profession.

The helpfulness to mankind, which is more conspicuous
in the activity of a surgeon, permits him to live out his
sadism without noticing it. The endeavor to assure the security of state order permits the attorney to give vent to his
unconscious tendency to inflict suffering upon others; his
official work keeps the unofficial work of the unconscious unnoticed.

We must bear in mind, that even as the socially useful act
is a resultant of many psychic motives, some of which are
partially criminal, so every criminal act is determined by
many motives, the majority of which remain buried in the
unconscious of the criminal. We can see, therefore, that only
a thorough knowledge of the psychic content of all motivations and their relative strength and efficacy will enable us
to understand fully a given criminal act.

The older psychology and also the superficial common
sense of the layman utilizes only the most accessible part of
the conscious motivations; the complex mass of conscious
and unconscious motivations are left out of consideration;
only the superficial thin layer of rationalizations is utilized.
On very rare occasions it may happen that the motives of
greatest dynamic importance may accidentally also be
grasped. The state attorney, the judge, the juror, the medico-
legal expert had until recently only the psychology of the
superficies at their disposal. It is no surprise, therefore, to
find that verdicts which are based on correct psychological
insight, and which are satisfactory to the common sense of
justice, have become exceptions rather than the rule; the
general confidence in our justice is thus in the midst of a

crisis which threatens to increase in scope and depth. Only extreme borderline cases can be understood more or less clearly, and, for practical purposes, correctly by means of our meager psychology of the conscious; these are cases in which the criminal motive definitely dominates our conscious Ego, and, therefore these conscious motives are from the practical point of view the most important; this is also true of those more rare cases in which a socially noble motive appears to be the dominating impulse to commit a crime; for instance, the killing of a chronically ill person out of pity. However, all other cases are too complex and remain unexplained; this despite the desperate attempts to bring into court expert medical men trained in psychology. The sense of justice of the public cannot be satisfied by these measures. While it is true that no one can exactly state what dissatisfies him and why, we must remember that every human being possesses an inner perceptive organ by means of which he understands unconsciously, or feels at least the unconscious of others.

This feeling of dissatisfaction comes from the fact that the verdict usually fails to take into consideration the unconscious of the offender. One feels that the offender was convicted for something which was constructed, but for which he was not responsible subjectively; one feels without knowing that the offender must have intended something different from what the court says he meant by his offense. Yet this "something different" remains out of reach, impossible to express in words, because it belongs to the unconscious. Psychoanalysis found it possible to formulate scientifically this obscure "something." Only the influence of psychoanaly-

sis on the court of justice will, therefore, be able to throw some light into darkness, and thus show the way out of the present crisis. At any rate, the physician, in his role of a medical expert was unable to perform this task. We shall have the opportunity to come back to his rather inefficient role in the court. We agree with Wilmans[1] when, in agree-

---

[1] Wilmans, *Die Sogenannte Verminderte Zurechnungsfähigkeit* (Berlin: 1927).

ment with so many other prominent psychiatrists, he states that the judge of today is incapable of understanding the personality of the criminal, and yet the understanding of the personality is absolutely necessary for a just verdict. We believe, however, that the psychiatrist of today is also incapable of such understanding unless he is trained along the lines of deeper psychology.

It is undoubtedly a sign of progress when men like Aschaffenburg, Wilmans, Bonhoefer, Leppmann, etc., come to the view that a great number of offenders of the law, who do not permit of a definite diagnosis (the so-called borderline cases), are to be considered mentally sick. They designate such cases as psychically defective, psychopathic personalities, hysterical or epileptic or cyclothymic personalities—or in general, borderline cases; they find it difficult, if at all possible, to delimit such cases more definitely and to diagnose them more precisely.[1]

Thus, even without the help of any deep psychological knowledge, they feel it necessary to consider the most striking cases as mentally sick, yet a deeper understanding of the personalities of such cases and their behavior is impossible without a deeper analytical knowledge. Just as histology is unthinkable without a microscope, so is living human psychology impossible without psychoanalysis. However, the appearance of criminal psychology side by side with the old criminal-biological theories which searched vainly in every criminal for gross never-to-be-found biological defects is a gratifying phenomenon. As a rule, this psychology touched only the very surface; many contemporary writers, however,

---

[1] How unreliable a gross psychiatric diagnosis is can be shown by the following: A prominent German medico-legal expert officially considered a certain imposter and swindler as legally irresponsible. He rendered this opinion twice in two separate trials of the case. At the third trial, however, the same medical expert considered the same offender as legally accountable, despite the fact that the clinical picture had in no way changed. It so happened that he forgot his previous testimony which he disowned even when definitely faced with it. This case does not surprise us, since testimony which is not based on an analytical understanding of the personality is devoid of any scientific foundation.

while still preoccupied with the platitudinous intelligence tests, began to recognize the importance of emotional factors in criminality.

The psychoanalyst cannot be satisfied with the formal psychiatric statement that this and that case is a "psychopathic personality," and yet the older type of psychiatrist can do little more than make this statement; the psychoanalyst cannot be satisfied with the latter because he can go further and point out the important and specific psychological mechanisms which are hidden behind these *too general* scientific designations. It cannot be emphasized too much that a great number, perhaps the greater number of these so-called borderline cases cannot be even recognized as such without the deep insight which psychoanalysis provides.

The demand voiced by Liszt that we should consider not the crime but the criminal could not be satisfied until Freud made the investigation of the human personality an exact scientific procedure. The introduction of psychoanalysis in the courtroom will be the first step toward the fulfillment of the requirement made by Liszt.

CRIMINALITY AS A GENERAL HUMAN

MANIFESTATION

WE INFERRED ALREADY THAT ANY ATtempt to establish definite criminal types, biologically discernible from the normal personality, fails to take into consideration the great number of the more or less asocial individuals. The relatively very small number of individuals who, as a result of degeneracy, i.e., hereditary or prenatal defects of development, are incapable of social adjustment, do not represent characteristically the class of criminal individuals.

The majority of criminals are not different physically and grossly psychologically from the normal individual; the deviation from the normal is a matter of development, which depends more on the life history of the person than upon heredity; in other words, the greatest number of criminals could under different circumstances have developed into normal individuals. The attempt of Lombroso and his school to draw a sharp line between the normal and the criminal comes from the narcissistic wish of the scientist to separate himself and his normal fellow men from the criminal, as if the latter belonged to a different race of beings, different biologically and recognizable through definite, easily discernible physical signs. Any attempt to cross out this artificial line of demarcation is met with the same affective opposition as was the Darwinian theory of evolution, which injured the human pride by making man evolve from a line of animals.

The psychoanalytic study of unconscious psychic life leads to the conviction that every part of the human personality, which is socially adjusted, represents a later and comparatively labile product of a special evolution.

However, within the innermost nucleus of the personality, which is both quantitatively and dynamically much more powerful, it is impossible to differentiate normal from criminal impulses. The human being enters the world as a criminal, i.e., socially not adjusted. During the first years of his life, the human individual preserves his criminality to the fullest degree. His actual social adjustment begins only at the time after the Œdipus complex is overcome. This happens during the so-called latency period which was described by Freud. This period begins between the ages of four and six, and ends at puberty. It is at this period that the development of the criminal begins to differentiate itself from that of the normal. The future normal individual succeeds (mostly in the latency period) in partly repressing his genuine criminal instinctual drives, and thus cuts them out of motor expression, and partly in transforming them into socially acceptable striving; the future criminal more or less fails in carrying out this adjustment.

The criminal carries out in his actions his natural unbridled instinctual drives; he acts as the child would act if it only could. The repressed, and therefore unconscious criminality of the normal man finds a few socially harmless outlets, like the dream and phantasy life, neurotic symptoms and also some transitional forms of behavior which are less harmless, like duelling, boxing, bull fights and, occasionally, the free expression of one's criminality in war.

No better proof for the general criminality of mankind could be found than the proof which would be brought about by the daring experiment of depriving, say, the Spanish nation of its bull fights, the Americans of their boxing and football games, old Europe of its soldier game and the world of its penal codes. The universal criminality of man of today demands violent, purely physical outlets; without them it would become transformed into a battle of all against all.

The only difference between the criminal and the normal individual is that the normal man partially controls his criminal drives and finds outlets for them in socially harmless activities. This power of controlling, and of the domestication of the primitive, unsocial tendencies is acquired by the individual as a result of education. In other words, criminality, generally speaking, is not a congenital defect but a defect in the bringing up; this statement does not cover certain borderline cases which should be considered separately. Our contention will become clearer if we could imagine that all the children of the world between the ages of two to six should suddenly become physically superior to the adult and were thus able to dominate the adult to the same degree as the adult dominates the child. These children, let us imagine further, would then set themselves to act out all their phantasies. These Gulliverian giant children dominating a world of dwarf-like adults would present a hundred-per-cent criminality in action.

The first drive in relation to the outside world which the newly born individual experiences is the drive to grasp, to dominate. This drive in its earliest expression appears in the form of the cannibalistic possession of the breast of the mother, a sort of a partial eating up of the mother. The psychic content of this drive on this level is known in the psychoanalytic theory of instinctual drives as the *oral-sadistic* phase of development of the individual. The pregenital sexuality of the suckling finds its satisfaction in the mouth activity while sucking the mother's breast, the nipple or the bottle or the thumb. In this phase one is naturally unable to find any trace of the future social attitude, i.e., the tendency to consider the interests of others.

Disturbances in the normal functioning during this instinctual phase, particularly any educational mistake in the process of weaning, might influence the educability of the individual along the lines of social relationships. Individuals who at every frustration of a wish show a tendency to violent action, who react to any postponement of a pleasure with uncontrollable impatience, prove frequently to have been orally spoiled children; these individuals serve as a proof of how exceptionally long indulgence during the period of sucking reappears with a vengeance in an adult.[1] But weaning must inevitably come some day, and such spoiled babies respond to it with spiteful resistance; they do not want to give up a rightfully acquired habit. Abraham and Alexander[2] consider that the deepest roots of kleptomania are to be found in the history of this period.

 The child finds itself compelled for the first time to submit to the wishes of the adult when it begins to be taught habits of cleanliness. At first the child experiences a definite pleasure in relation to its excretory functions; this pleasure consists either of holding back or expressing the excreta; this pleasure, as well as the coprophilic tendencies of the child, is considerably interfered with when the adult begins to present demands for orderliness, cleanliness, and propriety.

Interference with its primitive instinctual drives brings the child to the realization that its sovereignty is badly encroached upon; it becomes impossible for the child to utilize the excretory processes whenever and in whatever manner it wishes, and thus to derive pleasure from them whenever it wishes, in whatever manner and degree it wishes. One of the chief characteristics of this anal erotism is that it gives one a sense of power, a feeling that one's pleasures do not depend upon others; for, in contrast to breast or bottle, which can and are always taken away and therefore are connected with a feeling of insecurity, the excrements are products created by the child itself, and take the place of the breast or bottle as a source of pleasure. In other words, the source of oral pleasure is always in the hands of the adult, while the fecal masses, hidden within the body, are outside the reach of grown-ups who want to dominate.

---

[1] Cf. Abraham, *Collected Papers* (London: 1927).
[2] Cf. Alexander, *Castration Complex and Character* (1922).

The psychoanalytic literature has not yet considered with sufficient detail this strong drive for independence, the spite with which it is connected, and the high self-esteem of the anal phase of development. It was first recognized by Freud as stubbornness of the anal erotic; it is a sort of overcompensation for the sad experiences met with in the oral phase in which the child depended for pleasure on the whim of the mother.

However, sooner or later, the child learns to control and regulate its sphincter activity, because it is afraid of being censured and punished by the adults. The first crime which all humans, without exception, sooner or later commit is the violation of the prescription for cleanliness. Under the rule of this penal code of the nursery, man for the first time becomes acquainted with the punishment which the world metes out to individual transgressors. Ferenczi,[1] therefore, is right when he speaks of the "sphincter morality" as the beginning and foundation of adult human morality. As a prototype of certain refractory criminals who persist in their spiteful rejection of social demands, one can imagine a baby sitting on its little chamber pot persistently rejecting any demands coming from the outside; it sits in this sovereign position and feels superior to the grown-ups.

At the moment when the child begins to impose inhibitions on the demands of its own sphincter, it makes the first decisive step toward the adjustment to the outside world; at that moment it creates an inhibitory agency within its own personality, and this agency from now on demands from within what the outside world demanded heretofore. In other words, a definite part of the child's personality identifies itself with the demands of the person who is bringing it up. We thus deal here with an identification with a *demand*, i.e., a partial identification with a person; at a later phase the child will identify itself with an adult *person* as a whole instead of with a demand only.

---

1 Ferenczi, "Psychoanalysis of Sexual Habits," in *Collected Papers.*

This education to cleanliness becomes a prototype for the future restrictions of instinctual life; a disturbance during this phase of development may naturally serve as a cause of a future disturbance in one's social adjustment.

The anal character traits which were described by Freud, Jones, and Abraham, in their exaggerated form present a number of anti-social and criminal characteristics.

The exaggerated, unsocial, stubborn bluntness of some violators of the law corresponds to the unyielding persistence of infantile anal spite. The characteristic self-centered stubbornness of the anal character acquires in the majority of criminals the form of proud, inaccessible spite, which is directed against all humanity.

In the course of the development of every child we find that its interests gradually broaden, and in addition to its relationship to its own physiological processes it tries to establish a relationship with the outer world. The instinctual drives in the phases of oral and anal development which were just mentioned were psychologically concerned with intake of food and its elimination; instinctual pleasure was derived from these two processes. However, in view of the fact that they begin to be directed toward objects of the outer world, they approach for the first time a psychological level of the adult individual. As is to be expected, the first objects of the outside world toward which the child's interest is directed are the immediate members of the family. Thus, the relationship of the child to father, mother, brothers and sisters, becomes the central problem of the future adult individual. The psychological management of these relationships on the part of the growing human being becomes definitely the decisive factor in the whole development and functioning of the adult person. After thirty years of therapeutic work and psychoanalytical research this point may be considered definitely proved. The way in which the child overcomes the conflicts arising from this situation determines whether it will develop into a healthy or sick individual, or whether his general behavior will be that of a socially ad-

justed person or that of a criminal. We should like to
emphasize now, and we shall be able to prove later in these
pages, that psychoneurosis and criminality are defects in
one's social adjustment; they hardly differ from one another
in their respective psychological contents; the differences are
those of psychological dynamics. Both the neurotic and the
criminal fell victims to their incapacity of finding a socially
acceptable solution of the conflicts which the relationships
to the various members of the family engendered. The neurotic expresses symbolically by means of his symptoms, which
are socially innocuous, the same things which the criminal
does by means of real actions. This important fact opens to
us a promising method of study; we can understand the
psychological content of a criminal act through the psychoanalysis of the neuroses.

We thus come to the fundamental problem as to which
are the circumstances responsible for the fact that, in some
individuals, the unconscious criminal phantasy finds it sufficient to come to expression in the substitution form of a
neurotic symptom, while in other individuals it demands
the motor expression in the form of criminal acts. This problem requires the consideration of the economic and structural
characteristics of the psychic apparatus; it is a problem dealing with the relative strength of inhibitory psychic agencies
as compared with the pressure coming from the undomesti-
cated remnants of our instinctual drives. We shall be able
to throw light on the problem if we consider the data acquired by psychoanalysis with regard to the structural and
dynamic development of the human personality.

It is self-evident that, in order to gain an understanding
of criminality, we shall have to investigate the process by
means of which a socially adjusted Ego develops out of a
great homogeneous reservoir of instincts which originally
were unsocial; this reservoir of instinctual drives is called
the Id.

The two pregenital phases of adjustment which were described above, oral and anal, are but preparatory to the first

great necessity, which demands that the object relationship
to parents and siblings be transformed into relationships of
a social nature.

The problem which the child has to solve is this: it must
bring his original sexual attitude toward the parent of the
opposite sex into some sort of harmony with its attitude
toward the parent of the same sex. The little son, for instance, who had dropped the objectless pleasure-seeking of
oral and anal nature, lives under the pressure of a sexual
wish for his mother; although this wish does not always appear in consciousness, it is always and definitely present in
the unconscious. Under the pressure of this wish the little
son is thrown into sexual rivalry with his father, who becomes his sexual competitor, as it were.

The fear of the father, who is stronger, comes to expression as castration anxiety; this anxiety inhibits the active
masculine drive; the passive feminine tendencies which are
always present in man as a result of his natural biological
bisexuality and of oral fixations may, under the pressure of
castration anxiety, come to the foreground; hence, a passive
feminine attitude toward the more powerful father may set
in. One and the same person may thus be simultaneously
loved in a passive feminine way and hated because of competition. The little boy finds himself in a state of conflict
due to ambivalence of feeling. This situation which is
charged with such conflicting emotions presses the boy to
find a way out. He then attempts to look upon his father as
the prototype of what he himself wants to be; he wants to
become like father, i.e., to identify himself with him. This
identification is originally presented by a phantasy in which
the child hopes to replace the father in the latter's sexual
role; however, this identification carries with it also the following consequences: the role of the father as a person who
rules and forbids is taken over by the personality of the
child; the prototype father is thus introjected and as a result
a new partial personality is erected within the personality of
the son; this partial personality acts as a representative of the

father, as it were, and functions as an organ inhibiting the primitive instinctual impulses of the boy.

The child, at the time, is not yet physiologically mature and is as yet unable to function sexually as the father does; the full expression of this function must therefore wait; the *inhibitory* functions, however, become effective *at once*. Thus the first real social adjustment appears to be a result of a compromise between a drive toward a lustful pleasure and the prohibition of this drive. In other words, the individual succeeds in restricting the expression of instinctual impulses in the hope that in the future real gratification will be secured. This compromise is not satisfactory to the psychic life of the child, which for the time being is guided only by the pleasure principle; it must be accepted, however, under the pressure of fear of pain, which unavoidably arises at the very moment when an attempt is made to obtain the gratification of forbidden instinctual demands. Hence a complete identification with father becomes impossible; for physiological incapacity and castration anxiety prevent it; this identification does not go beyond the function of inhibition and a few sublimatory reactions.

The child has to console himself with the hope that a complete identification will be achieved at some future date ("When I grow up, I will ... etc.") ; for the present, he finds consolation for his renunciation in that he is loved (by father).

The wish for being loved, according to Freud, plays a greater role in the life of the girl than in that of the boy; the boy's wish is stimulated mainly by the fear of the punishing father.

Our investigations are substantially limited to those of men, because men continue to play a dominant role, not only in criminality, but in the general structure of society. Our conclusions, however, are valid for both sexes.

The fear of the father, the wish to be loved by him, and the tendency to take him as a model, thus represent the main springs in the process of identification as far as its inhibitory effect is concerned—an effect actually wished by the son. This identification produces an inner psychic agency which represents simultaneously an inhibitory function and an ideal to be achieved. This part of the personality, i.e., the social part of it, we call the Superego; it is differentiated from the rest of the Ego.

In summing up, we may say that the differentiation of the Superego from the rest of the personality could be described as a process which is dominated by the pleasure principle. Fear of punishment and of loss of love; in other words, the avoidance of real pain, and the craving to obtain positive pleasure by means of being loved, the hope that the future will provide many possibilities for gratification through complete identification with the educator, present the instinctual springs for the formation of the Superego.

As a result of this new formation within the Ego, a part of this Ego accepts and incorporates within itself the social demands of the environment, of the parents and of all other persons who have to do with the education of the child; this part of the Ego functions as a Superego and inhibits the forbidden instinctual impulses. The relationship between the Superego and the rest of the personality is thus a sort of a replica of the relationship which originally existed between the child and the adult who brought him up. Thus the original conflict between parent and child becomes transformed into an inner psychic conflict between two parts of the same personality, the Superego and the Ego. The fear of real punishment (castration anxiety) becomes transformed into fear of one's own conscience, i.e., the fear becomes internalized; the Ego feels it facing its Superego. In the same way, the wish to be loved by one's parents becomes internalized as a striving to remain in harmony with one's own conscience.

It is characteristic of all psychoneuroses and of the majority of criminals that the formation and proper organization of a Superego within their respective personalities remains imperfect. The organization of the Ego and the Superego into a harmonious unit fails, the Superego remains a sort of a foreign body within their personalities; there is a constant persisting tension between the Ego and the Superego; the Ego strives to regain its original independence and to follow as it once did the primitive, unsocial impulses of the Id. This striving for independence, however, is always thwarted by the threatening presence of both reality and the demands of the Superego.

This existence of the Superego as a foreign body within the personality can be best observed in a child during the early period of Superego development. One can observe a definite period, during which the Superego is still greatly dependent upon real persons, who serve as prototypes for its development. The brilliant observations of Anna Freud[1] proved that during this transitional stage the child behaves according to a sort of double standard; in the presence of the parents it behaves in accordance with their demands for good behavior and thus follows the pressure coming from its own Superego; yet when alone it returns at once to its primitive unsocial nature. We had the opportunity to observe this phenomenon in a three-year-old child. As it was getting off its chamber pot it looked on its own feces with unconcealed delight and exclaimed, "It smells so nice"; at that moment it noticed its mother and added with a guilty conscience, "No, whee!" During this period, when the Superego just begins to become an integral part of the personality, but is not yet entirely incorporated into it as a solid unit, one may best observe how the Ego tries to rid itself of this burdensome inhibitory agency. Only gradually and under the constant educative pressure from the adults is a successful introjection accomplished.

It must be borne in mind, however, that in the majority of adults, and throughout their lives, there always remains a certain dependence of the Superego on its prototypes. As soon as confidence in authority is lost, the inner power of the Superego becomes shattered. It would undoubtedly be

---

[1] Anna Freud, *The Technique of Child Analysis.*

difficult to find a man who would persist in remaining righteous if the whole world about him were violating all social restrictions.

Let us return to and clarify our considerations of the role of the sense of justice, which we reviewed above. We pointed out that, when the sense of justice is sufficiently injured, the inner restrictions of our instincts weaken and a number of repressed impulses break through; we stated that injustice was perceived by the Ego as a breaking of a silent social contract; the powerful restricting agencies of social life not having made good their promises, the Ego feels that it need not continue the policy of renunciation. The details of this social process become clearer now; it is under the pressure of the Superego that the Ego agreed to accept all the most important and fundamental restrictions on the instinctual impulses. The Superego is the inner representative of reality which demands renunciation; its inhibitory power, as we have seen, is more or less dependent upon the relationship which exists between the Ego and authority; when the Ego loses its confidence in those representing authority, the Superego, as the latter's psychic representative, loses to the same extent the power which it holds over the instinctual life of man.

We may then describe the regressive phenomenon which takes place in case of injury to the sense of justice as a process in which the Superego loses its inhibitory power over the Ego; the Ego then unopposed follows the tendencies of the Id. The remarkable thing in this, like in any other regressive phenomena, is the tendency to expand. The injustice may be related to a very insignificant matter, but the reactive breaking-through of repressed impulses not infrequently upsets the oldest and the most fundamental cultural restrictions. Michael Kohlass, who unjustly lost two horses, derives from this minor injury the right to kill. Such manner of thinking is reminiscent of that of the youngster who says: "When the parents are unjust, I have a right to do everything." We now can see clearly that our psychic apparatus took over the restrictions imposed by civilization reluctantly and, in fact, unwillingly.

Those instinctual restrictions which are developmentally the oldest, and which are most fundamental in the process of social formations, come entirely from the inhibitory power of the Superego and not from any prohibitions imposed from the outside. We may say incidentally that these fundamental social trends of man are derived chiefly from the tendencies which come from the Œdipus complex. We shall consider later the details of this interesting phenomenon.

On the whole, however, the civilized man of today still continues to follow the pattern of his childhood, and most of his self-renunciations are due to the fear of punishment. This inhibitory fear is covered by a thin layer of moral, but not yet quite organized inner inhibitions, which come from the youngest fringes of the Superego. The reason why the breaking-through of the repressed instinctual impulses has the tendency to expand is that, in case of even a relatively minor injustice on the part of the constituted authorities, the deepest, the apparently solidly organized inhibitions become threatened and loosened. Thus, for instance, we observed the following phenomenon: A political criminal in prison, who naturally considered his punishment unjust, had during his prison term vivid incestuous dreams accompanied by nocturnal emissions. Even the inhibition of incestuous wishes was thus lifted while the man suffered at the hands of what he thought the unjust law; it was as if the prisoner had said to himself: "If my father (the State) treats me in this fashion, then I don't need to respect his privileges and may take mother." Children use this mode of thinking quite readily, in order to weaken the moral authority of their parents; neurotics and neurotic criminals utilize the same method in order to weaken their own conscience, and thus to grant the Ego a free hand in the matter of gratifying its anti-social tendencies. As one of the writers expressed it elsewhere, they bribe or disarm their conscience by means of a voluntary acceptance of some suffering. All forms of psychoneuroses are based on this "bribery" mechanism; they represent a compromise made by the Ego in order to obtain simultaneous gratification of both the prohibited Id drives and the demands of the Superego.

In other words, in a neurosis the unadjusted Id tendencies succeed in gaining a substitutive gratification, despite the presence of a strict social agency within the personality. The same mechanisms which are at work in the production of a neurosis are operative in the behavior of the greatest majority of criminals. The difference between the neurotic and the criminal consists in the following: the neurotic symptom is a gratification which permits of no complete expression in action and is only of subjective significance to the neurotic himself. The neurotic suffering has the meaning of a self-inflicted punishment; the criminal gratification, however, is obtained by means of a real act which is directed against the outside world, and the consequence, the punishment, appears to be inflicted by the outside world. The neurosis thus appears to be a later development in the evolution of man, a sort of intrapsychic replica of the more primitive process—crime and punishment.

A neurosis, like the history of a crime, consists of two phases: in the first, a gratification of a wish which is not acceptable to reality or the Superego takes place; in the second, a punishment, a suffering sets in as a reaction of society or the Superego against the forbidden gratification.

The large group of criminals who show a psychic organization akin to the one of the neurotic patient, i.e., those who show the presence of an inner conflict between the social and anti-social tendencies of their personality, we shall call the group of *Neurotic Criminals*. Under this designation, we shall group those criminals who show unconscious psychic processes that might have led to the development of a neurosis. Modern psychiatry calls such criminals psychopathic personalities, hysterical or epileptic personalities, who, according to Aschaffenburg and other psychiatrists, make up the bulk of all transgressors of the law. The only difference between them and the psychoneurotics is that in the latter the tension between unconscious tendencies and repressing forces is resolved *autoplastically* (symptom), while in the former it is resolved *alloplastically* (criminal acts).

Later on we shall attempt to prove that this type of criminal is neither frightened away, nor inhibited, nor made a better person by the reaction of present-day society, i.e., by punishment, for in such cases of neurotic criminality punishment acts as a temptation to crime, and criminality is thus furthered instead of stopped.

Thus we may definitely recognize the existence of a group of criminals in whom the prototypes of social behavior remain foreign to the Ego.

There are also criminals who betray no tension between their instinctual drives and social demands; from the practical point of view this type is very important. Aichhorn, in his book *Wayward Youth,* describes this variety of criminal, particularly the young one. Aichhorn came to the conclusion that these individuals have not only a criminal Ego, but also a criminal Superego; they are well adjusted to the criminal prototypes of their social conscience and to their criminal environment; hence they live in accordance with the dictates of a special criminal morality; this means that they did carry out the process of identification with the interests of a community, but this community is not that of law-abiding citizens.

We must remember that the normal, non-criminal individual does not share the ideas of the whole community to which he belongs, for, as a rule, he belongs to a certain class, to a sort of a caste that has a special ideology of its own. The psychological content of the ideals and of the Superego of a proletarian differs considerably from those of an aristocrat; those of a pacifist and a militarist are also different; what one considers criminal, the other considers as a postulate of the highest ethical type. The psychological structure of the criminal mentioned above does not differ from that of a normal individual. He merely belongs to a social class that lives by different standards. We shall call this group the group of _Normal Criminals_. It will be again noted that these individuals are well adjusted to a totally different community, and that within the limits of that community they are normal social beings. The internal conflict between Ego and Super-ego is not present, or, at any rate, not greater than in the case of a normal person. Only the exaggerated conceit of a scientist, who is bound and determined to defend the standards of a definite social organization, will make one seek biological points of differentiation between these individuals and ourselves.

We think, therefore, that these criminals are to be looked upon as normal persons who had the misfortune of adjusting themselves to a weaker part of the community. Many of these, if they were brought up outside the criminal environment, would have grown up to be highly adjusted social individuals in our sense of the word. Nothing shows this point clearer than the romantic literature dealing with the criminal; all its traditions and literary presentations bear witness to bravery, spirit of sacrifice, sympathy with the weaker, chivalry, etc.

Thus we have two groups of criminals, one which is psychically sick and another which is psychically healthy, but socially abnormal; there is a third group which, as compared with these two, includes but a very small minority of criminals; yet forensic medicine has been and still is paying greater attention to this minority. We have in mind those criminals who were either retarded in their development because of defective biological growth or those whose psychological personality was destroyed by some organic processes (idiots, paretics, schizophrenics and epileptics).

The transition from this group to that of the neurotic is not easy to denote. To take schizophrenia as an example—it has not yet been definitely established to what degree constitutional factors and the general history of the individual are respectively responsible for the disease; in some cases, it appears one factor is more responsible than the other; in other cases, the reverse appears to be true. To cite another instance, we may refer to epilepsy, which appears to present a sort of a transitional form between psychoneurosis and organic disease.

At any rate, the criminals belonging to this group are not so much products of the psychological pressure which environment or life circumstances exerted on them, as they are victims of organic processes or heredity; we shall designate them as *criminals who are organically conditioned.*

We thus delimit three large classes of criminals:

I. *The neurotic criminal,* whose hostile activity against society is a result of an intrapsychic conflict between the social and anti-social components of his personality; this conflict, like that of a psychoneurosis, comes from impressions of earliest childhood and from circumstances of later life (psychological etiology).

II. *The normal criminal,* whose psychic organization is similar to that of the normal individual, except that he identified himself with criminal prototypes (sociological etiology).

III. The criminal whose criminality is conditioned by some pathological process of *organic* nature (biological etiology).

These three classes consist of individuals who, as a result of some definite, organic or psychic factors, become criminals; they are *chronic criminals;* there exists in addition a number of normal individuals who, under certain specific conditions become *acute criminals.* The criminal act of the *acute type* is not characteristic of any special group of people; as a matter of fact, every human individual, without exception, under certain conditions and situations is capable of a transgression of the law. The outstanding factor in such crimes is not the peculiarity of the person who committed it, but the singularity of the circumstances which lead to it. While such criminals cannot be fitted into any special typological scheme, and while they are least of all important from the social standpoint, psychologically they are extremely interesting. Moreover, from the standpoint of pronouncing a just verdict, it is of greatest practical importance to make a correct diagnosis of a crime of this type; for in such cases one need not undertake any special treatment, or take any measures in order to avoid the repetition of the crime.

All these classes and forms of criminality which we have just outlined fall between two extreme types of criminality, which occupy the opposite poles of our scheme and which are conceivable only theoretically.

On the one end we find the pure criminal, who had not formed any Superego to represent the demands of society within him; this criminal, when and if he does restrict his anti-social tendencies, does so without any inner urge and unwillingly; he does it merely because he is afraid of the outside authorities. At the other extreme end of our scheme we should find the perfectly adjusted social individual, who without any inner conflict considers the interests of the community before he considers his own; in other words, his Superego and Ego would be fused into one. In reality it is impossible to find these conflict-less individuals; only intermediary types can be found. These intermediary types (every single civilized individual belongs to one of the intermediary types) do not possess a homogeneous psychological organization; they always experience a certain tension between the primitive and socialized parts of the psychic apparatus.

In so far as these pages are devoted to the psychology of the criminal, we shall consider chiefly the *neurotic* and the *acute* criminal. The *normal criminal* and the majority of the professional criminals belonging to this type shall occupy our attention only in so far as we shall attempt to review critically the whole problem of criminality. As to the criminals whose criminality is based on pathological organic conditions, they belong to that chapter of penal jurisprudence and legal medicine which best succeeded in solving the problem of diagnosis and treatment; for such cases a strict scientific psychology may be dispensed with; gross descriptive psychiatry usually suffices.

THE PSYCHOANALYTICAL THEORY OF NEU-
ROTIC SYMPTOM FORMATION AS THE BASIS
FOR A CRIMINAL PSYCHOLOGY

As HAS BEEN STATED, THE PSYCHOLOGICAL understanding of crime and of the criminal is based primarily on the data obtained from our psychoanalytical knowledge of the neuroses; before beginning the special consideration of our problem we shall, therefore, state briefly the principles of the general theory of the neuroses.

The fact that we learn to understand crime through the understanding of the neuroses is an anachronism not infrequently found in the history of science; the neurosis presents the intrapsychic inheritance and parody of primitive criminality; in other words, the criminal act can be understood through the study of the psychic fossils of man. Is not a neurosis of a civilized man a sort of living out of his primitive anti-social tendencies, this living out having been pushed out of reality into the domain of psychic life? From the standpoint of its psychological content and structure it presents a true reproduction of primitive, prehistoric penal traditions. Crime and punishment is *the* meaning of a psychoneurosis, except that all this takes place not in real life but in the unconscious world of phantasy, and is represented by the neurotic symptoms. The study of a neurosis yields unconscious material which makes it possible for us to reconstruct not only the spirit of primitive justice—the talion principle, but also the nature of the primitive social problems, i.e., the primitive crime of incest and murder of the father and even the primitive punishment—castration.

The medical man whose studies have been confined to purely biological facts receives a remarkable, and at first a rather strange, set of impressions when he gains his first acquaintance with the psychoanalytic theory of the neuroses; he suddenly discovers that these diseases are described in terms to which natural sciences are not accustomed; he finds that the descriptions are couched partly in literary terms, partly in the language of a jurist and that they are based on a number of criminological concepts. He will read, for instance, about the Œdipus complex, the content of which embraces the primitive crime of murder of the father and incest with the mother; he will hear about castration anxiety, i.e., the fear of that singular punishment which represents the deepest fundamental source of all our human renunciations in favor of a social order; this same anxiety is the primary condition of the general structural development of our psychic apparatus, that divides our psychological functions into conscious and unconscious. He will also hear of the *sense of guilt* and *expiation,* of *sacrifice* and *penance,* of *bribery,* of the *severity* of certain unconscious psychic agencies, of the *need for punishment* and the *compulsion to confess* one's sins.

The medical man studied and learned all about the bones and muscle system of the human body; he learned about blood circulation and the physico-chemical processes of the human body; he learned to consider the body as a complicated heating machine—and suddenly he finds that psychoanalysis leads him into a sort of courtroom where the most primitive spirit of primitive races, or children, rules supreme; he suddenly learns that this singular court is deeply imbedded into the unconscious of the human personality. Psychoanalysis then assures him that many neurotic symptoms, which frequently appear in the form of physical

symptoms and which he always thought are due to physico-
chemical disturbances in the body, are due to those singular
intrapsychic processes which we have just sketched; he also
learns that these symptoms present a secret gratification of
forbidden anti-social tendencies and that these symptoms,
the pain and the discomfort of a neurosis, present at the very
same time the punishment for these transgressions. Thus, a
peculiar metamorphosis must take place; the medical man
in order to understand and to cure certain diseases had to
go through a thorough training in biology, chemistry, etc.,
now he suddenly faces the necessity of becoming a criminologist; he has to gain an understanding of criminal
psychology, and delve deeply into the spirit of a remarkably
primitive, barbarian penal code, the chief subject matter of
which is murder, incest, and castration. Thus, the road from
the psychoanalytical theory of the neuroses to the courtroom
appears to us much shorter than the road to anatomy and
physiology of the brain or to the physical chemistry of bodily
processes.

The psychoneurotic symptom consists either of physiologically useless deficiencies and disturbances of innervations,
or of psychologically meaningless, and groundless psychic
reactions.

The first group of physical symptoms which are psychically
conditioned, such as vomiting, constipation, difficulties in
breathing, cramps, paralyses, or the psychologically conditioned blindness, deafness, abnormalities of sensation, or lack
of sensations in various parts of the body are called by
psychoanalysis *conversion symptoms,* and are most characteristic of *hysteria.* They are the expression of unconscious
psychic processes, which, like all neurotic symptoms, partly
serve as a gratification of forbidden impulses and partly play
the role of self-injury as a punishment for the forbidden
gratification.

Disturbances of purely psychological nature such as fears,
inhibitions, depressions, self-accusations, all founded not on
reality of fact, but on intrapsychic conflicts, also the un-

founded changes of mood and apparently meaningless compulsions which appear foreign to the conscious personality—all these symptoms have proved through psychoanalysis to be the result of the play of unconscious forces generated by repressed instinctual demands and inner moral reaction against them. These disturbances comprise the symptomatology of *anxiety neuroses, phobias, compulsion neuroses* and *manic-depressive states.* As to the multiform morbid pictures of psychoses, i.e., the pathological falsification of inner (psychic) and outer reality by means of delusions, hallucinations, and even complete disorientation, and a resulting complete withdrawal of all interests in, and all relationships to, the outside world—all these symptoms acquire a definite meaning only if we think of them as psychological regressions to primitive forms of thinking and feeling.

Psychiatry was well acquainted with this whole mass of pathological psychic reactions: the purely external manifestations of these illnesses were described many times and arranged in numerous systems; however, the meaning and significance of these symptoms remained unknown till Freud propounded psychoanalysis. The discovery of unconscious mental processes and of the psychoanalytic technique for the study of these processes offered at once a clue to many mysteries which dwelt until then in the field of medical psychology. In the history of science one is able to find but few examples of such a sudden growth of a branch of scientific knowledge; in a very short time it explored successfully and in many respects even conquered a region which until then seemed so obscure and inpenetrable. As a result of therapeutic efforts and by means of the technique of free associations and of dream interpretation, and as a result of the understanding of the affective relationship between physician and patient, a new anatomy and physiology of the human mind was created. When toward the close of the Middle Ages the *inside of the human body* stopped being taboo and dissections were finally permitted, the founding of the science of anatomy was carried out within a comparatively short time. In our day we overcame a similar resistance to looking *inside* the human psyche, i.e. the unconscious part of *our personality;* this made it possible to gain knowledge of the structure of the human Ego in a comparatively shorter time. The neurotic symptom, be it the purely physical conversion symptom or the purely psychological symptom, acquired a meaning as soon as the unconscious motives which they were covering up were discovered. The incomprehensible, seemingly meaningless and useless symptom, like the seemingly meaningless dream can be understood as the product of interplay between two psychodynamic forces, the product of repressed wishes which the conscious personality rejects, and of the reaction against them on the part of the socially adjusted part of our personality. A symptom is, therefore, a compromise between the repressing and the repressed forces.

Psychoanalysis succeeded at first in uncovering the unconscious anti-social content of symptoms; this content was described in general terms as a combination of sexual drives and hostile impulses which were directed against the various members of the family, chiefly the parents. It took two decades of psychoanalytical research to prove conclusively that the Œdipus complex presented the chief unconscious psychological content of neurotic symptoms. It was found that all those psychological undercurrents which the adult person usually represses are affectively connected with the Œdipus situation of early childhood; these physic currents, after they are repressed, continue in the unconscious, tied as with a navel cord to the infantile Œdipus complex.

The first investigations dealt mainly with the unconscious repressed psychological content. However, the *repressing forces,* i.e., the reaction of the Ego to these forbidden ideas were not so well known. In a general way it was known that there exists in every individual a tendency to cover up the real meaning of our unconscious ideas by means of the mechanisms of dream and symptom formation; this tendency was generally recognized as a defense reaction on the part of the Ego. The first concept was that of two mutually antagonistic forces; the unconscious containing the primitive antisocial tendencies and the conscious Ego, i.e., the socially and ethically minded part of our personality. In other words, our Ego and our *instinctual* life, i.e., the *unconscious* and the *conscious* were considered as the two opposite poles of our personality. The manifest dream content and the neurotic symptom were considered as the expression of the repressed, which was clad in a harmless, unintelligible form in order not to disturb the socially fastidious, conscious Ego.

This first presentation, crude as it was, proved fundamentally true; yet it soon became clear that this simple formula failed to describe fully the reaction between the Ego and the repressed. Soon after he published his first communications regarding hysterical symptoms, Freud saw clearly that the neurotic symptom presents not only the disguised Ego-alien wish, but also a tendency directed against the Ego itself, an ethical element, a sort of self-punishment. If the symptoms were nothing more than a disguised gratification, then it would be impossible to understand why the neurotic suffers, why he complains that he is not well, or in general why a neurotic symptom should be unpleasant. Many neurotic states, such as the deep depressive states, for instance, show a great deal of suffering; they also show definitely the tendency to self-punishment; in severe cases it leads to self-destruction. The recognition of the feminine masochistic (homosexual) gratification, which permits a person's turning against his own self does not appear to be sufficient to explain this phenomenon, although such an erotic (masochistic) admixture is not only always present, but at times plays the main role in depressions. These observations on the self-punishment and suffering of neurotics gradually brought forth a sufficient amount of evidence which led Freud to assume the existence of an unconscious need for punishment; it remains unconscious and is most intimately bound with the ethico-social part of the Ego, that is, the Superego.

To cite a definite example of how deeply seated this inner need for suffering is, we may mention the following well-known clinical fact; many neurotic patients begin to feel subjectively worse as soon as they sense a slight improvement in their symptoms or even at the very beginning of the analytical treatment; they then develop severe anxiety states and at times even a weird drive for self-destruction; one could observe clearly in such patients how they cling with at least the same persistency to the suffering as they clung to the gratification which the symptoms usually provide. It is the immanent sense of guilt which apparently comes from the gratification alien to the Ego that forces the neurotic individual to carry his cross. One of the writers definitely established that neurotic suffering is one of the fundamental conditions of unconscious gratification.[1]

An observation made by Freud on manic-depressive patients could be applied to the general theory of symptom formation. Freud stated that frequent alternations of manic and depressive states in the same individual depend upon an alternation of unlimited gratification of unconscious wishes with unconscious self-punishment. The unbridled gratification of forbidden wishes which takes place in a manic attack causes an accumulation of feelings of guilt and the need for punishment; the satisfaction of the latter relieves one from this feeling of guilt. This need for punishment dominates the picture of a depression which follows a manic attack. The suffering, as a result of self-inflicted punishment, the unbridled raging of conscience in an attack of depression leads into a fresh manic attack in which, as in a revolution, the instincts too severely restricted in the depression break through with renewed vigor of self-assertion.

The very same individual who, while in a severe depression was constantly playing with the idea of suicide, may in a manic attack become dangerous to the lives of others.

When viewed in the light of the fundamental conditions

---

[1] Alexander, *Psychoanalysis of the Total Personality.*

leading to the development of a neurosis, the relationship which exists between the gratification of an unconscious wish and the subsequent reactive need of suffering, could be summarized as follows:

Each gratification of a repressed wish obtained through a symptom arouses an unconscious *anxiety before one's own conscience,* i.e., an anxiety experienced by the Ego in face of the socially adapted part of it, the Superego, which latter is to a great extent also unconscious. This anxiety is the intrapsychic continuation of the child's fear of the older person who brought him up; it is an internalization of the infantile fear of punishment and the fear of losing the affection of others. It is, in other words, the same anxiety which the child once had when facing the adult mentor; the individual carries over this anxiety into adulthood and experiences it when facing his conscience; the latter, we shall recall, developed as an inner representative of the parents with whom the child identified itself. This is seen with particular clearness in cases of depression, who couch their pathological self-reproaches in the same words that were used by their parents reprimanding them in childhood.

The gratification of forbidden wishes, even if carried out in a disguised form of meaningless symptoms, arouses a fear of the Superego. *The need for punishment* is a direct result of this unconscious anxiety. The various types of self-punishment and suffering have this dynamic significance: they tend to raise the pressure of the inhibiting conscience and thus open the way for a subsequent free gratification of forbidden wishes. The spirit of that criminal code which claims that punishment expiates a crime is thus made eternally active in the psychology of the neurosis; the neurotic Ego makes one step further in this logical causal chain; it considers the imposed punishment as a moral justification, as a license to indulge in new gratifications of forbidden wishes.

In the light of these considerations certain observations which did not seem clear before or which were not quite in accord with the general theory, could be explained. Dis-

guising the unconscious meaning of symptoms is apparently
not a satisfactory means to obviate a moral protest and to
avoid the neurotic anxiety. If this disguise were sufficient for
the escape from one's own conscience, then the self-punishing
tendencies and the suffering accompanying a neurosis would
prove superfluous and unintelligible. Moreover, the theory
based merely on the mechanisms of covering up one's unconscious tendencies would totally fail to explain certain phobic
states of inhibition. In these states, the patients anxiously try
to avoid performing simple, harmless things such as walking
in the street, riding on a train, writing, etc.; all this because
these simple activities have for them an unconscious symbolic
sexual meaning. This unconscious meaning is so deeply hidden in the manifest act that one cannot see it; why then
should certain neurotics react to such things with so much
anxiety? Mere disguise in such cases is apparently of little
help; it is the judgment of the Superego that continues to
generate anxiety. On the other hand, in such phobic states
one does not find, as a rule, the usual "self-punishment technique" or "the bribery maneuver" which, through suffering,
tend to disarm the inhibiting Superego. That is apparently
the reason why one finds in these cases of phobias that the
usual unconscious gratifications are also absent; the illness
consists of a direct inhibition, which is brought on by anxiety. On the other hand, the majority of the obsessional
neurotics show such a high degree of development of the
"bribery policy" that even the most forbidden unconscious
trends, like murder and incest, appear in consciousness un-
disguised; these patients acquire their freedom of thought
through formal self-control and self-restriction, like over-
punctilliousness, exaggerated conscientiousness in small
things, and through painful compulsions to wash constantly
and to perform all sorts of neurotic ceremonies, which represent an exaggeration of the orders given to them in childhood by those who trained them in cleanliness, orderliness,
etc.

Thus it may be said that the general condition of every

neurotic symptom formation is the satisfaction of one's own moral demands, by means of unconscious self-punishment; this satisfaction is combined with the concealment of the sense of the repressed wishes. While this disguise aims to conceal the real unconscious meaning of the symptom from the *conscious* part of the personality, the *unconscious* moral inhibitions find themselves disarmed by virtue of the fact that the need for punishment is also gratified.

Thus the structure and the content of every neurosis stands out as a partial repetition of the primary event of the primitive society, i.e., the first primitive crime and punishment; all this is internalized and deeply buried in the unconscious. Crime and punishment may appear today as changed both in form and content, but the deeply emotional connection with the principle of considering the punishment as an atonement is still highly effective even today. Anyone who is acquainted with the practical administration of justice today knows very well that the attempts of modern justice to consider punishment as a factor in prevention of crime are hardly more than of purely theoretical importance.

In the courtroom today, as of yore, we find that the principle of atonement is still the dominating principle; anyone who commits a crime must suffer a punishment proportionate to the severity of the crime; the establishment of the degree of punishment as well as the gravity of the crime is, strictly speaking, still not a matter of scientific knowledge, but a matter of feeling.

It is possible that as an individual, man of today may have progressed a little ahead of the spirit of primitive man, but as a social being, as seen in the function of his Superego and also in many of his public institutions, particularly in the spirit of his justice, he continues to remain on the level of primitive society.

Thus it would appear that the criminal and the law, taken together as a social phenomenon, perform the same task together as the neurotic does alone, by means of his psychic reactions and symptoms; to wit, crime and atonement. There is another parallel between the two: the neurotic utilizes the atonement (the suffering) as a license for his transgression (symptom formation). In the case of a number of criminals, whom we designate as neurotic criminals, punishment frequently serves the purpose only of lifting their moral inhibitions. The forthcoming punishment or the sentence already served is for the neurotic criminal the necessary condition for the performance of his transgressions, in particular for the repetition of his crimes. In cases of such criminals the most effective mode of treatment would prove the one which Victor Hugo imagined in *Les Miserables,* in the case of the priest who was attacked by a robber. The priest, instead of imposing punishment, which the criminal unconsciously hoped to obtain, responded to the crime with kind deeds. This mode of action, we believe, would prove in the cases under consideration a much more effective preventive method than any form of punishment; for punishment results in little more than the fact that the criminal experiences a sense of relief; it gives him a sense of having expiated his sins and thus reduces his inhibitions; kindness, on the contrary, would increase still further the inhibitory power of his Superego, which is fundamentally so excessively strong in a neurotic criminal.

THE PROBLEM OF RESPONSIBILITY AND THE ROLE OF MEDICAL EXPERT OPINION IN THE COURT

WHAT HAS BEEN SAID TILL NOW PERmits us, we believe, to make bold and enter the Augean stables of philosophy of law and attempt to make a psychological analysis of the concept of responsibility. We shall try to avoid the traditional tying up of the problem with religion and with the philosophical problem of free will. We shall first approach the concept of *responsibility* from the purely psychological point of view.

Psychoanalysis considers the human psychic apparatus as a system which is fully, and without a single gap, determined by psychological and biological causative factors. If we accept this viewpoint, then the religious and philosophical side of the problem of free will becomes a matter of no importance; for human acts are determined and overdetermined by a host of conscious and unconscious motives. What is usually called "free will" is equivalent to the conscious motives found in the Ego. These conscious motives are in themselves very complex derivations of unconscious, instinctual motives, which only after having passed a series of various psychic censorships became capable of entering consciousness; the recognition of this fact might enable us, perhaps, to throw some light on the problem of free will.

Even in the case of a normal, healthy person one can find that the motives which appear right to the Ego, and which are capable of becoming conscious, are not always victorious; that is to say, they are by no means always the decisive moments for a given act; many other motives, mostly unconscious, affect them and frequently even thwart them. The best proof of our contention may be found in our slips of the tongue and other forms of involuntary mistakes; consciously we intend to say or do one thing, but a different impulse comes from the unconscious and we say or do another thing, which betrays not our conscious but our unconscious intentions. We believe that the concept of free will is an expression of the narcissistic wish, or even the postulate of the moralists that the Superego does, or should rule, supreme and unlimited in the psychic apparatus of man; the believers in free will claim that man always had a free choice between good and evil; this idea of free choice is the foundation of the concept of responsibility; when we act wrongly we are responsible for the wrong, for we could have acted rightly if we had chosen to. This would be true if the actual constellations of psychological forces were different from what they are. The constellation of psychological forces that determine a given act depends in reality on the total life history of the given individual and his constitution. If he had a different father, a different bringing up, had he drunk one glass of beer less before he started, his act would have ended differently. The free will, of which moralists and philosophers tell us, represents not only an expression of a one-sided understanding of our conscious motives; it also presupposes the existence of a moral force which floats about freely in this world and which is capable of influencing our mental life at any given moment, and which at the same time leads a free life, independent of any influences.

A purely empirical, psychological answer to the quest of free will could be formulated as follows: A given human act is determined or conditioned by a host of factors and not by a single one; it is over-determined. Besides the purely physiologic determinants, we know of three dynamic psychological systems which are active within the human psychic apparatus; the Ego, the Superego and the Id. Each one of these systems contributes its share dynamically to any given act. The actions of normal individuals are resultants of the following process: the dynamic instinctual forces of the Id are brought into harmony with the dominating motives of the Ego, so that the Ego and Superego are joined into an important unitary system. In pathological states, however, the influence of the conscious Ego is curtailed in favor of the unconscious instinctual motivations.

The concept of responsibility thus acquires a purely *practical* meaning. The conscious Ego is that part of the psychic apparatus which assures contact with the outside world. Consequently, it is also that part of the human personality which we, as a rule, try to influence when we come in contact with our fellow-men. We try to do this when we reproach them or praise them, when we ask something of them or when we make them a promise, when we forbid or allow a given thing. In this sense, we may for practical purposes hold the individual responsible for his acts; that is to say, we assume an attitude as if the conscious Ego actually possessed the power to do what it wishes. Such an attitude has no theoretical foundation, but it has a practical, or still better, a tactical justification. For instance, the mayor holds his police commissioner fully responsible for the city traffic; from the practical (educational) viewpoint it is reasonable, but from the theoretical standpoint it is absurd; for the police commissioner cannot be considered actually guilty for each neglect of a traffic policeman or for each traffic accident. Yet it is the duty of the police commissioner to maintain law and order in the city, and in order to bring it about more effectively the mayor must hold him as fully responsible as possible. Freud remarked once that one may postulate that man is responsible even for his dreams, i.e., for his unconscious wishes. When asked whether we must bear responsibility for our dreams, Freud answered: "Who else can take over this responsibility?" After all, the individual himself is closer to his own unconscious than anyone else, even though one perceives one's self very distant from and foreign to it.

Psychoanalysis makes it possible for the individual to increase the scope of power of his conscious Ego, extending it into regions where only the unconscious reigned heretofore. The founder of psychoanalysis has thus a right to impose on us the responsibility for the unconscious, because he made it possible for man to gain the upper hand over the unconscious by means of the conscious part of his personality. Hence, society, before imposing responsibility, ought first give the transgressor of the law the opportunity of being able to assume the practical responsibility for his actions; this can be achieved only if society would first treat psychoanalytically those transgressors who are, more than the normal individual, under the influence of their unconscious trends. Only after one has been psychoanalyzed may one be considered responsible for his dreams; only then may one consider the neurotic responsible for his symptoms, and the neurotic criminal answerable for his actions. As long as the unconscious remains isolated from the conscious and thus leads an independent existence, as it were, it remains a more or less autonomous power; in its relationship to the conscious Ego it is then similar to those functions of our body which cannot be influenced by our conscious will.

The practical concept of responsibility can thus be replaced by the *scientific* concept of the degree and mode of *participation of the Ego in a given act*. Only the definite knowledge of the degree of this Ego participation should be considered the decisive factor in the choice of our methods of dealing with the given criminal. If one would insist on the use of the term "responsibility," we may say that an individual can be held responsible for his action only in so far as his conscious Ego took part in it. This would mean, then, that by means of warning, explanation, punishments, or threats, we may succeed in influencing the future behavior of a given criminal only in so far as his conscious Ego has influence on his behavior. We must bear in mind that the effect of education on the unconscious part of the personality is lasting only in children; in cases of adults, only psycho-analytical treatment can produce the same results. If we are to expect a lasting effect of the measures which are taken against the criminal, we will have to produce some definite changes in the structure of the criminal's Ego. The mere punishment of a criminal is, as a matter of principle, equivalent to the burning of the hysterical women or men in mediæval times. When psychiatrists of the older school, like Aschaffenburg,[1] supporting the principle of atonement that dominates our justice today, continue to believe that even in cases of limited responsibility, like in hysterical personalities, punishment has a therapeutic effect, then we must recall that punishment gratifies the need of punishment under which the neurotic labors, and thus may produce at times a certain temporary and purely symptomatic improvement; however, the fundamental disorder within the personality will remain untouched by punishment; the personality can be cured by punishment to the same extent that a chronic kidney disease can be cured by aspirin, although the secondary symptom of the illness, headaches, may very well be relieved for a time by the drug. Thus, to consider punishment a therapeutic measure is equivalent to the treatment of symptoms and not of actual diseases; such a method of treatment succeeds only in blurring the picture of the illness; it is a method that contradicts the best trend of modern medicine, which insists on the treatment of the causes and not the symptoms of a given disease.

In the light of the knowledge provided by psychoanalysis, the present-day legal definitions of complete or limited responsibility are indeed untenable. To cite but one instance, one may point out Paragraph 51 of the German penal code, which was conceived in full ignorance of the role the unconscious psychic processes play in the development of criminal-

---

[1] Aschaffenburg, *op. cit.*

ity. This paragraph first admits that those who commit a crime while in a state of unconsciousness or in a state of general psychic disorganization, are not responsible; this principle is applicable only to the comparatively rare cases of epileptic or hysterical twilight states, or to cases of severest intoxications.

The reference made by the same Paragraph 51 to pathological states, in which the individual's free will is impaired, has no scientific meaning; for there is no free will in the common sense of the word; we must remember that unconscious mental processes may and do affect our conscious motives and decisions, and, therefore, in every individual act a variable degree of influences coming from the unconscious is inevitably present. Moreover, not only pathological states, but also acute emotional states, may at times quite considerably impair the individual's capacity of exercising his so-called free will. Thus it is clear that only borderline cases of severe mental diseases are covered by the article mentioned above; yet these cases play a relatively unimportant part in practical criminology. The modern medico-legal expert, who follows only the traditional forensic psychiatry, is unable to find any exact formulation of limitation of responsibility, except for the few and extreme cases of the type covered by Paragraph 51. It appears, then, that the chief task of a modern medico-legal expert becomes reduced to nothing more than the making of a diagnosis of epilepsy or any other severe mental illness, when such a diagnosis is warranted by clinical facts.

Of recent years some attempts were made to mitigate the absurdity of this state of affairs; thus, when a case definitely shows pathological mental characteristics and yet permits of no definite psychiatric diagnosis, the vague concept of psychopathic personality is applied and the case is therefore considered not entirely responsible.

All such attempts scientifically to delimit the cases in question by way of introduction of such psychological concepts as "limited responsibility," provide us with little means for a clear understanding of the individual case, for these con-

cepts are created without the consideration of unc
mental processes. Theoretically speaking, every hui
ing's responsibility is limited, because no human act ...per-
formed under the full control of the conscious Ego. We
must, therefore, always evaluate the *quantitative* distribution
of conscious and unconscious motivations of every given act.
Only such evaluation will provide us with definite criteria
for purposes of diagnosis, or of sentencing, or of any other
measure which we might consider necessary to take in regard
to a given act. The task of the judge of the future will be
the establishment of such a psychological diagnosis; the
measures resulting from such a diagnosis will, therefore, be
founded on the psychological understanding of the criminal.
Rational measures are impossible without such a psychological understanding; why, for instance, should a pickpocket, who steals a watch, be sentenced for one or two years
imprisonment? This type of sentence is based neither on
empirical experience nor on psychological considerations. It
is clear, therefore, that in order to acquire any meaning at
all, such a paragraph as Paragraph 51 of the German penal
code should not continue to be limited definitely to a very
small number of borderline cases, but should be based on
the broad considerations of the whole problem of criminological diagnosis; otherwise the coöperation of the medico-
legal expert with the court is of little value. Such a psychological criminological diagnosis, i.e., the evaluation of the
relative parts played in a given criminal act by the conscious
Ego and by the unconscious, would have to become in the
future the chief task of the court and the medico-legal expert;
in other words, it will present the very basis of each court
procedure before sentence is imposed. It would be simple to
choose a correct sentence if the diagnostic investigation be
correctly done.

We doubt whether the medico-legal expert of today, who
is trained only along purely medical lines, will ever be able
to make such psychological diagnosis as we have described
above. On the other hand, the judge of today who is totally
unfamiliar with deeper psychology is just as little fit for the

task as the medico-legal expert. As matters stand now, in doubtful cases the judge expects some enlightenment from the physician, which the latter is unable to give him. We shall remark in passing that the more we learn to sense the psychology of the criminal the more numerous become the so-called doubtful cases.

We do not believe that the physician, his equipment being what it is, can find much that is of value to him in the court-room; too, we do not believe that the task of the medico-legal expert of the future will be to teach the judge the psychology of the criminal. Psychoanalysis should be one of the most important parts of the technical equipment of the *judge* himself; he, himself, must be the *expert* in the understanding of human behavior.

The concept of "limited responsibility" shows quite clearly how fluid and indefinite the concepts normal and abnormal, sick or healthy, are in problems of social, as well as of any other nature. We consider an individual sick when, despite a completely developed intelligence and judgment, he lives and acts under constant pressure of unconscious motives, which are not accessible to his conscious Ego; that individual is sick who is unable to change his behavior even when he himself condemns his actions and sincerely wishes to change his behavior, and is yet unable to do so even when he is punished. In order to understand the behavior of such an individual it is necessary to be in possession of the same knowledge as that which is needed for the understanding of the normal individual, the knowledge of the psychic apparatus. The judge who is called upon to understand human behavior, and judge it, ought to be able to understand clearly the healthy as well as the pathological transgressor of the law. He will need in the future, as he does in the present, the help of the medical expert in cases where the psychic disturbance is a result of organic disease. However, the cases which present-day forensic medicine considers borderline cases, and as only partially responsible, are very numerous and of enormous practical importance; no organic pathological processes can be found in these cases; they present pathological conditions of social adjustment, i.e., disturbances within the psychic apparatus. To make a proper diagnosis, i.e., to understand and evaluate the transgressor of the law, is the supreme task of the judge; if he is unable to perform this task without the help of medical experts, then he is probably unable to understand and judge any human action.

We should not wish, however, to give the impression that we are overoptimistic, we do not believe that the *official recognition of the unconscious* will take place in the near future, for the human being is so constituted that he finds it unbearable to recognize, not only the content of the unconscious, but even the mere fact that along with conscious motives, inaccessible and unknown psychological forces are constantly at work within him. One should not underestimate the fact that man fears his own instinctual life, and that the conscious Ego has the narcissistic aim of appearing to be the only master in his own house.

We are reminded of the many experiments with post-hypnotic suggestions, which were carried out years ago; psychoanalysis was unknown then; it was very striking to see how the individual who, while in a hypnotic state, was ordered to perform certain things, would then come out of the hypnotic state and carry out the orders, and then attempt to rationalize the suggested actions and explain them as his own. Thus, for instance, it was suggested to a woman in a hypnotic state that one hour after awakening she should leave her room, go downstairs, turn around as if to return to her room, and only then turn around again and leave her house. In her waking state she was, of course, unaware of the orders which she received while under hypnosis, but at the appointed hour she carried out the orders which had been given her when she was in hypnotic sleep; as she was leaving her house she was asked why she was going away and she instantly responded: "I must go to see my seamstress." When she was asked why she turned around on the stairway, she stated that she had forgotten her handkerchief. Actually something was driving her from within to act in a certain

way, but she did not know it and rationalized. Many transgressors of the law act in a similar fashion; the criminal
commits a crime precipitated by unconscious motives which
are unknown to him; then he goes on and invents and re-
constructs in perfectly good faith a number of motivations,
which he presents to the judge in order to "explain" his acts
to the court as well as to himself. Some criminals make a
number of contradictory statements at various stages of their
trial. They do this most frequently, not because they wish to
appear in the best light possible, but because they do not
know the most active unconscious motives for their crime
and, therefore, they keep on groping for some conscious
motivation and find themselves compelled to invent one at
every cross-examination.

The prosecuting attorney is right when he assumes that
the lawbreaker *does not* at first tell the truth; he *does lie,* but
he is often driven to tell lies by the same necessity as the
individual who is carrying out a post-hypnotic suggestion; he
must invent untrue motivations for his action, since the true
ones are hidden from him, buried in his unconscious; man
is never willing to admit that he may act at times without
conscious intentions. And yet the various lies and contradictions which are brought to light at a court trial are not infrequently taken as a proof of the suspect's dishonesty, spite
and craftiness. All members and attendants of the court of
justice are unwilling to recognize anything but conscious
motivations; therefore, when investigating a crime they look
only for these motives, as the only ones which are capable of
furnishing a rational explanation of the crime. One finds
judge, prosecuting attorney and even the suspect all in complete agreement and alliance on this point; faithful members
of a conceited humanity, they are unaware of their own
deepest weaknesses; they strive to appear the real sovereign
masters in the realm of their own personalities; yet unawares
they fall extremely short of this sovereignty. So it comes to
pass that occasionally when a criminal is asked by the court,
"Why did you do this or that?" he answers with a sort of

resignation, "I do not know"; such an answer appears to offend everybody's self-respect and no one believes these words; yet often these are the only sincere and true words pronounced during a trial. For man, the crown of creation, insists that he *must* know what he does and *why* he does it. It is to be borne in mind that, the more the civilized man of the Western world learned to master the forces of nature, the more he lost knowledge of his own self; having become master over space and time, he finds it so offensive to his self-respect to be called upon to admit that he *is* the slave of his unconscious instinctual life.

In contradistinction to the oriental fatalistic philosophy, the Western theory of the freedom of the will is a typical product of man's life-long denial of his inner weakness; and the greater this weakness, the stronger the striving to deny it. That is why the illusion of free will is so indispensable to our technical, materialistic civilization. In this illusion man finds a substitute for that power over his own inner life, which he had still possessed to a great extent during the Middle Ages, but which he lost.

Those who accept psychoanalysis accept and recognize the power of the unconscious; such recognition, however, signifies not a denial of, or a bowing to, the unconscious forces; it is instead the first step toward the real mastery of them. The reformation of our whole penal system is possible only when approached from this angle. If the existence of unconscious motivations of human actions is recognized, then medical treatment and education will naturally take the place of punishment. The illusion of free will and the institution of punishment present the two most powerful tools in the policy of repression to which modern man is addicted; he prefers to accept responsibility blindly, and permits himself to be punished rather than to recognize the power which his own unconscious has over him. Law statutes, judges, prosecuting attorneys, defending attorneys, medical experts and criminals themselves are all united in mutual support of this work of repression.

THE PART PLAYED BY THE EGO IN VARIOUS

MENTAL PROCESSES AND IN CRIME

THE EGO EXPERIENCES A CONSTANT PRESsure on the part of anti-social tendencies; this is true even of the socially adjusted individual; a number of psychic processes bear proof that these anti-social tendencies seek expression in a variety of ways; at times the expression of a phantastic or hallucinatory nature suffices.

The study and subsequent understanding of dreams, daydreams, wit, slips of the tongue and other mistakes, met with in everyday life, permitted Freud to establish the fact that the unconscious forces of the Id, which play such an important role in neurotic symptom formation, are also found at active play in the normal individual.

These unconscious forces, while presenting a definite criminal trend, are not infrequently brought to expression, but under a guise which is not prejudicial to society; the form of expression in such cases has only a subjective meaning; objectively it does not appear as socially detrimental. In other words, the unconscious trends may be and, as we shall see, actually are of the same psychological content as those of a real criminal; they differ from those of a real criminal only in one respect; instead of breaking through into definite anti-social acts, they are gratified by means of phantasy only; only the various slips and mistakes, the various minor acts, which come from carelessness, the apparent "accidents" of everyday life, which every one of us experiences, present a transition from phantasy to action. At times these are met with in criminal practice; they are known as crime committed as a result of carelessness.

It is characteristic for the dynamic inhibitory power of the Superego, that even the apparently harmless phantastic presentations of our anti-social tendencies, which appear in dreams, are shrouded in a guise that conceals their real meaning from the conscious Ego. In most of the cases the manifest dream content appears to be either beyond suspicion or unintelligible, while the latent content of such dreams either presents a definite criminal trend or has, at any rate, a definite meaning that has been rejected by the Ego. The normal individual, who is socially well adjusted, does not permit himself even in dreams to think that he has criminal tendencies.

The investigation of the dream life of man yielded highly valuable results for the understanding of neuroses. As a matter of fact, dreams are the most direct source of our knowledge of neuroses. If we wish to visualize the unconscious criminality which is universal, and if we are to obtain some light on the origin of criminality, we must have a definite understanding of the mechanisms of dream work.

Psychoanalysis of a Dream Containing a Concealed Criminal Wish

A middle-aged man, father of a family, an exceptionally kind-hearted person, who characterized himself as a man who *never* was able to hurt even a fly, while under analysis, brought the following dream:

> "I am taking a walk with one of the ranking officers of the Russian army. I become aware that it is the Tsar. Suddenly a stranger with a sword appears and wants to kill the Tsar. I want to jump in between the stranger and the Tsar to save the latter, but it is too late; the Tsar is killed."

In accordance with the technique of psychoanalysis, the dream, in order to be analyzed, is broken up into separate parts and the dreamer is asked to tell what comes to his mind when reminded of those parts separately. By means of this method one succeeds in reconstructing the dream work, i.e., the process of concealing the original repressed dream content. The original ideas, which are concealed under cover of the manifest content, can thus be brought to light, because the various parts of the dream, taken separately, appear to the dreamer quite innocuous; only in their relationship to one another do they represent the forbidden wish. The dream, we must remember, is a compromise between the drive to bring to an hallucinatory expression a certain repressed trend, and the pressure exerted by the psychic forces which try to repress the trend and to conceal it from the Ego. By means of free associations to various isolated parts of a dream, one is able to see more clearly what the unconscious seeks to express; only the meaning of the dream, as a whole, is concealed, not the unconscious presentation of an isolated part of the dream, which is torn away from the rest of the content. All this will become clearer when we return to the dream cited above.

Associations to the Dream

Tsar: "Tsar is called by the Russians 'little father'—father."

Officer of the Russian Army: "During the World War I used to shoot at Russians. It seems *strange* to me to think that I was then capable of such cruelty, for in normal life I'd never kill a fly. When not advancing, there existed between us and the Russians a silent agreement: we would not shoot at one another unless there was general fighting; we would calmly look at one another so frequently that we knew some of our enemies quite well. I cannot understand why, despite all this, I used to shoot at those Russians with particular cruelty, especially during these periods of quiet on the front.

I thought that the Russians wanted to kill our wives and children, and therefore my behavior was justified."

Stranger: The patient hesitated to give any association to the word "stranger." Nothing would come to his mind. He stated repeatedly that he did not know who the stranger was. He was then told that the stranger in the dream might mean no stranger at all, but the patient himself; i.e., by the stranger the patient tried to present the *strange* part of his own personality which commits murder. It was also pointed out to him that he already used the word "strange" when he described how unlike his kind character it was to shoot at the Russians. The patient protested violently and answered: "How could it be myself when in the dream I tried to save the Tsar?"

It was then explained to him that he himself was the sovereign author of the dream and, therefore, he could have successfully saved the Tsar, if he had really wished to. Thus, in his waking state when made to face the murder wish, which was presented in the dream, the patient made use of the same hypocritical maneuver as he used in his dream, i.e., he emphasized the gesture he made supposedly to save the Tsar.

Two mechanisms were utilized by this patient in order to conceal his murder wish.

(1) He chose a stranger to represent one part of his personality; i.e., he utilized the mechanism of projection and at the same time represented to some extent the true state of affairs, for the murder wish was actually foreign to his Ego, which was moral and sensitive; however, when in war this wish to kill could be gratified without a sense of guilt, he did gratify it.

(2) In addition, he concealed his criminal wish by means of a hypocritical gesture; he "tried" to save his victim; this is an overcompensation; the latter served the purpose of quieting his Superego and thus enabling him to carry out his murder wish undisturbed.

The object of this murder wish is concealed in his dream

more thoroughly than any other element. What takes place in the dream is not a simple murder, but the murder of the father. Already, in the beginning of the dream, the Russian officer became the Tsar; then by way of association, Tsar, "little father," father, the patient thought of his own father. This last association was able to enter the patient's consciousness at the very beginning of the analysis of this dream, because it appeared quite innocuous, since he was not yet at the moment aware that the stranger was the patient himself; did he not appear in the manifest dream content as the man who tried to save the Tsar?

This dream is a good example of how extraordinarily and carefully one is able to conceal one's latent murder wishes. The dreamer himself does not do any killing; he tries to save; the fact that the patient himself is the murderer is thus totally denied. But this does not quite satisfy him; in order to assure himself that he will be considered free of any suspicion, he puts a former enemy in place of his own father; this is the mechanism of displacement. Molded into this form the dream easily passed the censorship of the Superego, no matter how definitely it represented the murder of his father.

*   *   *   *   *

The *dream* then, like the *neurotic symptom,* represents a purely intrapsychic outlet for our anti-social tendencies, an outlet to which the outside world is naturally indifferent. The Ego participates in the formation of the dream only in so far as it utilizes its inhibitory capacity, in order to disguise the real meaning of the dream, and also in so far as it finds expression for its moral reaction (tendency to punishment, moral overcompensation, etc.) .

The transition from dream or neurotic symptom to action is presented by certain *daydreams;* in them the phantasy of the individual roves freely and revels not infrequently in criminal ideas, the realization of which is practically impossible. The schoolboy thus beats the teacher who annoys him; the soldier curses his superior officer and kills him off for his severity; the married man commits adultery; in short, every single individual creates for himself a phantasy as an outlet for his forbidden wishes.

If we compare the daydream with the dream in sleep, we find that the daydream represents characteristically not so much the behavior which the individual himself inwardly forbids himself, but rather those wishes that the individual would carry out in reality were he not afraid of real consequences. That is to say, that the daydreamer admits the presence of those wishes, but is, however, unable to carry them out. Thus, while the dream expresses the unconscious criminality of man, the daydream demonstrates his actual criminal propensities. The daydream being only a phantasy, the individual permits this phantasy to reach the full expression of that criminality of which the daydreamer would have been actually capable, if he were not afraid of the consequences.

While modern justice considers that thoughts may enter our minds free of duty, as it were, we may recall that, under the *corpus juris canonici,* people could have been brought to answer before the court for their forbidden thoughts.

As has been said, the Ego functions in the dream and in the formation of the neurotic symptom as an inhibitory agency, excludes the latent wishes from consciousness, and also prevents their direct motor expression; in the formation of daydreams the Ego takes quite an active part, but as far as motor expression is concerned, it keeps the forbidden wishes in check. It is difficult to say what part the Ego takes in slips of the tongue and various "accidental" acts; for the conscious Ego usually controls the motor expression of ideas; slips of the tongue and action, presenting as they do a motor activity directed to the outside world, could not actually be performed without some sort of participation of the Ego. One could say that the pictures of our dreams and the spontaneous flow of daydreams go on rather freely, the Ego being relatively powerless to prevent the process; the sovereign domain of the Ego is first of all the control of the innervations of our voluntary musculature; in the case of slips of the tongue and action, it does appear, however, as if the unconscious trends had become transformed into action by way of some short circuit, avoiding the influence of the Ego; the latter could be reproached, as it were, for not having fulfilled its function, in that it had failed to interfere where it could. The usual excuse offered by those who make a slip is that they "paid no attention" to what they were doing or saying; they were tired, distracted, upset, or preoccupied with other thoughts, and were therefore unable to think, etc. These excuses are well founded. The Ego was actually preoccupied with other things and that is the reason why it was unable to repress the trend which was coming up from the unconscious; it was unable to check its motor expression. Thus we may conclude that slips of the tongue and action usually take place when the impulse coming from the unconscious part of the personality catches the Ego unawares and breaks through to action. When we compare an accidental crime, i.e., a slip which results in a criminal act (manslaughter) with other crimes, we shall find that the characteristic thing about the former is that the Ego in such cases does not participate actively; that is why the mechanisms, which tend to win over the Ego, and which we shall describe later, are not utilized. The Ego, in such cases, is merely overcome by heretofore repressed tendencies; this happens at a special moment, which is characteristic for this psychological accident. We shall recall that when the Ego finds itself suddenly weak (over-fatigue, distractibility), when it is preoccupied with a specially difficult task and is thus concentrated on one special point, then many slips of the tongue and action occur; the Ego has, as a matter of fact, a double function; it is the perceptive apparatus, which keeps contact with reality, and at the same time it fulfills the function of keeping in contact with our inner life, keeping our instinctive life under control. The Ego fulfills best this double function of a perceptive organ, whose business it is to keep account of both outer and inner impressions, when it keeps our motor apparatus under its full control; only those instinctual demands are granted the right to expression which are in harmony with the demands of reality; when one of the two parts of its perceptive function is especially taxed, the other becomes less complete; it is impossible to watch simultaneously, and with the same efficiency, both our outer and inner lives; that is why one may perform many slips when one is concentrated on something outside himself, and, reversely, one is unable to observe the outer world as sharply as usual when one's interest happens to be directed inwards. The speaker, for instance, who concentrates intensely on the content of his speech will easily make a slip of the tongue, which will thus give expression to an unconscious trend; the distracted, learned professor, who is absorbed in his own thoughts, drops for a while the testing of outer reality and performs a fabulous number of slips, which become the theme of numerous funny stories. In short, whenever especially preoccupied with either reality testing or with the control of inner impulses, the Ego becomes relatively weaker than when it functions in an atmosphere of normal equilibrium. Its active participation in the performance of a given slip or mistake is small; it merely reduces its watchfulness for a moment and thus permits the Id tendencies to break through. The sin of omission is of great importance to reality, for unlike the dream, symptom, or daydream, a slip may carry with it serious consequences. It is supposed that the law punishes only the bad mistakes, which are the result of carelessness (lack of attention), but the real punishment is at times severer than simple lack of attention would warrant. It appears clear that people feel the unconscious intention of the careless person and they react affectively in a manner as if they actually wish to strike at this unconscious trend, by means of the severe punishment. In other words, the unconscious of the criminal is taken into account; in other cases, however, as in the case of the neurotic criminal, the suspect is hardly given any credit for the hopeless battle which his conscious personality leads against his own anti-social tendencies; and yet in other cases the law fails to take into account the moral attitude of the unconscious, the unconscious need of punishment.

We thus see that the ignorance of the relative participation of the conscious Ego and of the unconscious in a given crime should cause a great deal of confusion; the criminal, under these circumstances, receives hardly any rational treatment at the hands of the law; he appears to be a prey of the irrational unconscious reactions of his judges.

The accidental crimes belong to those few criminal cases, to whom a severer attitude than that accorded to them by juristic theory would be practically justified. In practice, the judge behaves often as if he actually knew well Freud's theory of the unconscious motivation of the slips and mistakes; however, only the precise knowledge of psychodynamics of all criminal cases would bring both law and the practice of it into one harmonious whole; only such knowledge would free the judges of affective, subjective reactions, and would permit a rational treatment of the criminal.

When we now turn to the consideration of those antisocial acts which are carried out in reality, we shall have to admit that the Ego participates in such acts much more actively than in dreams, daydreams, or everyday mistakes; yet, even in these cases, one could establish a scale which would indicate the degree to which the Ego participates in a given act.

The lowest place on that scale will then be taken by the *neurotic criminal,* who acts under the strong pressure of unconscious motives.

The characteristic thing about the *neurotic criminal* is that he identifies himself only partly with the criminal act he commits. Not infrequently he rejects the crime unconsciously, and this rejection is brought to light through irrational self-injury, which serves the purpose of self-punishment. His Superego forbids the neurotic criminal to commit the crime, yet by means of a complex chain of intrapsychic processes, which we shall consider later in detail, the bond between the Ego and Superego is loosened and thus a criminal act becomes possible. In some cases of neurotic criminality one can see clearly that the transgressions are of a compulsive nature. These criminals are very similar to the individuals who suffer from a compulsive neurosis. The compulsion appears to the conscious personality as something foreign, the Ego perceives the impulse and despite that it perceives it as something foreign, it is unable to stop it from motor expression. Kleptomania, pyromania, compulsive lying, and betrayal, belong to this type of crime. These cases which cause doubt and misunderstanding in the minds of many of the medical and legal profession, present a transition between a real neurosis and neurotic criminality. The degree to which the Ego participates in the acts of such individuals is only slightly greater than in the case of slips of the tongue and action. In the case of the latter, the Ego shuts its eyes, as it were; it is preoccupied with other things; in the case of a compulsive neurosis the *perceptive power* of the Ego remains intact, but its inhibitory power is paralyzed. Despite the fact that it perceives the impulse and rejects it as something foreign to it, it is unable to suppress the carrying out of this impulse.

However, the majority of neurotic criminals show that their Ego participates to quite a high degree in the carrying out of their actions; in this they are to some extent like the criminals whose crimes are committed with full awareness of what they are doing, for the Ego of the neurotic criminal accepts the crime *at the moment when the crime is being committed*. It is to be noted that this type of criminal acts impulsively; the influence of unconscious motives on his action is much stronger than in the case of a normal individual, and he is therefore unable to give a very definite account as to why he committed a given crime. The Ego is not fully torn away from the social part of the personality; there are trends within the Ego of the neurotic criminal which, even though unconscious, try to oppose the criminal act. The loosening of the dependence between Ego and Superego and the submission of the Ego to the leadership of the Id is accomplished by means of psychic mechanisms, which are similar to those operative in the formation of a neurotic symptom; these mechanisms remain concealed from the conscious personality of the neurotic criminal. We shall later examine more closely these mechanisms by means of which the Ego is won over in favor of the criminal act. It will then become clear that even in those cases where the Ego appears to be totally in favor of the crime, many unconscious processes brought about this very labile acceptance of the act by the Ego. The Ego allows itself to be turned in favor of the crime and tries to justify itself by means of the same mechanisms which we know from the general theory of the neuroses: rationalization, projections, self-punishment, etc.

We may sum up by saying that the individual who makes a slip of the tongue or action, the person who suffers from compulsions and the neurotic criminal, all have one part of their personality taking the side of society; they are inclined to ally themselves with their Superego rather than with their Id; only certain of their psychic processes, which are to a greater or lesser extent outside the control of consciousness, permit some of the tendencies of the Id to break through and find motor expression. In the normal criminal, however, the whole conscious personality takes the side of the criminal act, facing with a combative attitude all the social demands of the community.

In the normal individual, who commits a crime under special circumstances, and particularly in a state of affect, the active participation of the Ego in this crime is not smaller than in the case of a normal criminal; at the moment of the criminal act the whole Ego is identified with the act, but this psychological state is acute, accidental; it is brought about by some influence of the outside world, while the Ego of the normal criminal is chronically allied with the Id tendencies.

The results arrived at on the basis of facts, which heretofore have been considered, thus lead us to the conclusion that there exists in all human beings a large reservoir of anti-social or criminal drives, that all human beings have the tendency to carry out these anti-social or criminal wishes, that the various forms of outlet for these drives or wishes are determined by the degree to which the Ego of a given individual frees itself from the Superego and puts itself in the service of the instinctual demands, the Superego being the representative of social demands within the individual himself.

Thus the degree to which the Ego takes part in the criminality of a given individual, may serve as a basis for classification of criminality. The following scale could be grossly established; it is arranged on the basis of the increasing participation of the Ego in the criminal act:

Criminality in phantasy	Dreams, neurotic symptoms, daydreams.
Slips or mistakes resulting in crime	A transition to a fully expressed criminal act.
Compulsive acts	
Impulsive acting out accompanied by an inner conflict	The neurotic criminal.
Criminality resulting from an affective state or a special situation	Normal individuals.
Criminality without inner conflict	The normal criminal.

Excluded from the above classification remain those criminal cases who, as a result of organic disease or of toxic states, show a criminality with either a limited or no participation of the Ego.

GENERAL MECHANISMS OF CRIMINALITY

WE CAME TO THE CONCLUSION THAT, with the exception of the normal criminal, any individual commits a crime because the Ego's dependence on the inhibiting Superego becomes weak and is thus able to give in to the tendencies of the Id, which seeks motor expression. The psychological meaning of the process in which the Ego loses its dependence on the Superego and takes the side of the Id tendencies, can best be understood if we use as a point of departure those psychological situations in which even the normal individual feels freed from his usual moral inhibitions.

The extreme case of self-defense has already been mentioned; in this case the Ego feels freed from the necessity of sparing the life of another human being, since the one who attacks puts himself outside the law by threatening another person's life. The psychological situation in the case when the sense of justice is injured, is similar to the case of self-defense; it leads to rebellion and to the breaking through of primitive anti-social drives; one feels oneself threatened by the very authorities whose business it is to uphold the law. We saw that the Superego of adults is more or less dependent upon the individual's relation to those in authority; if the latter, by their injustice, destroy the confidence one has in them, the Ego at once loses its dependence on the inner representative of authority—the Superego.

In each of the two cases, in self-defense and in the case of injury to the sense of justice, suffering is either inflicted upon the Ego, is either threatened with suffering or suffering is directly inflicted upon it; this lifts the moral inhibitions. We already know that moral inhibitions originated, on one hand, by way of avoidance of pain and, on the other hand, by way of expectation that a certain pleasure will be gained in the future. It is quite natural, therefore, to see that a very great pain caused by the obedience of one's inhibition is able to lift these very inhibitions. To obey one's moral inhibitions at a critical moment, when self-defense is required, would be pure self-destruction. We must bear in mind that we became morally minded in order to live, i.e., in order to avoid extreme pain. In the above-mentioned critical situation, morality thus loses any sense; therefore it is discarded. The same is true of justified rebellion; those conditions under which the inhibiting power of the Superego were established cease at first to exist. The fear of pain, and compensation in the form of being loved, the two elements which form the basis for the existence of moral prohibitions, lose their inhibitory power whenever one is treated wrongly; to continue to submit to the law would, under the circumstances, mean only more suffering and no compensation for this deprivation. If it is true that the fear of pain (punishment) and the hope of being loved are the two basic psychological factors which move the Ego to the restriction of its anti-social tendencies, then it is quite easy to understand that an effective suffering, which is greater than the expected punishment, makes those two factors quite ineffective. If the suffering is too great, then even the compensation of being loved is not adequate; this is true not only of the relation of the individual to concrete people, but also of his relation to his own Superego.

These relations could be formulated in the following way:

When the Ego finds that it gains nothing from following the moral principles of the community, these principles are dropped; when one suffers under the circumstances, one's fear of punishment becomes smaller; one's Ego has nothing to lose. The greater the suffering, the weaker the dependence of the Ego on the Superego and on the powers that be; this is especially true when the suffering is caused by these powers. The threat of punishment has a sobering effect on the individual's instinctual impulses; the suffering itself, however, i.e., the suffering through punishment, has the effect of making the individual feel freer; for punishment means nothing but suffering. The suffering Ego has nothing more to lose and, therefore, when under the pressure of suffering the Ego tends to rise with courage or despair against the painful restrictions which are imposed on it, it tends to set itself free only in order to respond to the demands of the primitive tendencies of the Id.

The neurotic individual and the neurotic criminal present, respectively, the state of suffering and the state of rebellion; they free themselves from moral inhibitions. They deliberately, even though unconsciously, always bring about a state of affairs which, if it came about naturally, would have freed even the normal individual from moral inhibitions; that is, they bring about a situation which appears to justify their giving in to the demands of the Id, i.e., of their antisocial tendencies. Such situations are brought about in one of two ways; either the given individuals lead on the authorities to commit an injustice, or their own Superego is led to become extremely severe, i.e., unjust. If the child succeeds by means of clever provocation in making the parents or the teacher punish it too severely, then its Ego rebels and takes a free hand in giving in to the tendencies of the Id. When one is treated too severely one might at best be afraid of another punishment, and thus inhibit his instinctual impulses, but the inner, moral self-inhibition is lost.

In the case of a neurosis, a part of the symptoms serve the purpose of this maneuver of self-liberation, for symptoms play the role of both self-punishment and self-restriction. In the case of a neurotic criminal, the punishment which is actually meted out to him, and the difficult life situations into which such individuals get themselves unconsciously, but intentionally, play the same role of weakening the power of the Superego over the Ego.

One of the most significant forms which this exclusion of

the inhibitory influence of the Superego takes, is the projection of the sense of guilt which the neurotic criminal resorts to. This mechanism plays the most important role also in paranoid psychoses.

In a neurosis the suffering is brought about autoplastically, i.e., by means of symptoms; when the sense of guilt is projected, then the individual falsifies reality and becomes fixed in his belief that the world treats him badly. Reality is then misinterpreted in such a way that the sick Ego actually believes that it is in a critical situation, which justifies measures of self-defense; the guilty one then considers himself the victim and he considers the offended persons as the guilty ones.

In this situation, which is artificially created by the individual, a definite emotional state is created which the Ego considers as right and as fitting to the demands of the moment. Such a sick individual assumes that he is being attacked, or badly treated, or persecuted, or offended, and believes, therefore, that he may defend himself accordingly.

It is characteristic of the mechanism of projection that the motives which the individual ascribes to his opponent are actually motives which operate within the individual himself, but his own Superego rejects them and therefore he is blind to them. Thus the mechanism of projection of guilt represents not only a falsification of outer, but also of the inner reality. This falsification is brought about under the pressure of the Id tendencies, which can come, therefore, to full uninhibited expression.

Freud was the first to describe this mechanism as operating in the pathological jealousy of the neurotic; this mechanism is of decisive importance in a great number of crimes committed out of jealousy. In these cases, one of the marriage partners displaces onto the other his own unconscious, repressed criminal tendencies which offend his ethical and tender feelings; by means of this displacement he relieves himself of the burden of the sense of guilt; the jealous partner then thinks consciously: "Not I but he (or she) is untrue to me"; this situation, full of conflict, is at times so acute that the most innocent behavior of one partner is misinterpreted by the other in the most insane fashion. As a result of this jealousy, aggressive affects arise which are even more intense than those aroused in the case of actual adultery; too, quite frequently, marriages are broken up as a result of such a jealousy; the breaking up of the marriage signifies a victory of the unconscious adulterous trends of the jealous party, who thus becomes free and may realize these tendencies without any sense of guilt.

Such psychological methods free the Ego from the Superego; this is achieved through the falsification of outer and inner reality; there are also cases in which, as a result of a favorable accident, reality itself meets the Id tendencies halfway and thus even a normal individual might under proper circumstances commit a crime. Adultery may not necessarily remain a matter of phantasy. When one catches the unfaithful partner flagrantly in the act, the pain and the insult thus inflicted upon the Ego, by reality itself, become so intense that all moral qualms may fall by the wayside. The individual, under such circumstances, actually experiences the pain and the insult which the neurotic usually seeks in his phantasies; this may lead to crime. Even the law in such cases readily seeks a way to acquit the accused.

The various psychic processes in which the Ego abandons its dependence on the inhibitory influence of the Superego, have one common trait—intense suffering. There are three ways by which this suffering is brought about; it is experienced:

(1) In reality, without the individual's actual participation in the bringing about of the painful situation.

(2) By means of unconscious, intentional seeking and creating of the painful situation (the neurotic mechanism).

(3) By means of a living out in pure phantasy of a painful situation (the psychotic mechanism).

There is another method by means of which the Ego might be won over to committing an unsocial act—it is *rationaliza-*

tion. By rationalization psychoanalysis means that the Ego selects arbitrarily only those motives which are acceptable to it, and considers them as the only motives for a given anti-social act. There are, of course, a number of other motives which are not acceptable to the Ego and which played an important role in the act, but these are left out. In other words, only those motives which are acceptable to the Ego are singled out from the whole mass of determinants and per-ceived and recognized by our consciousness; the rest of the motives remain in the dark, since those which were perceived by the conscious Ego appear sufficiently to justify the given act.

The snob, for instance, in order to give himself a sense of importance, rationalizes his exclusiveness by emphasizing his great interest in various forms of culture; his cultural gain, however, is much smaller than the satisfaction he gets from his exhibitionism; but his exhibitionistic tendencies are not acceptable to his Ego and he does not want to recognize them. The bored lady of high society who is busy organizing pompous benefit balls will insist that she acts out of sym-pathy for the poor, while in reality this sympathy is much smaller than her wish to obtain some diversion; the latter motive, while being the more dominant motive of her action, she is unwilling to admit, however.

This mechanism of rationalization is found most fre-quently among the political criminals. These create for them-selves a special theory which permits them to give vent to their father-murder impulses in a more or less sublimated form, and without a sense of guilt. Such acts are frequently wrapped in illogical, transparent and threadbare rationaliza-tions. As a result of such rationalizations an innocent prin-cess, who has nothing to do with affairs of the State, might fall a victim to a terroristic act; this shows how our logical thinking, which is a function of the Ego, may be shattered by affects which come from the Id. Rationalization means a displacement of emphasis; behind the conscious motives, which are acceptable to the Ego, important unconscious mo-

tives which are unacceptable to the Ego are kept concealed.
We see and admit only the conscious determinants, and
hence a quantitative falsification of the psychic situation
ensues. The value of the conscious motives becomes over-
estimated, while the unconscious motives which reinforce
the conscious ones are denied.

In certain types of crime the inhibitory function of the
conscious Ego is eliminated by the following means: the
criminal act, like the neurotic symptom, appears to the consciousness of certain criminals as something meaningless.
Such crimes, which are substitutes for other unconsciously
intended acts, might be appropriately called *symptomatic
crimes;* the mechanisms that lead to such crimes are the same
as those which lead to the formation of neurotic symptoms:
displacements, allusions, symbolic equations, etc. Their
psycho-economic function is also the same as that of neurotic
symptoms, since both serve the purpose of relieving the
psychic tension by means of a gratification which remains
disguised and concealed from the conscious Ego.

Such cases represent a transition between criminality and
neuroses, particularly those of the compulsive type. When
lawbreakers of this type are asked to explain the reason for
their transgressions, they usually say that they acted under
an irresistible impulse; they don't know, they say, why they
did this or that; they insist that such transgressions are foreign to their real nature. And it is true, they have no conscious motivations to offer for these acts; the Ego in such
cases watches the transgression with perplexity, and only
afterwards tries to find some sort of a plausible reason for
the act. This attempt to attach to an incomprehensible act
retrospectively a number of plausible motivations is, as has
been already mentioned above, made not only because the
trial judge demands a conscious explanation, but also and
chiefly because the transgressor's own Ego demands it from
him; man does not want to appear in his own eyes a mere
plaything at the hands of his instincts; his own self-respect
demands from him some sort of explanation which would,

at least in some way, save for him his illusion that his conscious personality rules his instinctual drives. Thus, for instance, a notorious kleptomanic girl, who was treated by one of the writers "admitted" to the district attorney that she stole a cheap edition of "Faust" because she hoped some day to become an actress and, therefore, might some day in the future make use of the text. One of the writers, who was called to court as an expert witness and who had treated the delinquent girl before she was brought to trial, had no difficulty in convincing the court that the motivation given by the defendant was not the real one, but that the stealing of the book had a deep symbolic meaning to her and was a disguised expression of repressed, unconscious wishes.

It was interesting to observe how differently the girl behaved before the judge, as compared with her behavior toward the analyst in the course of her treatment. Only while under analysis was she really able to become sincere. She admitted to the physician that she was totally perplexed as to the reasons why she stole; she admitted that she was unable to understand why she acted as she did, she even ventured to wonder whether she acted as she did merely because she wanted to gratify an acquisitive desire. She had to reject this hypothesis, however, because it failed to explain why she preferred to steal simple pictures presenting a mother and child, while other apparently more valuable pictures failed to interest her; too, she frequently experienced certain aggressive feelings against those from whom she stole; she thought that these emotions might have had something to do with her compulsion to steal; she felt this particularly when she stole dresses, which she could not wear and for which she had no other use either; many other things she did could not be explained by this hypothesis.

The psychoanalytic treatment of this girl was successfully finished; she fully recovered from her trouble and has led since, for many years, a respectable and irreproachable life; the old affliction never recurred. The real unconscious motives for her pathological stealing came out clearly in her analysis. Stealing things meant to her committing an act of violence and the acquisition of something which life failed to give her. In her stealing she sought first compensation for the deprivation of parental love, later a compensation for the anatomical deficiency of the woman who envied man's masculinity, then for the frustrated desire for a child which she wanted, but which she was unable to have from her lover, since social convention and deeply seated inhibitions of a psychological nature made a pregnancy impossible. In the act of stealing, all these unconscious cravings received in a disguised form a substitutive gratification. The stealing of pictures presenting a mother and child gratified her craving to be a mother, the stealing of the book of "Faust" and many other important literary works had to her the meaning of the fascinating productivity of man, which she wanted to acquire; the stealing of clothes appeared as an act of revenge against her mother, who neglected her when she was a child; all these acts could serve as excellent examples of what we designated before as *symptomatic crimes*.

All the above-mentioned unconscious motivations were brought into the patient's consciousness by means of psycho-analysis; the patient learned to control her impulses, she learned to sublimate them in a manner acceptable to her Ego; she also learned to obtain real gratification in life in-stead of living on substitutive gratifications of a neurotic. Yet, despite all this, she found herself one day on trial; now, after the recovery from her illness, she was to answer for a crime committed before she got well; the situation appeared desperate; she considered it a hopeless task to attempt to explain her real motives to those who were officially called upon to understand her transgressions, so she decided to give in to the demands of the prosecuting attorney and present a conscious, generally intelligible motivation of her behavior. The psychoanalyst was pleasantly surprised to find that the court was able to follow the lines of thought, which are usually foreign to the legal mind. In medical circles one still finds such understanding rather infrequently; the court, in contradiction to the testimony of the official medical expert, acquitted the girl. The official medical expert was in general very skeptical; he would not consider kleptomania an illness; he contended that if it were an illness, one should be able to find in the girl the presence of some intellectual defect, of unusual perspiration and tremor of the hands, which should have come into evidence at the moment of stealing, etc. The girl, on the other hand, was a very intelligent, highly developed personality; such a person, the expert insisted, must know what she is doing. From the standpoint of the psychoanalyst, however, the contrast between the well-developed conscious personality, to whom the crime in question was totally foreign and the compulsive drive to steal, which acted like a foreign body in the conscious life of the girl, was the best proof that we were dealing here with a neurotic mechanism.

However, in the majority of cases, the unconscious tendencies do not break through into consciousness in the form of isolated circumscribed compulsions; instead, as we shall show later, the unconscious instinctual drives permeate the conscious Ego in its totality, so that the lives of such individuals bear the earmarks of fate, as it were; Freud said that the behavior of such individuals appears to be demonic in nature. All the mechanisms which have been described heretofore are operative in such "neurotic characters": mechanisms related to self-punishment, rationalizations, and symptom-like disguises of the real meaning of their behavior.

THE NEUROTIC CRIMINAL

I n a short communication, published in 1915, under the title "Certain Character Types Met with in Psychoanalytic Practice," Freud described several individuals whose lives always seem to run a singularly definite course; this course appears to bear the earmarks of a compulsive force, of a demanding fate, as it were; such individuals live under the pressure of certain unconscious psychic mechanisms, which do not depend upon their conscious volition; one of these types is called by Freud "The Exception"; this type of individual is usually fixed on some infantile situation and always, regardless of the possibilities presented by reality, such an individual insists on being treated as an exception. His whole life seems to be under the immutable influence of this irrational instinctive demand. Freud succeeded in finding a peculiarity in the early life of these individuals, which is common to them all. Says Freud: "Their neurosis was related to a specific experience or pain which affected them in very early childhood; at the time of this experience, they felt free of any guilt, and therefore thought that they were treated with unwarranted prejudice; this injustice made them insist on certain privileges, and as a result they developed an attitude of insubordination which contributed a great deal to making more acute the conflicts which later lead to the development of a neurosis."

It is quite easy to understand that individuals who insist on being exceptions in this world would find it very difficult to adjust themselves to the demands of social reality; that is why this group of individuals yield not a small number of criminals who, like the neurotic, although in a different fashion, fail to make a social adjustment.

Another type mentioned is "individuals who break as a result of success." These are individuals who live under the pressure of an unconscious sense of guilt; they are unable to stand success and, therefore, as Freud described it, right after success is achieved they develop a neurosis, or, as we have seen, they begin to seek out (unconsciously) all sorts of painful situations to get themselves into, in order to pay for their success, or else they impulsively begin to destroy and to squander the fruit of their own successful efforts.

While this type offers comparatively little that is of interest from the criminological standpoint, the third type described by Freud is of especial interest to us. Freud designated this type as "The Criminal Out of a Sense of Guilt."

These individuals commit a crime first of all because it is a forbidden act, and because the carrying out of the transgression causes them psychic relief. A sense of guilt of unknown origin and of long standing burdens them; they connect their sense of guilt with the crime they commit, and thus it is brought into consciousness in a fashion which is easier for them to bear. Their sense of guilt is the result of unconscious forbidden wishes, which their Superego condemns more severely than the transgression they actually commit. In other words, these individuals evidently possess a very austere conscience and therefore they are more afraid of their own inner moral judge than of the secular court. Their transgressions are usually of minor nature; at any rate their Superego considers them much more harmless than their forbidden unconscious wishes. The punishment for their transgressions acquires for them the value of a moral gain or victory, for through this punishment for a real crime they also pay for their unconscious wishes and are therefore able to rid themselves, temporarily at least, of the unconscious sense of guilt. Under the circumstances, they feel no need of bringing into consciousness the real causes of their feeling of guilt, these remain repressed and their roots are usually found in the Œdipus complex which they failed to overcome successfully; they thus succeed in displacing their sense of guilt from the unconscious causes onto the transgression actually committed.

The crime committed as a result of an unconscious sense of guilt is based on a combination of two of the psychological dynamic factors described above: that of disguise and of sense of guilt; the forbidden wish for which the transgression stands is brought to expression through this minor transgression and thus it is brought into consciousness, but in a fully disguised form. The punishment which was sought and successfully obtained calms the Superego, which, functioning as it does by means of inner perception, senses the latent true intent of the individual despite the various forms of disguise. The affective equation—unconscious wish equals the transgression of the law—is, according to Freud, made psychologically possible because both are forbidden things. In the majority of cases, one finds, in addition, a subtle symbolic meaning of the transgression, or even a hint at the real unconscious meaning of the act.

These criminals whose psychology is primarily based on the primitive talion-principle of punishment, a principle alive in our unconscious, are in a certain sense of the word overmoral; they possess an oversensitive conscience, despite the fact that in their unconscious they are a prey of archaic criminal tendencies, which they have never been able to overcome.

The early communications of Freud, dealing with these three types of neurotic characters, served as a stimulus for further investigations. Many observers studied these impulsive, irrational personalities; these investigations became of particular moment since the development of the analytical psychology of the Ego. Reik[1] and Reich[2] studied these types

---

1 Reik, *op. cit.*
2 Reich, *Der Triebhafte Character* (1925).

in detail, and Alexander[3] attempted to delimit the "neurotic character" as a clinical entity.

The latter's views are here outlined briefly.

Under the term *neurotic character* Alexander understands that type of pathological personality who fails to present any circumscribed clinical symptoms; instead, his whole life pattern shows typical deviations from the normal. The real neurotic, as is well known, is, as a rule, rather an inactive individual; the neurotic character is quite the opposite; he is a man of action, his life is very dramatic. The characteristic earmark of a neurosis, the autoplastic mode of instinctual gratification, is in the neurotic character frequently totally absent. Moreover, as has been said, the neurotic character is devoid of any symptoms; symptoms, it will be remembered, according to Freud, present a substitutive gratification of an instinctual impulse, which latter is unacceptable to the Ego, and this is the cardinal trait of a neurosis; the neurotic character is devoid of this trait. These individuals *act;* they live out their instinctual drives, even those drives which are unacceptable to the Ego, even the anti-social trends, and yet despite all this they cannot be considered real criminals. What differentiates them definitely from the real criminal is this: the personality of the real criminal is definitely and homogeneously anti-social, while that of the neurotic character is not homogeneous; a part of his personality condemns the impulsive living-out of his drives, even though he feels that he is unable to keep them under control. Within the psychic apparatus of the neurotic character there exists an inner agency which condemns their own actions. Many striking incidents of their behavior appear quite transparently directed against themselves; they present an irrational drive to self-injury and thus bear witness to the presence of a severe judge within their own personalities. In other words, the second fundamental trait of a neurosis, i.e., the presence of

3 Alexander, "The Neurotic Character," *International Journal of Psychoanalysis,* July, 1930.

a psychic conflict, of an unconscious battle between the two heterogeneous parts of the same personality, is character-istically present in the neurotic character. It is exactly this characteristic that allows us to recognize this type of per-sonality as pathological; their personality seems split in two; one acts impulsively while the other reacts to this impulsive behavior in a very moral, even overmoral fashion, for it not only tries to restrict the impulsive activities of the indi-vidual, it tries to inflict a self-injury.

We owe to psychoanalysis the fact that even the crude anti-social behavior of such individuals can be viewed now with the same *medical* understanding as a neurosis, or even an organic symptom is viewed. In the past our attitude has been limited merely to that of judgment and condemnation. We understand now that the neurotic character is as much a slave to his behavior as the neurotic or the physically sick are to their respective symptoms, for the motives for their behavior remain unconscious, and therefore the conscious personality is unable to gain access to or control of them. Fine admonitions, encouragement or punishment are of as little use as their own resolve to "begin tomorrow" a new mode of life, as little use as the decision of a diabetic to overcome his diabetes by means of will power. The power-lessness of the conscious Ego in face of the impulsive be-havior of a neurotic character is a common characteristic of this type of personality as well as of a neurosis and of a physical disease. We may state in passing that the apparent distance between the development of an organic symptom and that of a psychological one (anti-social or irrational be-havior) is so great that it is easy to understand why psycho-analysis and medicine failed thus far to fuse them into one unitary system. Too, it is not surprising that the neurotic characters are not yet generally recognized as sick people; instead, depending upon the age of the given case, they are turned over to a guardian or to the judge, but not to the doctor. We are accustomed to consider illness as something independent of the conscious will of man, as something like a *vis major* that the sick man must endure. On the other hand, we were accustomed to look upon human behavior as something for which the conscious personality must be held responsible. Only such cases as those covered by Paragraph 51 of the German penal code are relieved of this responsibility. It is hardly possible to hold some one responsible for a stomach ailment, but it is easier (and the experience of the last war proves it) to hold him responsible for his hysterical symptoms and still easier to make him answerable for the extravagance of his behavior, for his gambling, for his losing a great deal of money or for his inability to hold to any serious job. We must broaden our concept of disease and define it anew. We shall find it then not very difficult to see that such people *are* sick people; although some may regret this suggestion as one which places the physically sick person in rather bad company.

From the structural and dynamic point of view, we believe that irrational behavior, which is motivated by unconscious causes, stands closest to the neurotic behavior of a compulsive neurotic; the latter, however, is characterized by symptomatic acts which appear totally meaningless, while the former acquires the form of apparently rational acts; the example of the kleptomaniac will give point to our contention; the kleptomaniac steals as if to satisfy his acquisitive drives, but actually his stealing has a deeply concealed, thoroughly disguised, subjective, symbolic meaning. The singular impulse of the compulsive neurotic appears to his own conscious personality as something strange; in borderline cases, like kleptomania, it may even find its motor expression; the real neurotic character, however, always carries out his repressed impulses in real life, though generally under a modified guise; these impulses of the neurotic character overwhelm his Ego more diffusely than the specific and isolated compulsive acts of the neurotic; they influence the total behavior of the individual. At times they overpower his Ego to such an extent that the individual is unaware of any conscious conflict, i.e., he totally lacks insight into his illness; yet the ever-present unconscious conflict, i.e., the unconscious rejection of his own conscious conduct never fails to come to expression in the form of the tendency to self-injury. If we find that the unconscious moral reaction is definitely absent, then we do not consider such an individual a neurotic character; he then belongs to the group of normal criminals or to any other group of socially deviated personalities.

There is no doubt that the group of neurotic characters is of great medico-legal importance; for a very large number of these individuals, acting out neurotically as they do their unconscious drives, or driven by the impulse to be punished, come sooner or later into conflict with the law. It is one of the important tasks of psychoanalysis to be able to differentiate these individuals from real criminals; otherwise they continue to be viewed as criminals; the nosological concept of psychopathic personality, which was introduced into legal practice, fails to differentiate the neurotic character. Psychoanalysis will be able to fulfill the above-mentioned task concretely and successfully only if it is brought directly into the courtroom; this can be achieved either through expert psychoanalytical medical testimony or through special analytical training of the judge; only then will the law be able to make a step forward and away from the old mediæval spirit. It is striking how reminiscent of old witch trials some of our modern trials are; a man who committed a crime under the pressure of unconscious impulses is tortured by the fire of cross-examination, by means of which the judge and prosecuting attorney endeavor to bring out "real" conscious motivations where there actually are none.

The neurotic character, whether he does or does not get into conflict with the existing law, is a sick man who suffers from a neurosis without symptoms; the analytically trained eye recognizes him at once without any doubt, though it appears impossible to classify him in accordance with the existing diagnostic tables. These individuals have a very dramatic fate; they are driven through life by a demonic

impulse; symptoms are replaced by irrational behavior, the
unconscious meaning of which could be interpreted in the
same way as that of a neurotic symptom; as soon as their
unconscious drives are recognized, not only their isolated
acts, but the irrational nature of their life's course, as a
whole, acquire an intelligible meaning; certain adventurers,
for instance, belong to this group of people; their behavior
always betrays the rejection of the authority of the state and
its laws; they always succeed in being punished quite unjustly (unjustly at least from their subjective point of view)
by the Father-State, and they thus succeed in putting the
latter in the wrong; to this same group further belong those
who are designated by medico-legal authorities as morally
deficient, and whom Bleuler, in his textbook of psychiatry,
designates as psychopathic personalities; these are the ex-
citable, unstable, impulsive individuals, the eccentrics, the
liars and swindlers, the enemies of society, the querulous
fighters. Those who fall under the older rubric of moral insanity also belong to the group of neurotic characters. A great
number of these individuals betray their pathological nature
particularly in their love life. At this point, however, we
should like to warn against confusing two totally separate
classes of individuals; we must differentiate quite sharply
the personality whose behavior is neurotic, as far as social
organization is concerned, from those individuals whose impulses find expression exclusively in the domain of their love
life; we are aware, of course, of the fact that in some cases
the anti-social conduct stands out in the foreground of their
reactions, while in some cases their love life is more prominent. The description of the typical representatives of neurotic love life is beyond the scope of this book. Every one
knows the Don Juan types; they are always on the hunt for
an unattainable love ideal; not less known are those whose
love life is tinged with masochism and for whom love is a
sort of bondage; they live out their need for punishment,
not by an isolated masochistic perversion, but they weave it
rather diffusely into the whole pattern of their love life; the

primary condition for love and potency for these individuals is to make themselves slaves of a woman and serve her faithfully; they need these conditions for their happiness, as much as the pure masochistic individuals need the more overt forms of punishment; other individuals of the same group appear to be impelled to be attached to two women simultaneously and never be able definitely to choose one of the two. In such typical life situations the neurotic conflict finds its real and, at times, tragic expression.

As the distinguishing earmark of each and every neurotic character we may designate the fact that the tendencies which are unacceptable to the Ego possess a great expansive force. These individuals, unlike the neurotics, do not permit themselves to remain restricted to the domain of subjective symptoms; despite the fact that the socially adjusted part of their Ego disapproves of their impulses, they carry them out in the field of reality.

The relative strength of their Ego is undoubtedly smaller than that of the neurotic, but is not absolutely weak. Only the powerful expansiveness of their instinctual life makes it appear weak. We can see, therefore, that it is of decisive importance whether an individual's instinctive life tends to develop autoplastically or not; upon this depends the development of a neurosis or criminality. Without an autoplastic tendency, a neurosis is impossible. Without an alloplastic tendency no criminality is possible. The fundamental nature of the instinctual drives depends primarily upon constitutional factors. Because of the expansive nature of his instinctual life, the neurotic character is closer to the healthy rather than to the neurotic person.

The neurotic character *acts;* he does not let himself be driven by society into the phantasy world of symptoms. The neurotic, on the other hand, preserves the primitive infantile nature of his instinctive demands and is satisfied with the phantasy gratification which his symptoms give him. The normal individual prefers to modify his primitive unrealizable instinctive drives, in order to avoid giving up actual gratification provided by reality. The neurotic character, as we see, wants more than this; he wants to preserve his primitive drives and also carry them out unmodified; he wants both, i.e., the primitive anti-social gratification of the neurotic and the actual gratification in reality of the normal individual. Yet, a part of his own Ego opposes this attempt to obtain both forms of gratification and he therefore falls a victim of his own avidity.

As has been said, the expansive living-out of his instinctual drives distinguishes the neurotic character from the real neurotic and brings him closer to the normal individual. This feature also plays an important and favorable role in the problem of treatment of a neurotic character. The stupendous step from autoplastic introversion to action, a step which is well-nigh impossible for many severe neurotics, is for the neurotic character a rather easy matter. It is not necessary to force him into action. We aim instead to bring his expansive active behavior under the control of his conscious personality. That is why neurotic characters present a rather gratifying field for psychoanalytical treatment—if they would only come to an analyst. In their youth they usually have no insight into their illness; they appear often to be hale and hearty go-getters, who only gradually and after a series of long and bitter life experiences acquire some insight. That is why they reach rather mature age before the analyst finally makes their acquaintance.

These considerations make it clear that the neurotic character, unlike the real neurotic, has the same bio-psychological constitution as the normal individual. His deviation from the normal is not so much a result of a special, abnormal constitution, as a consequence of a special development and a special life history. Certain pathogenic factors, acting on a man endowed with constitutionally weak expansive power of instinctual drives, produce a neurotic. The same or similar factors lead the child who is endowed with normal expansive power of instincts to become a neurotic character. The neurotic character may, therefore, with some justification, be called a tamed primitive individual; this explains the re-markable and conspicuous unevenness of his personality; on the one hand, there is a persistent instinctive drive to actual gratification of primitive wishes, and on the other, an in-hibitory self-punishing, inner moral self-condemnation. This splitting of the personality is similar to that of a real neu-rotic, except that the gratification as well as the punishment for it is obtained through real acts and real life experiences.

One might even go further and say that a specially expan-sive and untamable set of instinctive drives yields with greater difficulty to demands of civilization and, therefore, it rarely compromises on mere substitutive gratification, or it rarely accepts any sublimations which usually domesticate our primitive impulses. Individuals endowed with such strong primitive natures find it most difficult to adjust them-selves to the conditions of present-day civilization, which imposes so many restrictions upon them; only those whose instinctual drives are less expansive find it easier to make the necessary adjustment; this being the case, we may say that what we call today the normal individual is an inter-mediary type between the expansive primitive man and the neurotic. Imposing considerable restrictions upon our in-stinctive life, our civilization, like any other civilization, tends toward the development of neuroses, i.e., it tends to a certain degeneration of our instinctive life. To possess a moderate degree of this degenerative weakness, to be able readily to accept various sublimations in lieu of direct grati-fication of primitive drives, means, perhaps, to possess the secret of mental health in the present-day sense of the word, i.e., the secret of adjustment to the complex conditions of life as they exist in the highly organized society of today. The individual and his individual instinctual impulses, his self-possessed intactness, the individual as a biological unit is today sacrificed in favor of the community as a whole. The socialized individual, if compared with the single, inde-pendent individual, appears from a biological point of view to be a sort of a product of deterioration. As far as the deeper instinctive impulses are concerned, the urbane individual of our highly organized civilization appears crippled as compared with the much less social man of primitive patriarchal days.

The neurotic character thus appears to fight the tragic battle of the individual against society. Some individuals belonging to this type openly reject the restrictive demands of society and thus become lawbreakers; on the other hand, there are individuals in the same group who are less daring; these keep up for themselves the illusion of individualism by becoming persistent addicts to various types of eccentricities; these individuals save their individuality through a special arrangement of their private lives; the passionate collector and amateur, the gambler, the daring record breakers, the daredevils who snatch every possible opportunity to stake their lives—all belong to this group. Behind the seemingly ridiculous drive of the eccentric to do something out of the way lies a half-concealed spite against society, which demands that man give up individual freedom of instinctive expression. The spite of the eccentric is more harmless and less challenging than that of the neurotic lawbreaker, but the psychic foundation of both is identical; it is a spiteful holding fast to one's individual primitive rights against the onslaught of mass formations.

Both types of the neurotic character, the *criminal* and the *eccentric* are frequently treated of by poets and writers. Dmitry Karamazov is the classical representative of the criminal type, while Balzac's *Oncle Pons* represents the eccentric. The *condottiere* image of *Casanova* is a good example of the *adventurer type*. Casanova, for instance, shows a rare accumulation of almost all the earmarks of a neurotic character; he is an extreme individualist, spitefully opposed to all forms of authority, secular or ecclesiastic, he always expresses his individualistic superiority; yet he does live under the pressure of a strong need for punishment. His own description of his arrest leaves no doubt as to the correctness of our contention; he refused to listen to the admonitions of his friends and to run away; he stubbornly rejected the help of his protector, Bragadino, and finally provoked his own arrest—Casanova had a deeply seated sense of guilt; this comes repeatedly to expression in his constant play with danger, a play he never abandoned throughout his life. One does not need to seek far for the reason why Casanova makes such a profound and fascinating impression on the reader of today. Man of today has neurotic tendencies, i.e., he usually gives up his impulse to act and to remain primitive; while Casanova *acts*, Casanova does not give anything up; he is the fighter for the freedom of his individual instinctual wishes, he boldly challenges the monotonously gray ideals of the community; he even succeeds in ringing a note of ethical protest when he starts his battle, for he appears to us as the heroic apologist of free thought, who protests against the tyrannical spirit of the Inquisition and the superstition of the church. Yet, even these catchwords, by means of which he hopes to justify his acts, do not allay his own unconscious need for punishment; he *must* be arrested. This arrest which he himself causes serves him as an atonement for his rise against those in authority, a rise in which he, like any other individualist, unconsciously and symbolically fights his first authority, his father.

In our anti-individualistic age one does not often meet a Casanova, who pokes such dramatic fun at State, church and other sundry authorities. Such individuals today would be a definite anachronism; they are less out of place in the lethal chambers of the palace of the Doges than in our colorless prisons. Even as the prisons of today became prosaic, so has the modern neurotic character of the adventurer type become more colorless; this type is found today among the organized parties of political opposition; still more frequently he appears in the guise of a captain of industry, a reckless money-maker, who, however, is driven by the same unconscious forces of self-destruction as his heroic predecessor of the days gone by; the frequent alternations of financial rises and falls, which are so characteristic of this type, are but the expression of the simultaneous operation of aggressive and self-destructive drives.

It will now be clear why the neurotic character has always been a source of inspiration to the poetic and literary imagination; is not the neurotic character mostly a very strong original personality, whose manner of life is at the same time prompted by deep social consciousness? He represents the active struggle between individual and society which is carried on, not by means of inconclusive intrapsychic processes, that lead to neurotic symptoms, but by means of a dramatic enactment of his own external life. That is why such individuals are born heroes, whose end is inevitably tragic. Their debacle represents the victory of society; the onlooker, who is himself inwardly split in two, is able to identify himself with the hero and thus gratify both sides of his own personality, the rebellious and the social.

We came to the conclusion that the neurotic criminal is but a special case of a neurotic character, whose impulsive behavior brings him in conflict with the law. We saw that other representatives of the same group lead a ridiculous, isolated existence of eccentrics; these find an outlet for their impulses and gratification of their self-punishment tendencies in a number of more harmless, socially less injurious ways. In some individuals these unconscious motivations of their life pattern are still less clearly distinguishable; their neurotic trends become frequently evident, but under special circumstances, such as in their married life, the often irrational course of their careers, or the apparently accidental ups and downs of their professional lives.

There is no fundamental difference between the neurotic criminal and all these socially harmless representatives of the group of neurotic characters; the difference lies merely in the external fact that the neurotic lawbreaker chooses a form of acting out of his impulses which is socially harmful.

These diagnostic considerations force upon us the following conclusion: the neurotic criminal, like any neurotic character, is an individual psychoneurotically sick, and as such he is curable and, therefore, it is imperative that he be given medico-psychological treatment. His illness is due to a disproportion between the power of his instinctive drives and the strength of the inhibitory function of his Ego and to an insufficient elasticity of his instinctual life. His illness is, to be sure, a paradoxical one; it is a result of the unusual primitive health of his instincts; it is a result of a healthy primitive state, which neither present-day society nor his own Superego can tolerate in this primitive form. At any rate, his socially harmful behavior is a result of unconscious drives to which his conscious will has no access whatever. To impose punishment on him is ludicrous, no matter what meaning one may ascribe to punishment. From the standpoint of the *theory of requital,* it is of no meaning, because we make him suffer for something over which he has no control. Too, the punishment with which he is threatened cannot intimidate him and therefore cannot deter him from his behavior, because of the simple fact that unconsciously he feels the need of punishment and therefore welcomes the severity of the law; quite often he even actively seeks punishment; as a matter of fact, in the case of criminals whose criminality is dictated by their unconscious sense of guilt, the expected punishment presents the main motive for the transgression. Thus the social advantages derived from the *general intimi-dation* ("general prevention of crime") appear highly questionable, for many criminals, i.e., all their neurotic fellow sufferers, derive the possibility of their neurotic acting out from the very punishment which is supposed to prevent it. Finally, we must say that punishment cannot make these individuals *better,* either; is it not clear that their conscious will power cannot overcome the forces which operate in their unconscious? To punish such individuals is psychologically meaningless and sociologically harmful.

Independently of these more or less theoretical considerations, psychoanalytic practice shows that these individuals are frequently, if not always, curable. They are full of unconscious conflicts; as in the neurosis, the socially adjusted part of their personality is in a state of constant conflict with the anti-social part of their personality. Yet, if their instinctual structure is not burdened with constitutional difficulties they are most gratifying subjects for psychoanalytical therapy. Unlike the real neurotic, whose tendency to introversion is due to constitutional factors, these individuals show that only the acquired layers of their personalities are pathologically affected. We must remember in this connection that psychoanalysis is most successful just in this field, for it is able to remove the results of pathogenic influences that took place in the course of the individual's life; it finds it much more difficult to bring about any essential change in the constitutional factors.

PERVERSION AND CRIMINALITY

THE SPECIAL PSYCHOLOGICAL FACTORS which made it pertinent that we consider the neurotic criminal apart from other criminals are still more in evidence in the cases of those who tend to *perversions*. If one insists on considering the conscious will power as the basis for responsibility, we will find ourselves especially puzzled when we face a transgressor whose crime is a *perversion*. Perverse drives, as is known, cannot be influenced by the responsible part of the individual's personality. The various codifications of criminal law confuse quite readily the great number of cases of incest, i.e., sexual congress between mother and son, father and daughter, brother and sister, with perversions, putting them all in one group of crimes against morality. Yet incest, it must be remembered, is deeply rooted in our natural sexual drive, it is the manifestation of sexual strivings which are characteristic of every human being and are the foundation of the Œdipus complex, which in turn is the cornerstone of human sexual development. The prohibition of incest is purposeful and intelligible; this prohibition does not demand from the individual that he give up his sexuality as a whole; it demands only that the individual give up his infantile object of sexual love. The real perversions, i.e., derivations from the normal sexual drives, should from the practical (not theoretical) viewpoint be considered as natural facts; as something akin to a physical anomaly which cannot be changed by any known mode of punishment. We may forbid the practice of perverse sexual *acts.* In some special cases, we have to do so; such as in the cases of sadists, whose practices acquire the proportion of an actual crime, but, in general, to forbid one the practice of one's perversion is tantamount to the prohibition of sexual gratification in general, for the sexually perverse individual is absolutely unable to obtain any sexual gratification in a normal way. Because of the peculiarity of his development he has no choice; he either gets his gratification through the practice of perversion or he must give up all hope for any gratification at all.

It is, of course, self-understood that society has a perfect right to forbid murder with assault; a murderer of this kind cannot be permitted to live out his sexual impulses in his own way, since the latter is so damaging to society. The same may be said of many other perversions which, although less extreme in their anti-social nature, yet present a threat to the rights of others or to the social order as a whole. Society, it appears, has been unable till now to find any other method than to use the threat of punishment for the purpose of prohibiting certain anti-social activities; this being the case, one might be tempted to resign one's self to this situation and agree that it is necessary to use threats and force in order to prevent certain particularly dangerous, perverse individuals from gratifying their perverse desires; one might then take a step further and state that one must deal with the problem with the greatest possible caution or forbearance, before the answer is found to the question as to who should be considered a socially dangerous perverse individual, and as to what kind of perversions should be considered merely the private affair of the given individual. Let us think, for instance, of the severe punishment imposed for sodomy, or let us consider that part of the project of the new German penal code which demands that bodily injuries in so far "as they violate public morals" should be punished even in the case when they were inflicted with the consent of the injured. Such punitive measures appear to us as unwarranted intrusions into the private life of citizens; they are devoid of any

far-reaching, imperative, sociological foundation, and are
nothing more than a meaningless and superfluous offense to
the general sense of justice.

These simple considerations become unusually complex
and difficult, if one tries to understand the genesis and meaning of perversions in the light of psychoanalytical knowledge.
Freud and many others dealt with this problem quite ex-
haustively, and explained this phenomenon in a great number of clinical presentations. For our purpose, it would
suffice to state that perversions do not depend on *heredity*
even nearly to the extent which, until recently, has been
claimed by medical science; furthermore, perversions are not
unchangeable defects which the individual happens to have
brought with him into life at the time of his birth; on the
contrary, they are rather the result of impressions made by
pathogenic influences, which operated or occurred during
the course of the individual's life. If we now turn our attention to the problem of measures to be taken in the interest
of society against a perverse individual, we shall have to think
very carefully. We must bear in mind that, generally speaking, acquired perversions are invariably a consequence of
too great interference with the normal sexual life of the
child. The point of departure in the development of a perversion is the type of prohibition imposed upon the child
for its first normally directed sexual desires; we have in mind
the prohibition of incest, which is the foundation of the
development of every human social organization.

We know that with the exception of homosexuality the
greatest number of perversions present a regression to an
earlier pregenital level of libido development. The fear of
the father, which in our unconscious, follows the talion principle, appears as castration anxiety, drives the little boy away
from his earliest, rather weak genital feelings, which are at
first directed toward the mother, and pushes him back by
way of regression to the sado-masochisitic level of libido development; hence, the instinctive striving for the sexual act
becomes substituted by the wish to cause pain or to experi-

ence pain. In the case of the sadist, which is so important from the criminological point of view, yet another mechanism is brought into operation. The sadist's original primitive aggression against his father becomes first displaced onto the woman; these aggressive trends become then blended with the sexual drive; the latter thus changes its primitive emotional content and becomes permeated with sadism. By means of this psychological mechanism the individual rids himself of the burden of hatred, which is directed against the father; however, he obtains this relief through sacrificing the original normal character of his sexual feelings. The following paradoxical formulation of the situation is thus justified: it appears that the perverse individual is the victim of the social order, for does not this order demand that hate of the father and the sexual wish for the mother be definitely given up?

It is to be regretted that psychoanalysts had no access to the case of Haarmann.[1] Yet, even on the basis of the few data concerning his childhood and the general development of the man, one may rightly assume that his hate of his father was never properly liquidated; this hate in Haarmann's case was quite unusual and permeated the whole life of the man; it finally came to expression by way of displacement on other persons, and specifically in the form of murder.

The same mechanism, although not in its erotized form, drove Cain to kill his brother Abel instead of his father. The

---

[1] Cf. Th. Lessing Haarmann, Berlin, 1925, p. 29.

"It is important for the psychologist to know that even as a little boy, he saw in his father a sort of a rival whom he hated and whose death he wished. This animosity against the father persisted throughout his life. The two mutually accused and threatened one another. The father threatened to put the son away into an insane asylum; the son, in turn, because of an alleged murder of a train engineer, threatens to get the father into prison. They abused one another and fist fights were frequent. The father accused the son of planning his murder; the son reciprocated with a similar accusation of the father; they constantly exchanged reciprocal accusations of intending to poison or to injure one another. In the meantime they committed many frauds together, or succeeded in saving one another from falling into the hands of justice. As to Haarmann's attitude toward his mother, it had always been highly enthusiastic; she was the only one about whom he could say something nice and kind; he always spoke of her with great sentiment."

desire to kill the father is forbidden by one's own Superego; such a murder becomes possible, however, when instead of the father another person is taken as a substitute, who is less protected by the Superego and who is also envied. We shall find a somewhat similar mechanism later in the description of the case of Mme Lefebvre; we shall see what an important role this mechanism plays in the cases of many neurotic murders.

This is not the place to go into the theory of all individual perversions. We must limit ourselves to the statement that the Œdipus complex plays the central role in the development of perversions, the latter being a regressive retreat from the Œdipus situation. The constitutional force of the various individual pregenital drives plays a specially important role in the choice of a given perversion.

It is of fundamental importance for our problem to emphasize that the most essential factor in the etiology of perversions is the mode of management of the child; *overgreat strictness* in the management of infantile sexuality, forceful measures which lead to *too extreme repression* of sexual feelings, and therefore to *insincerity* and *hypocrisy,* easily pave the way to perversions. Not every individual becomes perverse, but the fact that he did not become perverse is not to *his* credit but to the credit of his bringing up. Hence, we must state that the development of perversions is not the child's fault, but the fault of the bringing up. It is therefore offensive to one's sense of justice to impose legal punishment for a perversion; for the pervert is the victim of false methods of bringing up, for which society and not the pervert is responsible. According to Liszt, all criminals are victims of their environment and bringing up, but we must remember that in the case of the habitual criminal the conscious which takes part in the crime can be influenced to some extent, while the conscious will of the perverse individual is absolutely unable to change any of his perverse sexual drives. If we are more or less powerless, as far as a change of our *social structure* and its deficiencies is concerned, we can at least begin to introduce new methods of hygienic sexual education, methods which would be based on the knowledge of psychoanalysis, and which might tend to prevent the development of perversions.

A community which fails to undertake any reform of sexual education becomes an accomplice in the development of perversions.

The same conclusions are, in general, valid as regards *homosexuality;* we have in mind that type of homosexuality which is not caused by hereditary factors, but which is acquired in the course of the child's development. We shall consider this problem in detail, not only because homosexuality is so widespread, but also because of its great social significance.

While such perversions as sadism, masochism, exhibitionism, etc., present regressions to pregenital levels of libido development, acquired homosexuality consists of extreme sexual attraction to individuals of the same sex. Every single individual, as a matter of fact, every living being, is *bisexual* in its biological development; yet the majority of cases of homosexuality are not due to the congenital overpowering strength of one type of sexuality as compared with the other. The overemphasis of the *homosexual* component of one's sexuality, which develops in the course of an individual's life, is due primarily to a specific form of flight from the *Œdipus conflict;* the individual in such cases gives up his own sex. Here, as in the case of perversions, we cannot go into the details of the complex psychological mechanisms which lead to homosexuality; we shall merely refer to the fact that there exists a voluminous psychoanalytical literature on the subject, and the writings of Freud on the problem are of particular importance.

We shall summarize only those features of the problem which have a bearing on criminology.

The process of giving up one's hate of one's father always leads to an increase of the passive-feminine feelings. In normal cases, these passive-feminine strivings become an integral

part of submissiveness to the authority of the father; they
become desexualized, and in this desexualized form they act
as the first forces for social growth. The family, the germ
cell of society, as it were, is held together by the fact that the
sons look upon the father as their leader and consider one
another as comrades, as allies in the same battle of life; thus
the passive-feminine component of man holds the family
together; in other words, the passive-feminine, i.e., the homosexual component of man's nature in its desexualized, sublimated aspects, forms the foundation of social solidarity.
Freud, in his investigation of mass psychology (*Group Psychology and the Analysis of the Ego*), demonstrated the
fact that the formation of groups of individuals is based upon
the sublimated passive attitude of man to his father, and on
the desexualized erotic solidarity with his brothers. Homosexuality, then, as *one* of the components of our bisexual
organization is, in its sublimated form, *the* condition for the
formation of a social unit, its growth and its cohesiveness.
Some might, therefore, contend that homosexuality, when
it appears as a sexual perversion, that is, when it appears as
an extreme development of the grossly sexual side of the
homosexual component of our sexuality, fails to develop or
at any rate weakens the *sublimated forms* of the relationships
between father, brothers, and sons; society naturally extols
only the sublimated homosexual component of men, for its
existence is based on them; in frank, unsublimated homosexuality, it sees a danger to itself; if it were not so it would
be difficult to understand why society tolerates, as a private
affair of the given individual, such phenomena as masochism
or the homosexuality of women, but not man's homosexuality. Yet homosexuality, strictly speaking, does not threaten
anybody's rights; unlike sadism, it is harmless, and hurts no
one against his will; but, thinks society, if the fundamental
elements which keep the community together break down
into its grossly sexual manifestations, society incurs a definite
loss. The grossly sexual relationship is a relationship only
between two individuals and is not capable of holding a large

mass of people together; a fear of corruption arises akin to one which arises in cases of political scandals. When women, in so far as they remained primarily sexual beings, began to strive to gain higher public functions, and governmental positions, and in some cases succeeded, there arose at once the apprehension that politics might become influenced by sexual ties, or grossly sexual factors instead of by purposeful decisions. Evidently the same danger is sensed by society in those cases where sensual homosexuality appears in place of its sublimated form, for in the struggle between the desexualized and frankly sexualized instinctual drives, the former always fall victims to the universal immanent pleasure principle. When there is a conflict between duty and sensual pleasure, the latter usually wins an easy victory. These considerations make it easier for us to understand why homosexuality of women is so much more readily tolerated; has not this socially formative factor played until now too negligible a role in the cohesiveness of society to be considered a dangerous phenomenon? How long will women be treated with tolerance in this respect is another question, now that their public significance and role is so rapidly increasing.

These theoretical considerations, then, make clear to us why society is afraid of homosexuality and rejects it so bitterly. Experience, however, fails to justify this great fear. The average homosexual may very well show a typical deficiency in certain social virtues; for instead of a factual, somewhat distant attitude toward men, the attitude of the overt homosexual is more personal and is more colored with a sort of sexual code of behavior; it is similar to the private relationship which exists between man and woman. However, a great number of homosexuals, especially those of a high intellectual type, usually distinguish themselves by their especially great capacity for sublimations. This apparent contradiction shows only that the modern civilized man is so restricted in his primitive sexuality that he possesses an enormous quantity of sublimated and socially usable libidinous energy; the fact that he occasionally reconverts some of this libidinous energy again into grossly sexual, homosexual energy does not seem practically to affect his capacity for being and remaining a social human being. One should also bear in mind that because of the limitations of gratification which the homosexual has to face, he is forced to develop many sublimations. The general dislike with which his mode of sexual gratification is viewed drives him to sublimated productive activity, which is his compensation for the injury which society inflicts upon his self-respect. Only the great importance of sublimated tendencies for relations among people of the same sex, and therefore for the development of society, makes it possible to understand the unconscious motives which are behind the tenacious preservation of such laws as Paragraph 175 of the German code, which is directed against men homosexuals.

Even our psychoanalytical knowledge of the economic distribution of psychic energy does not warrant the suspicion that extreme growth of homosexuality might develop into a social menace; and we can say with certainty that punishing homosexuals for their homosexuality is meaningless and unjust. The only measure to apply for the solution of the problem is not the punishment of the adult, but the proper management of the child. Homosexuality, like any other sexual perversion, is a problem of child education and not a criminological problem. The perverse individual, as has been said, is the victim of his unconscious incest fear; defeated in his attempt to escape his unconscious conflict with his parent, he becomes the conspicuous victim of the demand for sexual repression which is voiced by society. The only effective means for the elimination of perversions are freedom for the normal sexual feeling, understanding of the demands and of the development of this powerful instinct of man, a change of the sexual atmosphere in the family, and an educational system of children based on the concepts of psychoanalysis. The revengeful attitude of society toward the victims of its own mistakes is cruel, useless and purposeless. As to the homosexuality of the adult, this must be tolerated; for with the exception of those cases which can be cured by analysis, one can do nothing; all other measures remain without avail. The eternal argument that homosexuals seduce youth is of little practical importance. The power-and-pleasure quality of the normal sexual drive is such that no seduction can affect it; if it is occasionally affected, it is because the psychological foundation for homosexuality is already laid in such cases. The damage, however, which legal prohibition of homosexuality causes is so much the greater, for the prohibition increases the unconscious incestuous meaning of the homosexual act, and therefore like any other prohibition, its effect is not the frightening away from the forbidden act but the increase in the attractiveness of it.

Congenital, genuine homosexuality is of relatively negligible importance. Like any other fact created by biological constitution, we must look on it with the clear awareness that we are helpless.

The only purposeful measure is, therefore, the following: *the sexual perversion of the adult must be tolerated,* the extreme cases which are dangerous to society should be isolated; at the same time we must attempt to institute preventive measures by means of rational, psychologically correct education of children, and by diminishing the repression of normal sexuality; those individuals whose perversions are accompanied by a *psychological conflict,* i.e., those who consider their tendencies as a sickness, are greatly helped by psychoanalytical treatment.

A PSYCHOANALYTICAL TABLE OF

CRIMINOLOGICAL DIAGNOSIS

(A Schematic Summary of Criminal Behavior)

Having attempted in these pages to describe the psychological conditions under which criminal behavior develops, we shall now present a brief summary of our views, which could find practical application in criminology.

Our analysis of the concept of legal responsibility leads us to the belief that this juristic concept should be replaced by a purposeful system of criminological diagnosis; the latter must be based on the consideration of the respective degree to which the conscious Ego and the unconscious of the criminal participate in a given crime. We considered criminality only from this point of view, and its schematic presentation follows. We differentiated the existence of (I) crimes committed by individuals who are affected by a number of criminal trends (chronic criminals); these are individuals whose psychic apparatus is so constructed that they tend to criminality. And (II) crimes committed by non-criminal individuals (accidental criminality).

(I) CHRONIC CRIMINALITY. This group can be divided in the following two subgroups, according to the degree of the Ego participation.

(a) *Criminal behavior* of those individuals whose Ego, as a result of *toxic* or other *organic destructive* processes is considerably damaged or totally paralyzed. All those cases, which are considered by legal and forensic medicine as not responsible, belong to this group. The degree to which the Ego participates in the criminal behavior of such individuals may fall to zero (idiocy, organic mental diseases, alcoholics, drug addicts). It must naturally be borne in mind that a toxic state may be brought about deliberately by the criminal himself for the purpose of excluding the influence of any inhibition which might interfere with the proposed crime; too, in other cases, like in drug addicts, the intoxication is a manifestation of a severe neurosis. Therefore only a certain number of crimes committed in a toxic state will fall under this heading. Intoxication is frequently only the immediate cause of the crime; the real cause of it is to be sought, however, in the neurosis of the criminal. In such cases, the toxic state appears to be the secondary result of the neurosis, and therefore the criminal belongs to the class of neurotic criminals.

(b) *Criminal behavior conditioned by a neurosis.* This behavior is prompted first of all by unconscious motives, and therefore it is impossible for the conscious personality to take any part in it. The Ego is won over to the carrying-out of a crime by means of special mechanisms, which loosen the Ego from the influence of the inhibitory Superego, or the Ego is deceived by means of various disguises and therefore it fails to appreciate the meaning of the criminal act. Depending upon the chief mechanisms at work, we can distinguish:

Compulsive or Symptomatic Crimes (kleptomania, pyromania, pathological lying). These are nearest to straight neurotic symptoms. The compulsion appears as a foreign body in the Ego, meaningless and isolated from the rest of the conscious personality. The Ego in such cases is overcome by unconscious tendencies.

Neurotic acting out of criminal tendencies, the total personality participating in it. The Ego is won over to the crime by means of psychological mechanisms involving suffering, or by means of rationalizations. The mechanisms involving suffering are either of a *neurotic* or a *psychotic* nature; in the case of the former the suffering is sought in reality for the purpose of moral relief; while in case of the latter the suffering is sought for the purpose of completing the phantasy which underlies the projection of one's own guilt.

Rationalizations, which are used also by normal people in their daily life, represent a quantitative falsification of psychodynamic relationships, an over-estimation of the conscious motives which are acceptable to the Ego; this serves the purpose of bringing the crime and the conscience of the individual into a state of harmony.

As an extreme example of criminal neurotic acting out, one may mention the criminal out of a sense of guilt; such a criminal commits a crime in order to tie together his preëxistent unconscious sense of guilt with an actual, relatively harmless transgression. The various mechanisms which are operative in other cases are set into action in these cases also (disguise of the meaning of the act and the seeking of pain). This schematic presentation, like all schematizations, is mostly true of borderline cases, in which a single one of the mechanisms described above plays the most prominent role.

(c) *Criminal behavior of the normal, non-neurotic criminal whose Superego is criminal.* We shall limit ourselves here to the restatement of the fact that individuals of this group form a special community that functions on the basis of a special moral code which is different from the usual; it is a special moral code of criminals ("honesty among thieves"). The whole personality of the individual belonging to such a community identifies itself with the crime. His anti-social acts are totally acceptable to his Ego as well as to his Superego. Tramps, beggars, gangsters (primacy of the pleasure principle), professional criminals like pickpockets, burglars, receivers of stolen goods, all belong to this diagnostic group.

(d) *The genuine criminal.* This imaginary type is mentioned only for the sake of completeness. This individual could be thought of as one who is not adjusted at all to social life, as one who lives on the primitive level of the primitive man; such an individual would carry out in action any of his primitive drives as soon as he would perceive them; he would not feel bridled by any inner inhibition; the only inhibition he would be able to recognize is the resistance with which the outside world would meet his behavior, i.e., he would experience only fear of reality which would threaten him with punishment; in short, an individual without a Super-ego. It may sound quite paradoxical, but it is none the less true that this theoretically conceived type of individual, whose actual existence is highly doubtful, differs only quantitatively from the average normal individual. As has been mentioned already, the majority of people resist some of their own tendencies toward anti-social behavior, not because of moral qualms, but because of fear of real consequences. We must remember that the changes within our psychic apparatus, which lead to the establishment of an inner inhibitory agency that puts itself automatically in the service of social demands, develops within us only in regard to certain, but not all, of our relations to society. The oldest social laws, which evidently present the basic conditions for the formation of communal life, the laws forbidding the murder of parents, incest and cannibalism, became inner human laws which do not depend any more upon the threat of punishment coming from without. These are almost the only laws which man, in general, obeys without police supervision.) All other inhibitions of our anti-social tendencies, inhibitions which were acquired in the course of our individual development, and which depend more or less on the moral code and convention of a given cultural age, may well have become more or less independent from prohibitions imposed by outside authority, yet we must recognize that they are very labile inhibitions; they appear to need reinforcement by means of fear of real consequences. Even murder is not quite intimately woven into our inner inhibitions, for under certain circumstances (in war, for instance) it will be committed by the soldier under orders; but the majority of people will not kill their father or eat human flesh even when under military orders.

Criminality must thus be recognized as a general human phenomenon, which is attentuated only through the coöperation of the fear one has before one's own conscience with the fear of consequences that reality has always in stock for one. Thus our task is reduced to the investigation of those conditions under which in certain situations the coöperation of the two types of fear, mentioned above, becomes weakened and insufficient for the prevention of an anti-social act.

II. ACCIDENTAL CRIMINALITY. This second group may be divided into two subgroups:

(a) *Crimes resulting from "mistakes"* (manslaughter). Under circumstances of severe taxation of the Ego an unconscious criminal trend may break through acutely and be carried out in action. The Ego totally rejects the latter.

(b) *Situational Crimes.* These are crimes which are committed under definitely exceptional circumstances, which bring about an exceptional affective state; the latter leads to a specific crime which is usually understood and forgiven by the community. In regard to the psychology of such crimes, we must remember that in such cases we always deal with a pain caused by a real situation; this pain causes extreme injury to one's sense of justice, so that the inhibitory power of the Superego, which usually functions quite normally, is put out of commission.

*   *   *   *   *

This cursory review of the various forms of criminality will show in a general way, we hope, what we think the principle of criminological diagnosis should be; such a diagnosis should present the foundation of the criminal justice of the future. The task of the future judge who is to be psychoanalytically trained will be not to fit the criminal under a given paragraph of the law, but to determine the correct psychological category to which he belongs.

The measures to be taken in any given case will not consist any more of meaningless, arbitrary, arithmetically calculated prison terms; those measures will clearly depend on and be dictated by the diagnosis itself.

The first group, that of chronic criminality resulting from toxic or other organic pathological conditions, belongs to the physician, the neurotic criminal to the psychoanalyst.

The criminal with the criminal Superego presents rather a problem of education. Proper preventive and educational measures, which could influence the Superego development, is particularly promising in cases of youngsters, as proven by the work of Aichhorn.

It goes without saying, that all chronic criminals will have to be isolated, or made socially safe in some other way, throughout the course of the period during which they remain a menace to society.

The punishment of the accidental criminal serves no purpose and is therefore superfluous. As to the normal criminal, the civil code which exists in all civilized states may suffice. Its principle of restitution is either adequate to deal with this type of lawbreaker, or it is elastic enough to be easily extended in scope; too, the introduction of compulsory labor, which would serve for making good the loss caused by the crime, could be considered. One must, however, bear in mind that these measures should not be applied without taking into account the role of the fundamental sense of justice, as well as the idea of intimidation.

PSYCHIC DETERMINISM AND RESPONSIBILITY

T HE PROBLEM OF RESPONSIBILITY IS ONE OF the most controversial problems of psychology. There was and still is a great deal of confusion on this subject because it has practical, forensic and ethical-religious implications as well as merely scientific ones. To discuss the problem from these different frames of reference without differentiating precisely among them, leads unavoidably to a logical impasse. From the legal and moral points of view it is inevitable that we hold a person responsible in principle for all of his actions and make exceptions only in certain specific instances such as in the presence of a psychosis or overpowering external coercion. And even in these exceptional cases a certain amount of responsibility will have to rest with the person; only the degree of responsibility can be questioned. Freud's answer to the question—"Should a person be held responsible for his dreams which are the products of unconscious forces over which he has no conscious control?"—was: "Who else but the dreamer should be held responsible for his dreams?" The concept of responsibility cannot be applied in a strictly logical fashion to all the processes which take place in the organism. "Is a person responsible for his high blood pressure?" does not sound like a very meaningful question. However, after a medical consultation in which advice was given to avoid salt-containing food, smoking and emotionally disturbing situations, the question becomes meaningful. Not abiding by this advice makes the patient at least partially responsible for a continuance of his high blood pressure. One acquires this responsibility, however, only after having learned how to control the blood pressure. A person who is in control of his behavior should be considered responsible for it.

At this point it is customary to bring into the discussion the question of psychic determinism. One argument is: if we accept the principle of causality in the field of human behavior, it follows that whatever a person does is determined by certain natural laws. Free choice, often called free will, is but an illusion. A decision is the result of certain psychophysiological causes, and there is only one possible outcome. Another school of thought maintains that whenever a person is in control of his mental faculties he can choose freely between doing right or wrong and he must be held responsible for his choice.

I shall not discuss the question of psychic determinism in a philosophical sense, but will try to demonstrate that independent of the theory one accepts, determinism or freedom of will, there is only one logical answer to the problem of responsibility.

Let us examine a concrete example, that of a skipper who, seeing his boat in jeopardy, decides to stay with it and advises the rest of the crew and the passengers to leave the sinking ship. The determinist would say that the skipper had no other choice, being the person that he is. The opponents of determinism may say that the captain deserves merit if he follows his duty and stays with the ship, and condemnation if he deserts it, since he had his free choice. Both answers appear logical, and the impasse in deciding which is correct comes from the fact that causal explanations and value judgments are not clearly differentiated. The whole problem is what the German philosophers call a *schein* problem, or in English a pseudo-problem.

To evaluate the skipper's action in a causal sense, we must know his personality. If we scrutinize it, we will find that he was indoctrinated with the ethics of navigation. He certainly was not born with this value system; he acquired it through the influence of those persons who shaped his personality in his early youth and those who taught him navigation later. The code of the sea was deeply ingrained in his personality—became as we say, his second nature—and he acted according to this acquired value system. If he had been a man who was never taught these principles or had not assimilated them so completely that they became stronger than his biological instinct of self-preservation, he would have deserted his ship in order to save his life. His behavior was determined by those ethical values which he incorporated into his personality. So far everyone will go along with the reasoning of the determinists. Can we, however, still follow them if they say that since the captain could have acted only in the way he did, he does not deserve any special credit, and similarly, if he had deserted the ship he could not be held responsible because he had not assimilated the code of navigation and therefore had no other choice?

This practical conclusion is obviously not only undesirable, but illogical as well. How did the skipper become a person who could control his instinct of self-preservation and act according to the ethics of his profession, which do not allow him to save his life even if his ship is sinking? Obviously, by educational procedures. These procedures, however, are based on the principle of responsibility. He was praised as a child when he acted according to the prevailing code and was reprimanded if he violated it. He was made responsible for his acts; he had to face the consequences of his behavior. This principle of holding a person responsible for his behavior has a deep effect in shaping the personality and eventually results in making the person what he is. It has an influence on all who are brought up according to these principles. If a "wrongdoer" is made responsible for his act, all the members of his group will be influenced by this. It would therefore be quite inconsistent to draw the conclusion that the skipper who deserts his ship should not be made responsible for his deed. Obviously, such an attitude would undermine the whole code of navigation and would be contradictory to all those educational principles which made him a good skipper.

The general conclusion, then, is that ethical standards are determinative factors in behavior. This is not the place to go into a discussion of all the complex psychological processes by which they become inculcated in a person. Identification with external authorities (parents) is of outstanding significance. One of the most important factors, however, is that a person is always made responsible for the consequences of his behavior.

At this point we must consider another argument. One may admit the practical desirability, as a means of education, of making children responsible for their behavior. However, adults are finished products. The captain who goes down with his ship does not need external rewards; he acts to satisfy his own internal code. And conversely, the deserting captain will not be made more ethical through punishment. His personality is already fixed, and if he has not assimilated the code by the time he is mature, he will not be able to do so in the future. This argument contains two inadequacies: (1) Public exposure may have a deep influence upon the deserter and may shift the equilibrium of conflicting forces in favor of the ethical principles which he holds but which are not sufficiently effective. His shame after being humiliated may become stronger than his self-preservative instinct and thus he may become a more reliable seaman. (2) It is certain that if his desertion is accepted with the fatalistic argument that he could not act differently and therefore is not responsible, this position would undermine the whole code of navigation.

An opponent might now try to contradict our position by the technique of *reductio ad absurdum*. He might ask: "How far do you want to go with your old-fashioned principle of responsibility? Is an accident-prone driver responsible for his mishaps? We know that our actions are determined more by unconscious than conscious motivations. One has no control over unconscious motivations. As far as conscious motivations are concerned, to make a person responsible for them may have some practical, educational or reforming value. This obviously does not apply to unconscious motivations. To set an example by punishment for deeds committed under the influence of unconscious factors cannot be effective." This argument contradicts Freud's position; he considered a person responsible even for his dreams. The basic error in this whole reasoning is that it treats the conscious and unconscious portions of the personality as two completely isolated systems without any intercommunication, like the left hand not knowing what the right hand is doing. This assumption is contrary to our knowledge. Slips of the tongue and other parapraxias are committed via our voluntary muscles, yet under the influence of unconscious motives. In such cases behavior is influenced by fully or partially unconscious motivations which infiltrate by various psychodynamic processes into a territory otherwise under the control of the conscious ego. The intercommunication between the two systems, conscious and unconscious, however, is a two-way traffic. Not only do unconscious processes influence conscious processes, but also conversely, conscious processes influence the unconscious. The best evidence of this is seen in psychoanalytic therapy wherein frequently the patient responds in his dream to an interpretation given by the analyst during the previous session. The method of free association also is based on the same intercommunication. The fact that the patient is asked to give up conscious control over his train of thought results in the greater influence of unconscious forces upon thought processes. Free associations are to a large degree influenced by unconscious forces which otherwise, when the vigilance of conscious censorship is intact, are less effective. Since both conscious and unconscious systems in the last analysis are parts of a whole cohesive system, the mental apparatus, it is not possible to make a person responsible only for what takes place in his conscious mind. An example may illustrate this point.

Some years ago a German court was confronted with a

difficult decision in a case of fratricide. A man, during deer-hunting season, shot his older brother by accident, mistaking him in the foggy dawn for a deer, a kind of accident not unknown in this country. During the trial it turned out that the older brother had married the divorced wife of the younger who had never reconciled himself to this marriage and harbored a deep-seated resentment against his older brother. The question was to determine whether the deed was murder or accident. Even though the act was evaluated as an accident, the question remained whether one could relieve the younger brother of responsibility for the act. No matter how different the legal and moral evaluation of this act may be, if it is considered either as an accident motivated by unconscious forces or as a premeditated murder, and no matter how different the disposition will be in either case, one cannot clear the perpetrator of responsibility for the consequences of his act, such as the economic security of his brother's widow and orphans.

In this case such considerations as trying to reform the brother by punishment are obviously not valid, yet there is no doubt that to make a person responsible for his acts has an effect upon his future behavior, even if his act was moti-vated by factors unknown to him. Punishment of careless drivers, even if their accidents are the result of unconscious motives, will increase almost every driver's sense of responsi-bility and consequently his vigilance over his movements. To eliminate punishment for accidents from traffic laws would undoubtedly result in an increase of accidents. On the other hand it would be quite erroneous to assume that fear of con-sequences, for example of punishment, will in all cases have a deterring influence upon criminal activity. The delinquent described by Freud as the criminal who commits his delin-quencies because of his guilty conscience, is known to react to punishment paradoxically. He is not only undeterred by punishment, but is encouraged by it to break the law again. One important reason for his criminality is his need for punishment by which he tries to relieve guilt feelings for deep-seated unconscious tendencies. To be punished for a smaller crime instead of the greater one he unconsciously wants to commit, is a good bargain for him. Moreover, punishment diminishes the restrictive force of his conscience. After being severely punished, he feels even with society and is freer than before to act antisocially. It would be erroneous, however, to draw the conclusion that such persons should not be made responsible for their acts. It only indicates that the disposition of different types of criminals must be individually determined according to the nature of the offender. Some may react favorably to punishment, others require incarceration along with therapy, and again with others there is no alternative but permanent custodial segregation from society. The fundamental principle, however, no matter what practical disposition is made, is that every person must be held responsible for the consequences of his acts.

The final conclusion of all these considerations is that the moral principle of responsibility is indispensable for society. A person reared according to the principle of responsibility will eventually internalize this feeling of responsibility towards others as a responsibility towards himself as well. This internalization of the feeling of responsibility is what makes him a social being. Only in a totalitarian society does the internal feeling of responsibility lose its meaning. Members of such societies have no freedom of deliberation. Their action is prescribed precisely and their education makes them automatons who act according to conditioned reflexes only. Since their behavior is not determined by any form of free deliberation, internal responsibility loses its meaning. They account for their actions only to external authority and not to their own conscience. The feeling of responsibility towards one's own self develops only in free societies. It is the basis of their existence.

Part II

SOME CRIMINAL CASES IN THE LIGHT OF

PSYCHOANALYSIS

PSYCHOANALYSIS OF CRIMINALS.

METHODOLOGICAL PROBLEMS

A PSYCHOANALYTICAL INVESTIGATION OF a specific criminal case presents certain specific difficulties which are different from those met with in the problem of interpreting a neurosis. The neurotic comes to the physician to get rid of his neurotic pain; he is ready to yield to the physician, whom he considers his ally, all his conscious and unconscious material; the criminal, when facing the representatives of the law, feels differently and is, therefore, less ready to give the necessary material. The relation of the defendant to his attorney is based, generally speaking, on a different set of psychological moments than that of patient and doctor; in both cases help is being sought, but it is not the same kind of help in both instances. The analytical patient knows that the doctor can help him only if, and when, the patient coöperates and tells his free associations. The defendant, however, while demanding that his lawyer bring his case to a successful issue, is by no means convinced that this success could be best achieved by telling the whole truth; therefore, the defending attorney is not always able to learn the whole truth about the transgression; instead, he has a report of the facts as given by the defendant, who tries to arrange them in a way which he thinks would best serve his practical interests. Any fundamental change in this state of affairs is possible, as has been already well emphasized by Ferenczi, only if and when our methods of dealing with the criminal are changed and if our mental attitude acquires a definite medico-psychological point of view. Only if the transgressor were certain that he is not threatened with any punishment or any other form of suffering, that instead there are those who want to understand him and help him, only then will his situation become comparable to that of a patient who comes to be analyzed. We may add that even if the defendant were absolutely frank and open with his attorney and the court, it would yet be impossible to apply the classical analytical methods for purposes of diagnosis, for some of the fundamental conditions of the psychoanalytical situation will still be missing; the psychic tension of one who expects sentence is not favorable for the smooth run of free associations which are the foundation of the psychoanalytical method.

It is quite natural that *after* the verdict is pronounced these difficulties disappear, especially if the defendant is out of prison. Here, however, another difficulty arises; neither acquittal nor the verdict of guilty create any favorable conditions which make the criminal accessible to psychoanalysis. Thus, for instance, one of the cases described below, immediately after he was set free by the court, was offered financial aid and a free psychoanalysis; this he rejected, saying that he was unable to accept charity. A criminal out of a sense of guilt *is* unable to accept the help of his defender, for such help is to him an act of charity which acts against the demands of his need for punishment; this need, as long as it remains ungratified, drives him to new transgressions, which will finally get him into jail.

Similar conditions cause Ferenczi to doubt the applicability of psychoanalysis in cases of criminals who are awaiting trial. If Ferenczi had in mind psychoanalytical therapy, we agree with him, for the atmosphere which is created by the present-day methods of dispensing justice makes it actually impossible for the defendant to be sincere, sincerity being the fundamental condition for psychoanalytical treatment; Ferenczi, however, believes that even a psychoanalytical understanding of the defendant is impossible as long as trial is pending. The cases described below were explained by means of psychoanalytical understanding before the verdict of the court was given; this fact will, perhaps, dispose of the necessity of going into too much theoretical discussion. We may add that the aim which therapy sets for itself is different from that of trying to understand the psychic motivations of a given crime and the total personality of a given criminal. Even in cases of neurosis, after a rather short time, occasionally after a few analytical hours, the analyst obtains a general picture and gains insight into the essential features of the origin and structure of the neurosis, but, of course, he is not able, for some time, to apply this knowledge for purposes of therapy; by means of psychoanalytical knowledge we are able to take the proper measure of the transgressor who is awaiting trial. The general attitude of the defendant, his denials, his confessions, the type and content of his rationalizations could be evaluated psychoanalytically. In general, the observation of a criminal made during the fatal hours preceding the trial, reveal to a psychoanalyst a great deal about the unconscious of the man; at times, even more is revealed than in the course of many empty weeks of a difficult analysis of a psychoneurotic. The dramatically concentrated expressions of the man's unconscious, just before and during the trial, are more convincing at times and much deeper than the protracted epic presentation which the unconscious uses in free associations. This, incidentally, was observed with inexorable regularity in the first case described below, a case of a man driven by his need for punishment. The defendant, facing the court, leads us through his crime and through his behavior in general; he carries out before our eyes a part of his own analysis in a very plastic fashion. The analytically trained attorney was able, in the case described below, to establish at times an atmosphere of confidential understanding which, from the point of view of obtaining unconscious material, was equivalent to the transference relationship between physician and patient.

AN OFFENDER THROUGH AN UNCONSCIOUS

FEELING OF GUILT

THE MATERIAL FOR THIS CASE BECAME available thanks to the relationship of mutual confidence which established itself between the defendant and his attorney, a relationship which corresponded to the positive transference occurring in the course of a psychoanalysis. Yet, for reasons given below, the material is rather scanty. The lack of the repressed infantile material is particularly conspicuous, because such material can be obtained only through the method of free associations; hence, only allusions suggesting certain reconstructions were obtained. Thus, while from the standpoint of therapy the etiology of the case is not clear, a number of valuable data gave us sufficient insight for the psychological understanding of the unconscious mechanisms, that led this man to repeated breaking of the law.

A thirty-four-year-old, cultured man, we will call him Bruno, was sentenced to prison for more than a year because of various petty thefts. He appealed to a higher court. Mr. Staub, who undertook his defense, visited him in prison and found him in a comfortable state of mind and rather pleased with his situation. It soon became evident that he was not the usual type of thief; neither his social position nor the general circumstances appeared consistent with Bruno's offense. For years he had been a surgeon in a university hospital; his medical diploma was a forged one, but his medical knowledge was well grounded; his superiors held him in great esteem and valued his work highly; his theoretical contributions and laboratory research were very successful; he published several original scientific papers.

In the course of his medical work in one of the large cities of Central Europe, he stole medical books from one bookshop and went at once to offer them for sale in another in the immediate vicinity; he neglected to remove the bookseller's labels from the stolen books. This was noticed and he was asked to return; before leaving the bookshop, Bruno gave them his correct name and address. The theft was naturally discovered, Bruno was arrested and it incidentally became known that he had no right to practice medicine and that his diploma was forged.

This theft, like all his former delinquencies, could not be explained by the usual motivations of an ordinary theft. In the bookshop in which he stole the books he had been known for a number of years as a steady customer; his credit was good and he could buy any book he wished; moreover, he was in comfortable circumstances, since only a short time previously he had acquired the well-paid position of assistant gynecologist at the university hospital. Because of the insignificance of the offense, Bruno was discharged on probation; he then went to Berlin, where he stopped in a hotel under his own name; he at once went to the medical quarter of the city, visited several bookshops, stole various medical books and without removing the bookseller's labels, offered them for sale in a shop in the vicinity; as formerly, it was quickly noticed; he was asked to return; he left his name and address and was again arrested. The whole episode was a true repetition of the previous one.

When the police commissioner examined the details of the affair, he told Bruno that in view of the comparative insignificance of the offense he was to be free temporarily. Bruno then volunteered the information that he had also stolen some parts of a microscope in one of the optical shops; the police even then refused to keep him in custody; at this Bruno made another confession. He stated that on his way to Berlin he stopped off at Leipzig at an exhibition and there he had stolen several porcelain figures, which he produced. He was then arrested and sent to jail to await trial. In jail he felt well, he even seemed free of any worry; his only wish was to obtain as many medical books as possible and he studied with great zeal. Throughout his detention in jail he appeared satisfied and happy, his deportment was excellent; he tried to establish contact with the prison physician, in order to help him in the prison hospital; the physician at first distrusted Bruno, but finally learned to admire his medical skill and scientific knowledge.

It soon became clear to Mr. Staub, Bruno's attorney, that he was dealing with a culprit whose acts were not prompted by purely conscious motives and that he dealt here with a case of neurotic acting-out of some unconscious impulse. Even a criminologist, untrained in the problems of deeper psychology, would have been struck by the irrational nature of Bruno's behavior. One gains a definite impression that Bruno wanted to get into jail and did all he could to achieve this aim. Unlike the ordinary thief, who acts with utmost caution and who does his best to avoid detection and capture, Bruno seems to have deliberately done his best to be discovered; such type of behavior can be explained only when we assume that Bruno acted under the pressure of an unconscious drive to be punished. He gained nothing by his petty thefts, he could and did only lose. His behavior with the police in Berlin, his confession of totally unsuspected offenses, which made it impossible not to arrest him, all bear witness to Bruno's unconscious but definite and effective need for punishment.

The next question which arises rather forcibly is, What were the sources of this relentless need for punishment? If we assume that he was driven to his delinquencies by an unconscious wish to do himself definite harm, we might be justified in thinking that his need for punishment was a reaction against his use of a forged medical diploma; as a matter of fact, his very first theft actually ruined his spurious medical career. However, the study of Bruno's life history made it clear to us that his unconscious sense of guilt, which was apparently closely related to his medical work, actually came from more primitive and deeper sources of his personality.

He committed his first offense at the age of seventeen, when he was a cadet in training to become an officer. At that time he stole some sweets; this happened in the canteen and within sight of those who had charge of it. In his diary he refers to this event as a very grave offense, which made him feel very guilty and which had justly caused him to be expelled from the cadet corps. Actually, however, he was not expelled at that time; he was to be punished by temporary suspension of leave, but he ran away and as a result was expelled. We were able to gain some suspicion as to the real source of Bruno's deeply seated sense of guilt in connection with his first theft, when we learned that he stole the sweets immediately after his mother, who was pregnant at the time, visited him; when recalling this incident, Bruno told his attorney that that pregnancy filled him with a frightful sense of shame, and that he felt at that time as if people were pointing their fingers at him.

This first offense bears all the earmarks of a crime committed out of an unconscious sense of guilt. He felt guilty for his mother's pregnancy, for in his unconscious phantasy he considered himself responsible for his mother's condition; hence he committed a relatively minor offense for which he was punished; he needed that punishment in order to be relieved of the unconscious sense of guilt which was awakened in him by the sight of his pregnant mother. That is why he took the comparatively insignificant transgression so deeply to heart; did it not serve him the purpose of relieving him of the guilt which was created by a much more serious and forbidden wish—to see his mother pregnant by himself? The deep emotions with which this wish was charged were thus transferred onto the minor miscreance of stealing some sweets. The question why he happened to steal sweets for the purpose of provoking punishment is answered by the following memory of an early age. Bruno's father was very strict, he was a stern puritanical person, who watched with most painful frugality every lump of sugar that young Bruno was permitted to have. Even now, an adult, mature person, Bruno cannot tell without bitterness how his father watched him that he take not more than *one* lump of sugar with his tea or coffee; his mother surreptitiously permitted him a second, but if his father discovered this, Bruno was thrashed with a whip. Thus the enjoyment of sweets became for Bruno a symbol of a secret relationship with his mother, which was forbidden by his father; a relationship, the discovery of which was followed by punishment. It should be recalled that in accordance with psychoanalytical experience, sugar and sweets in general appear to our unconscious as substitutes for mother's milk and are, therefore, perceived as a symbol of mother as a whole. The predilection for sweets, found in so many individuals, is a derivative of the oral fixation on the act of sucking, an act which presents the first sensual relationship between child and mother.

If we return now to Bruno's first delinquency, which occurred when he was a cadet, we shall observe that it bore the two characteristics which Freud described in the cases of crimes committed out of a sense of guilt: (1) the offense is carried out because it represents a forbidden act; the sense of guilt which had been active before the offense was committed, and which comes from the Œdipus conflict, is attached to the offense itself; (2) this offense has as its aim the suffering of punishment, which thus attenuates the preëxisting sense of guilt. The manifest transgression thus presents but a disguise for the Œdipus crime which was actually intended.

Bruno's unconscious sense of guilt was deeply seated; it arose early in his childhood; his infantile neurosis, which consisted of a phobia, was precipitated by a sudden occurrence when he was five years old. He was with his mother in the city, where they went to call for his father; two runaway horses suddenly dashed toward them; Bruno was so frightened that for many years afterwards he was afraid to walk in the streets. This excessive fear reaction can be easily explained in the light of general psychoanalytical experience; it arose as a result of the sense of guilt, which was awakened in the little boy escorting his mother, for he wanted to have his mother all to himself and wished to defer meeting his father for as long as possible; the scene with the maddened horses galloping toward him provoked such an excessive and lasting reaction because it occurred at the moment when the boy was in the throes of his psychological conflict; just at the moment when he was indulging in a daydream: "I shall remain alone with mother, father will not come," two wild horses suddenly rushed forth—a true enactment of the infantile zoöphobia; the animal, representing the father who appears to avenge himself upon the boy who wished his parent's death.

It is, therefore, worth noting how Bruno elevated the trifling incident of the cadet corps to one of the most important events of his life. By means of a feigned suicidal attempt he forced his parents to forgive his misdemeanor and he was permitted to return to school; previously he was taken away from school, as he had contracted various childhood diseases; the parents acted in this on the advice of their old family physician. This physician appears to have played quite an important role in Bruno's life. It was this physician who frustrated the boy's early wish to study medicine. This physician convinced Bruno's parents that in order to build up the boy's weakened health, he should choose a profession which required more physical than intellectual effort. This meddling was so much more a heavy blow to Bruno, because he had watched the old doctor for years and envied him his freedom of access to his mother's bedroom, his mother having been frequently ill. Thus, to become a doctor, which was forbidden him, came to mean freedom for unopposed physical relationship with mother; next to father only the doctor enjoyed this privilege. The parental prohibition contributed particularly to the boy's identification of the medical calling with the gratification of his infantile incestuous wishes; both modes of approach to mother were equally forbidden him.

Medical work and his infantile sexual curiosity and peeping trends were woven together in his mind; how intimate this relationship was could be demonstrated by the following incident: once, attending a lecture on anatomy he stole a camera from a girl student; as he did not even attempt to leave the lecture room, he was naturally found out at once. It is because of the sense of guilt which was in him, connected with medical knowledge, that he stole the optic instrument; acquiring anatomical knowledge was to him equivalent to peeping secretly at mother and it is *for this crime* and not for stealing that he sought to be punished. In other words, we again deal here with a symbolic act performed out of an unconscious sense of guilt.

It is clear now why Bruno always stole medical books and optical instruments. Medical work acquired for him the absolute emotional value of incest; that is why he *had* to acquire his medical knowledge, medical instruments and a medical diploma not in the usual legitimate way, but by means of an illicit struggle, by means of forgery and stealing. This method offered him two definite psychological acquisitions; on one hand, the spiteful defiant nature of his behavior helped him to associate medicine more completely with incest, and thus afforded him a more complete unconscious gratification of his Œdipus wishes; on the other hand, the sense of guilt arising from both medical work and incestuous trends were easily displaced on comparatively minor and frequently only formal transgressions. Is not the crime of the skillful and competent practice of surgery without a medical diploma, a minor and merely a formal transgression, as compared with the latter's unconscious meaning of sexual intercourse with one's own mother? This mechanism afforded him a particularly keen sense of pleasure. The extent of his joy becomes particularly clear when we read in his diary that without a medical diploma and in defiance of all laws he, Bruno, performed better operations than many diplomated and licensed surgeons.

However, Bruno was able to maintain these affects of spite

and defiance in a state of equilibrium only as long as he remained an unpaid assistant, i.e., so long as he could devote himself to his calling under duress of deprivation. When he rose higher in his career, when he obtained a well-paid position, working under an appreciative chief and, what is of particular importance, when he started to work in the gynecological division of the hospital, then the ground fell from under his proud defiance and the unconscious sense of guilt grew to a point of high tension.

It was at this stage of his career that he began to steal books, which led to his unmasking. To be prosecuted and punished for the mere formality of not having a diploma, and despite his being a competent and successful surgeon, afforded Bruno a particular relief from his sense of guilt; that is why he was so cheerful and so keen for work while in jail; for the whole situation made it possible for him again to put the world in the wrong and thus to recapture his sense of spite and defiance. After leaving prison he writes to his attorney and tells triumphantly that he bought a microscope; he acquired it legitimately; he paid for it with his own money; it was a much better microscope than the one he had once stolen, and "I shall prove to the world that I am not merely a dead weight in human society." We should note the striking overevaluation of the possession of a microscope; we should also note the defiant haste with which he acquired it immediately upon regaining his freedom. It is an additional illustration of how, by way of displacement, the possession of a scientific instrument became charged with the affect of the infantile peeping lust, which is a special manifestation of one's incestuous drive.

The theft of the porcelain figures which were new and actually of no value is more in the nature of a kleptomanic act. In addition to what we already know about Bruno, we obtained a hint as to the unconscious meaning of this theft in the following manner: as he was relating this part of his story he spontaneously recalled that his mother possessed a very valuable collection of old porcelain figures, which he liked very much. It is difficult to say which of the following two mechanisms played a more important role in the stealing of these porcelains. By gaining possession of the figures, he might have identified himself unconsciously with his mother, who owned similar objects; on the other hand, following the principle of *pars pro toto,* so characteristic of our unconscious, by appropriating the figures he might have gratified his unconscious drive to gain possession of his mother; from what we know of the man, it would seem that this latter determinant played a greater role in this minor theft.

In general, it would appear that the incestuous wishes had a tenacious grip on Bruno throughout his life; in spiteful defiance of his father he refused to relinquish his incestuous claims. His whole manner of life seems to be motivated by the drive to put the world in the wrong, i.e., all the unconscious father presentations; he always strove to compel them to treat him harshly and unjustly; he thus freed himself of his sense of guilt without having to give up his spite and defiance. He was able to tolerate only bad, harsh, unjust fathers; that is why he could not accept his kindly medical chief, or the help offered by his lawyer, or an analysis gratis, which was proposed. In his childhood he learned to know only one type of parent, that is, an unbending, non-understanding father; it is only when facing such a father that he is able to assert himself; his whole psychic apparatus seems to have adjusted itself only to the specific atmosphere of his childhood. For Bruno to meet a kind and understanding father means to meet some one he never knew, of whom he had never had any conception; it means to throw him into an unfamiliar and uncanny relationship charged with a sense of guilt; it means to break down the very foundation of the psychological structure in which he had always lived. That is why he preferred to flee as soon as his lawyer offered him assistance; then, more secure at a distance from this image of a good father, he wrote: "You want to know why I cannot accept your offer of help. Well, every account must be footed; the debit and credit totals of our account appears too much in favor of one side only. Should I accept your offer I would remain indebted to you for the rest of my life; I never was able to endure a feeling of indebtedness. I should have remained in prison; I was born under an evil star."

He found no difficulty in placing present-day justice in the role of his father and thus reëstablishing for himself the atmosphere of his parental home. This accomplished, it was easier for him to escape the moral influence of a father who was guided by a narrow-minded, bureaucratic code of morals, a father who showed himself repeatedly unjust and harsh and cruel, a father who forbade him the usual pleasures which a child should have, a father who treated mother badly and who deceived her; Bruno thus totally escaped any dependence on father and was therefore able to preserve his Œdipus complex in its infantile freshness. The educational methods of Bruno's father are characteristically demonstrated by such details as a beating for the use of an extra lump of sugar, or as the setting aside of Friday as the only day when the boy was permitted to play with his toys; this militaristic morality of duty and drill, which was dominant in pre-war Germany, very frequently made any identification with one's parents or teachers impossible and led to the formation of a Superego which was like a foreign body in one's personality. If we also bear in mind that this father maltreated and scolded his wife, who was his social and intellectual superior, in the presence of the children, that contrary to the morality he preached with such hypocrisy, he also deceived her—then we can understand why Bruno strove all through his life to place in the wrong any father image and thus easily free himself from the inner inhibitory influence of the father. We say easily, because the nature of present-day justice makes it really quite easy for one to see in it the reflection of a non-understanding father. At any rate, Bruno established this psychological association to its fullest possible extent. According to his lights, he, a capable surgeon, a physician with excellent scientific background, who had so unselfishly treated many people, was punished unjustly; this gave him a sense of unconscious triumph over society; it gave him a sense of profound gratification, which many normal people would envy despite their healthy sublimations.

Bruno thus appears to be a typical neurotic criminal; his misdemeanors are prompted by his unconscious sense of guilt and at times bear a kleptomanic tinge; the harm done society by such offenders appears to be comparatively small. We believe that a more adequate method of dealing with them would be temporary commitment to a special mental institution combined with an attempt to cure them by means of psychoanalysis.

Punishment by law, as it is practiced today in cases like Bruno's, is quite senseless; it is totally ineffectual in bringing about an improvement in the culprit's behavior; more than that, punishment in such cases is harmful from the social point of view, because it only serves to spur on such offenders to ever newer and newer transgressions. One could hardly do Bruno any greater favor than to put one's self in the wrong in his eyes; on the other hand, a kindness throws him into a state of confusion. So long as society continues to punish such individuals, i.e., so long as society continues to be taken in by their unconscious provocations, they are to some extent right when they refuse to be cured: why should they voluntarily give up so many possibilities of unconscious gratifications of which psychoanalytic treatment would rob them? The real will to be cured will awaken in them when society stops punishing them.

A NEUROTIC ATTEMPT AT MURDER

K ARL, A YOUNG MAN OF TWENTY-FIVE, had been chronically without a job, but his record, on the whole, remained unblemished. One evening he came to a transient hotel in Berlin with his mistress, a housemaid, and engaged a room; here he fired a shot into the girl's temple. He then collapsed, but soon regained consciousness, rang for a physician and called the police; he was taken into custody and it was then discovered that Karl and his mistress had planned a double suicide; they met that evening to carry out their plan; first they went to various inns and amusement places, then they wrote farewell letters and finally reached the hotel room, where they were to put an end to their lives. Karl had a revolver, which he had bought with the girl's money. As he fired at his sweetheart he lost his courage; he found himself incapable of firing the second shot at himself, and surrendered to the police instead. She was not killed. She lost the sight of one eye.

At first it was impossible to find any obvious reasons for the crime. Karl was a healthy and easygoing young man, with a weakness for alcohol and women. His mother died when he was yet a child; his father was an officer in active service; after the war he worked as an engineer and was continually away from home. Karl thus grew up under very little super-vision; moreover, at an early age he enlisted in the army, went to war and later served in the frontier guard; hence Karl's education was of necessity neglected and so he was not very successful in gaining a proper foothold in life; he became a clerk but worked only intermittently; he was without a job most of the time, yet he suffered no great need, living on the unemployment dole and occasional odd jobs. His mistress came from a provincial lower middleclass family, and was in service on the West Side of Berlin. She had known Karl for some months before the tragic incident described above. They entered a love relationship soon after they met. Before leaving her native town, the girl was engaged to a man favored by her parents; the engagement was not broken off; she felt she had to marry the man, because her parents wished it. She did not conceal this from Karl and he would frequently ask her whether she would not rather marry him; to this the girl would reply that if he had a steady job and could support a wife and if he would stop drinking and going about with other women, she would gladly marry him. However, her engagement did not seem to interfere with their liaison; as Karl earned very little, the girl paid for their amusements. Karl had no objection to this state of affairs. He accepted his sweetheart's engagement to another man and would console himself thinking that, of course, the girl had to marry the man, since her parents insisted on it; if she disobeyed them, they would disown her; if he, Karl, were in a position to support a family she would undoubtedly prefer to marry him. Yet the emotional equilibrium of both the young man and the girl appears to have been disturbed quite often; frequent ill humor in one would be reflected in the other by depression; these swings of mood seem to have been caused mainly by the girl's constant vacillation between her fiancé and her lover. One day she told Karl that it would be best if she married her fiancé while he, Karl, could remain her lover. Karl rejected the plan most vehemently; he considered it absolutely immoral and not worth considering. A depression followed in the wake of this exchange of opinion and the suicidal trend came to expression for the first time. He told his sweetheart that he would put an end to his life, that he was good for nothing, that he was unable to establish a home and a family, that he was in all respects weary of life;

the girl at once begged him to take her with him in death; she, too, she said, was extremely unhappy; she did not love her fiancé; her parents forced her to get married; she was ready to do her duty, but she knew beforehand that it would be an unhappy marriage; moreover, the girl added, she was tired of life; her nearest relatives misunderstood and mistreated her; her older sister had accused her, unjustly, of stealing; in short, the girl wanted to join him in death. Karl at once snatched at this idea, and told himself that he must save his sweetheart from an unhappy life and from a tragic future; thus the suicide pact was made.

It goes without saying, that the reasons for their decision, which Karl and his sweetheart consciously considered valid, were neither the true nor the most important reasons for their suicidal wishes. The motives for killing his sweetheart, which Karl related, can be easily recognized as rather transparent rationalizations which sought to cover up deeper and more effectual psychological determinants; too, the immediate occasion which precipitated in him the thought of suicide, appears striking. He knew that the girl had promised to marry another man; yet he considered it seemly to have a liaison with her; why then this sudden, vehement, affective defense reaction when it was suggested to him that she marry the other man, but continue to keep him, Karl, as her lover? Nothing would have substantially changed in Karl's relation with the girl, if this suggestion were carried out; it is not quite clear why this suggestion released a suicidal trend.

Our psychoanalytical experience tells us that being the lover of a married woman has, in the unconscious of this lover, the meaning of the fulfilled Œdipus wish; the infantile Œdipus situation is reënacted: a third person having no rights gains illicit possession of a woman who legally belongs to another man. His sweetheart's proposal had no other meaning for Karl than that of an invitation to reënact the Œdipus situation. His mother died when he was little; it is to be regretted that unfavorable external circumstances did not allow us to lift to any considerable degree the strong amnesia which covered so deeply his early childhood. As to Karl's attitude toward his father, he occasionally liked him, but frequently disliked and defied him. Now he lived with his father and then they became estranged and Karl would leave him; a distinct ambivalence thus appeared to control Karl's attitude toward his father. When, however, at the age of sixty, the father remarried and brought home with him a young wife who was almost Karl's age, the relations between father and son appeared to improve; the usual animosity between child and stepmother was strikingly absent in this case; on the contrary, Karl felt attracted to the young woman and soon a genuine comradeship bound stepson and stepmother together. Karl's attitude toward his father's home, which heretofore was rather negative, changed into one of the greatest harmony imaginable. The stepmother, who was delicate and ailing, was one day taken seriously ill, and she remained bed-ridden for a long time. Karl would spend the day at his father's home; he took care of his stepmother; he was cheerful, he prepared and served her her food; he chatted with her; he attended to various household duties. His father was working in the meantime; he would not come home till evening. As evening set in, Karl would leave to spend the night away from his father's home.

Suddenly, one evening, the father suggested that it would perhaps be better if Karl would not stay with his stepmother during the day, while the father was away working; people, he said, might misunderstand and gossip about it. Taken by itself, this suggestion appeared reasonable; it seemed to be nothing more than a precaution and an expression of respect for people's good opinion. Yet on Karl it had a devastating effect; he felt that his father was unusually unkind and unfair to him; he was brokenhearted that his father had such base suspicions about him; he therefore decided to leave his father's home for good; he did not again visit it until his stepmother died some months later.

This vehement emotional reaction, which was so uncalled for by the facts, appears striking in many respects. One thinks of the French saying: *Il n'y a que la vérité qui blesse*. Ostensibly there was not a single reason why Karl should consciously reproach himself for any improper intentions toward his stepmother; however, if we view the incident in the light of general psychoanalytical experience, it will appear to us more clear; evidently Karl was so painfully hurt by his father's suggestion, because it must have touched upon a most vulnerable spot; evidently Karl perceived the remark as a frank statement of something of which he was not himself aware, but for which he had an unconscious, yet very deep, yearning. Karl until this had had many love affairs; but they were all but of very short duration; in other words, he had failed until then to establish any real object love relationship with a woman; yet immediately after he left father's house he established a love relationship with the girl in Berlin, which lasted a number of months until the day when he fired the fateful shot at her. This girl was of the same age as his stepmother and of a similar physical build; in general, she bore such a striking resemblance to his stepmother that it was even evident to the untrained eyes of some of the witnesses who were called to testify in court. His sweetheart resembled his stepmother yet in other respects; for she, too, belonged to another man; was she not engaged and planning to marry? Moreover, in their relationship the girl played the role of a mother, as it were. She paid many of Karl's expenses, she found a job for his brother; in general, she appeared to be the giver while Karl remained the receiver. It appears that the whole relationship had for Karl the emotional value of his former attitude toward his stepmother. Too, all he wanted unconsciously from his stepmother he quite definitely brought to realization in this liaison.

We can understand another similarity between Karl's unconscious attitude toward his stepmother and that which he felt toward his real sweetheart. He reacted with similar depressions to his father's remark that people might gossip about him and his stepmother and to his sweetheart's suggestion that he remain her lover after her marriage; his attachment to both women was fed from the same emotional sources. The attachment to his stepmother, as compared with his relationship toward people generally, appears to have been unusually strong; it apparently came from unconscious incestuous wishes. Karl's Superego was sufficiently strong to inhibit any awareness of these wishes and still more their actual realization. It is not difficult to see why his father's warning had such a profound effect on Karl; even under normal circumstances it was difficult for Karl to keep his incestuous wishes constantly repressed, for they were unusually strong; now the warning uttered by his father touched a sensitive chord and thus seriously endangered the whole work of repression. He immediately made attempts to rid himself of the awakened unconscious feelings of guilt (he was conscience-stricken) and he did this by means of a projection, i.e., he distorted the meaning of the warning made by his father; he considered it a reproach; he thus insisted that father reproached him for something that he did not actually do; in other words, his father was unjust to him; Karl thus succeeds in putting his father in the wrong and leaves him. Actually, the father's words contained no reproach for his son's incest wishes; it is the son who read the meaning into his father's words. Like most projections, Karl's might have been justified; his projected affect may very well have been a reaction to his father's unconscious feelings; for the warning must have also been an expression of jealousy on the part of the father. Thus an affective reaction, which could not be explained by its conscious content, became quite intelligible when we took into consideration the dialogue which took place between the respective unconscious systems of father and son.

Although he projected his sense of guilt and thus rid himself of inner self-reproaches, Karl was yet unable to silence the voice of his unconscious incestuous drive; as a matter of fact, this voice should have and did become louder, since his unconscious sense of guilt was diminished, and therefore the inhibitory power of his Superego was weakened. Karl thus found himself under great pressure of his deeper instinctual drives; viewed in the light of this psychological tension, his liaison appears to have been an attempt to strike a compromise with his unconscious impulses: he chose an exogamous object on whom to live out his thwarted love; in other words, it was an attempt to solve his problems in a healthy, normal direction. However, this solution betrays primarily the unusual strength of Karl's incestuous wishes, for the object he chose bore a striking likeness to the mother who was forbidden him. The girl's suggestion that he continue to be her lover after she married another man, naturally reawakened Karl's unconscious sense of guilt. Up to that moment his unconscious inhibitory forces were in a temporary slumber, as it were; it cost Karl a great deal of effort and pain to keep them in that slumber. He succeeded in this by virtue of the fact that his love object was not in reality his mother, but a strange woman, i.e., an object which was not prohibited; this permitted his Id tendencies, which were tinged with incestuous wishes, to gain the upper hand and to find free expression; however, the girl's suggestion threatened to make too clear to his conscious the real meaning of his feelings; it threatened to undermine the whole work of repression and therefore aroused with increased force his unconscious sense of guilt. Karl was able to keep in a state of psychological equilibrium only as long as his mistress remained unmarried, and so long as she lived away from her fiancé; however, once married, the unconscious would see in their relationship a perfect enactment of the crime of incest—and this Karl was unable to bear. Again, an extreme state of tension ensued and as a short-cut solution of the problem arose the decision to kill the girl and himself. We shall presently be able to see also the deeper meaning of this decision.

Karl suffered from an extremely strong incestuous set of impulses, which were a result of an unsolved Œdipus complex. Although we are unable to prove directly that Karl was bound to his real mother by powerful incestuous wishes, his behavior and his psychological reactions leave no doubt in the mind of an experienced analyst that Karl's incestuous attachment to his real mother was and remained strong and psychologically active. At first he lived out this attachment in a sublimated form in relation to his stepmother; his father's warning disturbed the normal work of repression and closed this outlet for him; he then displaced his incestuous wishes onto his sweetheart, who served as a substitute. When, however, his repressed wishes were shattered at this point too, Karl naturally regressed to the sadomasochistic level. The wish of the couple to die together, like an hysterical symptom, presents simultaneously a gratification of their erotic wishes and a self-imposed punishment for this gratification; the popular expression "united in death" is suggestive of the erotic content of such a striving; the living out of one's incestuous wishes becomes possible under such circumstances, because the self-imposed capital punishment removes the sense of guilt.

Another determinant which caused Karl's depression appears to be the following: the girl's suggestion that she marry the other man signified to Karl that the father (his substitutive image, or prototype) won a victory over him; the decision to kill the woman meant, therefore, also the decision to rob the father of his wife. Both components of the Œdipus wish, that is, first, to rob the father of his wife, and second, to unite with her, could have been thus gratified.

Although we have gained some insight into the unconscious motives of Karl's action, the chief problem remains unsolved. We don't see yet how Karl succeeded in carrying out his plan to murder without any apparent sense of guilt. The attempt to kill must have had yet another unconscious meaning, which pacified his overdemanding Superego. Otherwise it is impossible to understand why he appeared undisturbed and without any definite signs of remorse, despite the fact that he had crippled his sweetheart and evaded suicide. This remarkable harmony which appears to have established itself between the gratification of the criminal impulse and the demands of the Superego is of particular psychological interest; some definite unconscious processes create this harmony; an understanding of this process would furnish us with a clue to the solution of the mystery why some people of definite moral sensibility at times commit very serious crimes without any sense of guilt.

Karl always lived under the pressure of his conscience, which influenced his behavior; his unconscious sense of guilt, which came from his incest impulses, made him restless and unstable; it finally drove him away from his father's home; it made any normal relation with his sweetheart impossible. He was repeatedly asked to tell what actually drove him to the decision to end his own life and that of his sweetheart. Karl would invariably give the same stereotyped answer: "I saw the marriage of my oldest brother." (Karl was the youngest of three.) "My brother works all day; he occupies a high position and earns a lot of money; his wife sleeps most of the day, dresses up, deceives him and spends all his money; it is a very unhappy marriage. I wanted to save my friend from such an unhappy marriage." The logical blindness of this argument is astounding. The example cited by Karl shows that it is the man and not the woman who is the injured party of the marriage; it is the woman who betrays the man and who is therefore the guilty one. Karl's argument would be quite intelligible if the woman he wanted to kill were an untrue and disloyal woman. Karl thus betrays his unconscious intention to kill a bad woman. Viewed from a certain angle, his sweetheart would actually appear to be such a woman; she deceived her fiancé, she spent her money on another man; in short, she did for Karl all that Karl unconsciously wished his stepmother to do, and that gave him an unconscious sense of guilt. Yet Karl decided to kill his sweetheart; apparently he identified himself unconsciously first with the injured man, fundamentally with his father, and then decided to avenge himself for the woman's unfaithfulness by killing her. Sweetheart and stepmother were strongly identified with one another in his unconscious; he thus was able to kill his stepmother in his sweetheart, as if it were the sweetheart and not the stepmother who was untrue to his father. Thus, in the end, Karl was able to play unconsciously the role of the avenging father. We can now see why Karl was able to free himself of his unconscious sense of guilt, which should have arisen as a result of incestuous gratification: he identified himself with the avenging father and he thus succeeded in luring his Superego to take the side of his Id. He was successful in this, only because he took over the role of the father who was being betrayed by his wife, and avenged himself upon her; the murder thus acquired a positive value and diminished the feelings of guilt. We thus have again a good example of the projection of the sense of guilt. His own incestuous wishes, which he had for his stepmother, he successfully projected into his sweetheart, who was a substitute for the stepmother. He was able to do so because his sweetheart was actually deceiving her fiancé. Thus playing the role of father, he wants to kill the unfaithful woman and feels free from any sense of guilt.

It is interesting to note that the girl herself unconsciously perceived Karl's act as one of vengeance; after the shocking incident in the hotel room, she turned violently against her lover; she married her fiancé; wherever and whenever she could, she tried to cause Karl trouble and to injure him; she insisted that she had agreed to die only because Karl drove her to that decision; that he wanted to kill her; she did not abandon her hostile attitude till the very last moment; only in open court, under pressure of the testimony of some witnesses and the evidence of the farewell letters written in her own handwriting, did she at last give up her violent hostility. This singular attitude remains unintelligible unless we perceive it as an instinctive reaction against the tinge of revenge, which she perceived unconsciously in Karl's deed.

These dynamic unconscious impulses which ruled Karl's mind could break through to active expression only after his conscious Ego was won over to this by means of various rationalizations. Karl therefore convinced his conscious Ego that he did the right thing, that to kill his sweetheart meant to free her of the disappointments, suffering and insults which life hurled at her.

As to his decision to commit suicide, we have seen that through the act of self-destruction his unconscious would have achieved several aims; he would become united in death with his sweetheart and thus gratify his Œdipus wishes on the sado-masochistic level; he would identify himself with the avenging father, and free himself from his own sense of guilt by killing in himself the son who committed the crime of incest. There is another important unconscious motive in Karl's suicidal trend; by killing himself he would gratify another Œdipus wish, namely that of killing his father within himself. This identification with his father was made possible by the role he unconsciously ascribed to his sweetheart; as if to say: the man who possesses his mother should be brought to death by self-destruction. Thus suicide acquires the significance of getting rid of the Superego (again the introjected father), which as the main source of Karl's feelings of guilt had to be silenced once and for all. Freud was right when he insisted that every suicide presents a disguised murder of another person who has been introjected.

It remains for us now to explain the psychological circumstances which prevented Karl from actually committing suicide. We already observed that after shooting the girl he showed no striking sense of guilt; he felt rather righteous; he defended himself with great energy and tenacity and was reconciled with his father.

By killing his beloved he avenged his father's honor, as it were; he punished her for unfaithfulness; in other words, he acted as if to please his father; moreover, he also punished himself by sacrificing his own love object. Thus the sense of guilt with regard to his father was considerably reduced; it became quantitatively too weak to overcome the natural, instinctive will to live. Moreover, the depression created by the girl's suggestion of a suicide pact should have naturally disappeared, since his accomplice *permitted* him to kill her; was she not in perfect agreement with the suicide pact? More

than that, by getting rid of the woman he succeeded in identifying himself with his father in a tragic setting. His father's
first wife (Karl's mother) died; Karl, too, sacrifices the object
of his love; this sacrifice is at the same time an act of self-
punishment. Having played this tragic and painful role, Karl
felt his father's equal and, with the sense of guilt disposed
of, he could make peace with him.

The unconscious sense of guilt which Karl felt toward his
father and the unconscious homosexual fixation on him, were
the strongest feelings which lived in Karl; they were stronger
than any heterosexual drive. This is proved by the final
psychological result of the act, of which his sweetheart was
the victim. Karl tried to rid himself of his mother (his sweetheart), whose existence formed a rift between him and his
father, in order to be able to stay with father undisturbed;
in other words, the passive homosexual component of his
drive to separate father from mother played the most decisive role in Karl's shooting the girl. His aggressive attitude
toward women, which he gives vent to in his criticism of his
brother's wife; his general attitude toward women, to whom
he never was able to establish any deep emotional attachment; his attempt to kill his sweetheart, and finally the subsequent reconciliation with his father—are all definite
expressions of Karl's unconscious homosexuality. He was
able to give up the gratification of his incestuous wishes,
which he would have obtained by following the girl in
death, chiefly because he was able to flee into a passive homosexual relationship to his father. This relationship meant a
gratification of the reversed Œdipus wishes, i.e., the wish
to be united with father. That is why the life instinct gained
the upper hand and Karl could go on living.

*   *   *   *   *

We have dealt here with a criminal act which was *not*
dictated by *criminal* motives; the main motive power in this
crime came from unresolved extremely strong unconscious
feelings of guilt; in other words, it was a crime motivated by
unconscious *ethical* emotions. Karl is a *neurotic criminal,*

whose conscious Ego was unable to give a satisfactory explanation of the crime. Any punishment, any enforced suffering was in this case purposeless and ineffectual. Karl is a subject for psychoanalytic treatment, he does not belong to the prison community. Psychoanalytic treatment in such a case would resolve the Œdipus complex, and therefore would produce a cure and make a return to normal social life quite possible.

We may mention, in conclusion, the oddity of the singular, purely formal aspects of Karl's case; according to the German penal code (other penal codes are not free of similar incongruities), the accomplished murder of a person upon the latter's expressed wish is punishable by a relatively short prison term; an attempt at such a murder is not punishable at all. If, however, as in Karl's case, the victim escaped death, but the attempt resulted in the loss of an eye then, in accordance with paragraph 225 of the penal code, a much severer sentence must be imposed!

THE PSYCHODYNAMICS OF THE CASE

OF MME LEFEBVRE[1]

In august, 1925, mme lefebvre, a well-to-do French middle-class woman in her sixties, shot her daughter-in-law. The murder occurred while taking an automobile ride, the son driving. The victim was in her sixth month of pregnancy. Mme Lefebvre was tried and sentenced to death; the sentence was commuted to life imprisonment. Since then she has been living a religious, quiet life in prison, comparatively free of remorse or any other conflicts. It was hard to find any obvious reasons for the crime; the usual psychology of the superficies appears unable to explain it. The woman herself told the court and a year and one-half later the psychoanalyst, Marie Bonaparte, that she always had the feeling that she did her duty by killing her daughter-in-law. She still believes that she killed her as one "destroys a weed, or uproots bad corn, or kills a wild animal." When she was asked in what way the daughter-in-law was like a wild animal, she was unable to give any satisfactory answer; she would now say that her daughter-in-law once instituted a law suit against her own mother; then, she would state that the young woman once had an exchange of words with her (Mme Lefebvre) and said among other things: "I am here, and you will have to take me into account." This is about all Mme Lefebvre ever had to say in justification of her crime. Evidently these reasons appear sufficient to the

---

[1] The material here used is taken from the psychoanalytical study of the case made by Marie Bonaparte (*Revue Française Psychoanalytique*, Tome I, 1927, No. 1).

culprit, for even several years after the murder she continues to feel that she has done no wrong; to put it in her own words, she freed herself of a nuisance and therefore all is well now, and hence she sees no reason for having any remorse. Apparently, she even thinks that her crime was in complete harmony with her religious ideas, for she said once that the murder was a righteous deed, which could not have happened without the will of the Lord.

We note in this case the same remarkable and irrational absence of conscious conflict which we observed in the previous case.

Mme Lefebvre was apparently of the opinion that her daughter-in-law had committed a capital crime against her and that she only meted out justice in putting her to death. If we are to believe Mme Lefebvre, the crime committed by her daughter-in-law consisted of the somewhat threatening remark: "I am here and you will have to take me into account." The meaning of this expression is quite clear. It means no more than the words "I am here," and this implied the crime. A young woman, a stranger, came and stole her son. The popular supposition that an illicit relationship between mother and son must have been the reason for the crime, proved true psychologically, even though not justified by fact. As a matter of fact, this crime can be explained only as one resulting from the Œdipus situation.

We know from the history of the trial that Mme Lefebvre decided to buy a revolver when she first suspected that her daughter-in-law was pregnant. She bought the revolver as soon as the pregnancy became a certainty. To herself and to her family she explained that she bought the revolver in order to protect her home against thieves, who frequently broke into houses in the neighborhood. Marie Bonaparte was struck by the similarity between this explanation and the unconscious content of the reproach which Mme Lefebvre made to her daughter-in-law; it will be recalled that she felt the latter had stolen her son. The analyst established further that the pregnancy of her son's wife was so unbearable to this well-to-do French bourgeois woman that she was driven to commit a crime which took her away from her peaceful, well-ordered family life, from her husband, her home and her children and which might even have cost her her life.

The jealousy with which Mme Lefebvre reacted to her daughter-in-law's pregnancy, was particularly strengthened by the specific symbolic significance which pregnancy always has for women.

Girls must solve their castration complex (the fear of losing the penis) in a way which is different from that of boys. In contradistinction to the boy, the girl is compelled very early in life to reconcile herself to the inevitable fact that she is different anatomically; she is forced to recognize the fact that she is a woman, i.e., a castrated being, and she gradually learns to give up her infantile hopes to become a man; in addition she knows instinctively that nature gave the woman a substitute and compensation for the masculine organ; namely, a child, which will grow in her body; she loves that child in her doll. A child thus acquires for the mother the unconscious meaning of a substitute for the masculine organ which she lacked. Marie Bonaparte found that one of the unconscious determinants of the hate which Mme Lefebvre felt so keenly against her daughter-in-law was to be found in the feminine castration complex. The daughter-in-law stole her son who represented to his mother's unconscious the substitute for the penis. The mother was unable to suffer the fact that her own son gave her daughter-in-law a baby, a fœtus; her own son thus appeared to her unconscious as that fœtus, the feminine substitute for a penis, which the daughter-in-law had stolen.

The reaction against the pregnant daughter-in-law,[1] according to the findings of Marie Bonaparte, represents also a revival of an old hostility which Mme Lefebvre had felt in

[1] It will be recalled that the daughter-in-law was killed while riding in an automobile, Mme Lefebvre firing the shot. Automobiles and pistols are not infrequent symbols of masculine genitalia.

her early days against her own mother. The latter was pregnant twice during her daughter's childhood. First her brother Charles was born; then, when she was four years old, came her little sister Nelly. The arrival of this second sibling must have aroused the typical jealousy in the little girl. This reappeared so many years later and repeated itself in the crime which she committed. Apparently, like all children in this situation, she bore unconscious death wishes against her mother, which she later displaced onto her sister.

A childhood memory, which Mme Lefebvre told her analyst, shows the very typical psychological circumstances just mentioned. The children loved to play church services. Little Charles played the priest and said mass; they played funeral; the procession would follow a path in the garden; they would bury dead little chicks; cigar boxes served for coffins and a special corner served as a cemetery; they would decorate the graves with small crosses made of daisies. Marie Bonaparte recognized in this childhood game the psychological prototype of Mme Lefebvre's future crime. The dead little chicks —symbols of the death wish against the youngest child[1]— were being buried with religious ceremony, the little brother playing the role of accomplice. We shall recall the remarkable fact that Mme Lefebvre chose to kill her daughter-in-law in the presence of her son, who was driving the automobile; apparently she needed his presence as a setting for the murder.

We agree with Marie Bonaparte that the crime was an expression of jealousy and hatred; Mme Lefebvre hated her daughter-in-law, because the young woman, being pregnant by her son, had thus "stolen" the substitute penis from her; in the light of this psychological situation, we are able to envisage the deepest roots of this tragedy; they are to be found in the childhood Œdipus situation of Mme Lefebvre. The jealousy was originally directed against her own mother,

---

1 The usage of the chick or chicken is suggestive: poulet (French) =kuken (German) =little girl. Compare the slang meaning of "chicken" in English.

when the latter was pregnant and when she later gave birth to a little sister; the whole set of these complex infantile feelings were later displaced onto the daughter-in-law.

Marie Bonaparte rightly states that other very powerful motives must also have been operating to bring about a recrudescence of the infantile Œdipus conflict just at the moment when the daughter-in-law became pregnant. Throughout her life Mme Lefebvre had suffered from very many hypochondriacal complaints; these had become much worse during the ten years which preceded the crime, i.e., since the beginning of the menopause. It appears that genital functions having come to a standstill and conception having become impossible, she developed a number of persistent physical symptoms which were symbolic presentations of pregnancy. It also appears that since she entered the menopause she clung with desperate tenacity to her right to motherhood. For twelve years, from the age of forty-eight to sixty, she suffered constantly from digestive disturbances, which had to her unconscious the meaning of anal pregnancy phantasies. The hypochondriacal individual, who is unable to turn his interests (his libido) toward the outside world, withdraws these interests and concentrates them on his own organs; from this time on these serve as a means of expression of his instinctual wishes. This withdrawal of the libido from the outer world and the turning of it onto one's own person is performed with very great ease by those individuals who, in the course of their development, failed to reach the complete adult genital level.

In the case of Mme Lefebvre, Maria Bonaparte saw clearly that two factors led her to a severe regression to the anal erotic level: on one hand, it was the jealousy awakened by the pregnancy of her daughter-in-law, who had stolen her son, i.e., her phantastic penis, from her; on the other hand, the menopause brought about a complete loss of genital feminine function; hence the regression mentioned above. She wanted to be in full possession of her son in the capacity of a *mater familias;* she wanted to be the possessor, the sole proprietor of her blood relations; under these circumstances the appearance of a daughter-in-law appeared to her an intrusion, a violent appropriation of her son by another woman; she perceived it as a painful robbery. All these violent narcissistic injuries aroused in her the old, repressed Œdipus wish, the wish to kill her mother, which was rekindled with renewed violence; we shall recall that this wish was very early displaced onto her little sister. From the standpoint of psychodynamics, it appears that by shooting her daughter-in-law Mme Lefebvre carried out the deeply repressed wish to kill her own mother.

It remains, however, unexplained how these unconscious drives were brought to such a pitch that they overturned her Ego and made the murder possible.

Marie Bonaparte believes that the answer to this question could be found in the following mechanism. Mme Lefebvre believes that she committed no crime, that she has done her duty and relieved the family of an unwelcome intruder; this is a paranoid falsification of reality which fused her Superego with her Id. This singular modification of the normal psychic structure eliminated any possibility of a conflict; the crime could be carried out because the unconscious, the conscious and conscience became harmoniously united. According to Maria Bonaparte, an identification with a strict domineering mother might have been the first reason why Mme Lefebvre's Superego was so easily turned off its usual path.

This *identification* is assumed by Marie Bonaparte, but no details are given. We shall attempt to prove, first, that Marie Bonaparte's intuitive assumption is correct and, second, that it is this identification that offers us the real clue to the full understanding of the murder.

To understand the deep change in the Ego structure of Mme Lefebvre it is important, according to her analyst, to bear in mind her general demeanor since the murder. Mme Lefebvre feels very well; she is comfortable and free of remorse; she has no desire to see her son; she does not feel that she did him any wrong; more than that, unconsciously she feels that he was her accomplice; even as her younger brother was in the symbolic murder of her little sister—that unwelcome intruder into the family of Mme Lefebvre's childhood; her little brother helped her then to bury the little sister and to hallow the act by religious ceremonies. The role of brother and son Mme Lefebvre then shifted to God-Father; she wrote her husband from her cell: "Till my last day, I shall remain at the foot of the Cross, even as Mary Magdalene."

This conception of the dynamic reconstruction of her Ego becomes reinforced when we recall that Mme Lefebvre utilized the same set of psychological mechanisms of displacement, even in her childhood. Her little brother had for her, then, the same psychological meaning as her son acquired later in her life; in her childhood she endowed him with the attributes of a father; he dressed up like a priest and carried out the funeral mass for the little chicks. We thus see that since her childhood Mme Lefebvre tried to displace on her siblings the forbidden wish to unite with father and to get rid of mother. She was apparently unable to solve her Œdipus conflict; so under pressure of the Superego she projected the whole conflict on her siblings; thus the younger brother became the father-image (brother, too, had a penis), while the younger sister became the disturbing element in their relations, as her mother had been in the relations to her father. Thus in that childhood funeral game, the child realized her repressed Œdipus wishes. The murder was a striking repetition of the old game of childhood, where roles were distributed in a somewhat similar way. The daughter-in-law was the chick, i.e., the little sister, the son played the role of the little brother. The murder, thus, brought her the same sense of relief as the game in childhood—the game which simultaneously gratified her hatred and also the demands of her Superego (religious ceremonies). Moreover, the gratification of her need for punishment, which she obtained through being imprisoned, adds to her feeling of contentment.

Thus the unconscious motivations of this murder could be summarized as follows:

The proverbial jealousy which all mothers show in rela-

tion to their daughters-in-law is deeply rooted in the unconscious of women; it comes from the unconscious meaning
which the son has for the mother; he is to her a substitute
for a penis. Usually when the mother reaches the menopause
and thus loses her genital femininity, her daughter-in-law's
pregnancy causes extreme narcissistic pain and thus increases
the pangs of jealousy to the utmost degree. This painful
sterility is in many psychological aspects similar to the sterility of which the little daughter is aware, when she compares
herself with her mother; this circumstance aroused in Mme
Lefebvre the primitive Œdipus complex, which she had repressed with so much difficulty. Her psychological relation
to her son, in addition to his being a penis substitute, had
also the emotional value of the repressed wishes which she
had toward her father. The jealousy originally directed
against her mother was totally displaced onto her son's wife.
It is the murder of the mother that Mme Lefebvre committed when she killed her daughter-in-law. It is through
these considerations that Marie Bonaparte succeeded in reconstructing the psychic processes which led to the murder.
The question that remains unanswered is why and how did
it happen that these human tendencies, common to all
women, i.e., the jealousy a mother feels in relation to her
son's wife, should have broken through in the case of Mme
Lefebvre and found motor expression in the act of murder.

We shall now attempt to describe in detail those psychic
mechanisms, which, as we learned from the analysis of other
criminal cases, paralyze the influence of the inhibitory Superego and thus permit the Ego to commit a crime. We shall
incidentally see a noteworthy similarity between these mechanisms and those which we have described above, in the case
of the neurotic attempt at murder.

Through her daughter-in-law's pregnancy Mme Lefebvre
found herself in the same situation as when a little girl she
saw her mother pregnant; she could observe it, but real
motherhood was denied her. She also found herself in the
same situation which would have obtained had she, as a little

girl, been able to fulfill her Œdipus wishes. In other words, the daughter-in-law brought to realization what Mme Lefebvre had wanted when, as a child, she watched her mother, to wit: the daughter was now pregnant and not the mother! Thus Mme Lefebvre succeeded in identifying herself with her own mother and reacted, therefore, in the same way as she was afraid, in her unconscious, her mother would have reacted toward her; it was thus she should have reacted, following the dictates of her Superego. This *identification with her mother* permitted Mme Lefebvre to carry out the vengeance of the mother who was robbed of her child. Unconsciously Mme Lefebvre played out the game which she had begun in her childhood and which she brought to its logical conclusion in ripe middle age. When a child, she successfully concealed her Œdipus wishes, but gratified them symbolically; now by way of identifying herself with her mother she could also carry out the act of hatred for the crime of incest. One can understand this psychic process only if one bears in mind the laws which govern *identification* and *projection*. Those Œdipus wishes which were directed against her mother she projected into her daughter-in-law; those Œdipus wishes which were directed toward the father, she displaced onto her son. As to the unconscious sense of guilt aroused in her as a result of her Œdipus wishes, she rids herself of them by the following means: she identifies herself with the injured mother, who took revenge upon the woman into whom she projected her own Œdipus wishes. This paranoid method of shifting and exchanging roles permitted the complete living out of the Œdipus complex; it also explains the psychological triumph of Mme Lefebvre: was not justice finally done? Were not the criminal Œdipus wishes punished? We understand now why Mme Lefebvre feels free of discomfort and why she shows no signs of remorse or regret. The murder had to her unconscious the meaning of punishment for her own Œdipus wishes; the unconscious talion principle was fulfilled; the guilt was atoned.

The meaning of Mme Lefebvre's rationalizations also becomes clear now. We understand why she wanted to kill her own daughter-in-law as one "destroys a weed, or spoiled corn, or as one kills a wild animal"; we also understand why she spoke reproachfully of her daughter-in-law, saying that "she wanted to bring a law suit against her own mother." We see clearly whence her conviction that her crime was a benevolent act and why she considered her daughter-in-law a criminal. In Mme Lefebvre's unconscious phantasies, her daughter-in-law was the incarnation of her own infantile unconscious, illicit personality. All her hostility toward her daughter-in-law corresponded to her own unconscious infantile hostility toward her mother. By hating her daughter-in-law she turns outward those inner forces, which in her childhood were directed against her own Œdipus wishes and which helped the work of repression.

The psycho-economic characteristics of the crime also become clear now. The repressed instinctual drives were freed and those forces which until then were directed inward and acted as inhibitors, turned outward and were lived out in a sadistic act. Mme Lefebvre thus appears the victim of extreme repressions, of the austere religious atmosphere of her childhood. The murder was a result of coöperation between two sets of forces, i.e., between the *repressed* aggressions and the *forces of repression;* this coöperation became successful only when these forces, instead of being turned inward, and on her own instinctual drives, were turned outward and on her daughter-in-law; thus the *repressed* and the *repressing* trends were turned into one and the same direction. The menopause is the most suitable moment for this change of direction, which turns the repressing forces outward. The severe repression made Mme Lefebvre frigid; she never experienced any sexual gratification. Therefore we think that this crime should be charged up chiefly to the extreme intensity of the repressing forces which were operating in the woman. One can obtain some conception of this intensity from the sharp criticism which she directed against her daughter-in-law, for this very criticism she had herself directed before against her own impulses and thus repressed them.

The *punishment* imposed upon her by a court of justice Mme Lefebvre perceives as a benefaction; she could not feel otherwise, for through this punishment she rids herself of the last remnants of the sense of guilt which she had partly quieted by means of projections. Hence her feeling of well-being in prison; all her physical complaints disappeared; when Marie Bonaparte saw her in prison, her whole habitus appeared rejuvenated. The pleasure she derived from all this consists of the final union with her father, of the symbolic fulfillment of the Œdipus wishes. From now on she is united with God, her father; she has rid herself of her rival and nothing can disturb this happiness. Any attempt on the part of the Superego to interfere is automatically neutralized, for she killed her own evil wishes in the person of her daughter-in-law. This complete harmony between Superego and Id is not even disturbed by conscious reasoning, because she chose her rationalizations very carefully and they silenced the cry of conscience. Thus, under the cloak of deep religious feeling she disguised her final union with her father—the supreme realization of her Œdipus wishes.

We may add that this crime had yet another determinant which originated in the woman's infantile situation. As a child she witnessed an experience similar to the one in which she found herself before she committed murder. Her *grand-mother,* too, had to stand aside and see another woman steal her son. This grandmother appears to have become to her the true positive mother ideal; she always had something negative to say about her mother; she covered her hatred rather poorly; however, she appears to have concentrated all her love on her grandmother. The latter became for her the prototype of a good mother; Mme Lefebvre considered her as the mother ideal, as the head of the family. It is quite easy to understand that the little girl felt as if her grandmother had experienced the same jealousy as she, as if she had seen reflected in her grandmother the things she herself felt in regard to her mother. Moreover, she was able to identify herself with her grandmother much more easily, for they were not rivals, one because of youth, the other because of old age being deprived of any sexual gratification; in other words, they were allies in their suffering. The great harmony which one finds between grandparent and grandchild is primarily due to the fact that their psychological status in life is identical—therefore jealousy cannot disturb their relations.

Hence, her crime completed for Mme Lefebvre her identification also with her grandmother, who hated Mme Lefebvre's mother (daughter-in-law), for having stolen her son's love. The unassailable kindly personality of the grandmother, as she appeared in Mme Lefebvre's memories, and the strong negative criticism of her mother made the identification with grandmother still easier; it is this that helped her to such a great extent to rid herself of any sense of guilt; the mother then was equated with the daughter-in-law, the guilty woman, while Mme Lefebvre was the grandmother, i.e., the kind, pure, unjustly injured woman who she thought had a right to avenge herself; hence the murder was an act of righteous vengeance to her, a righteous deed.

We thus see how the struggle of the Œdipus drives were raging within Mme Lefebvre throughout her life; she clung to her repressed wishes which, instead of being given up, remained under the persistent pressure of the Superego and were constantly displaced from one person onto another. She finally succeeded in realizing fully the Œdipus wish, but she did this by means of the projection mechanism; she finally killed her mother and reunited herself with her father without any sense of guilt. The Id tendencies were lived out, the demands of the Superego satisfied, the conscious Ego wrapped in rationalizations, and as a result complete happiness was achieved—an harmonious union with God, the father.

*   *   *   *   *

We believe that many murders which are committed under the influence of unconscious motivations are prompted by similar psychological mechanisms. The crime committed by Cain, the first neurotic murderer, appears to justify our view. The first murder in the Bible is not a father murder. Instead of killing the father, the older brother kills the younger. Cain felt that the younger brother bore the same jealousy toward his parents as *he* felt toward his *father*. Therefore he was able to kill Abel, thus *killing in his brother his own jealousy of his father*. In this way he got rid of a rival; he could do this without any sense of guilt, for he identified himself with his father and avenged the latter for his own Œdipus wishes. Cain killed in Abel the prohibited part of his own Ego, i.e., his own Œdipus wishes. The murder committed by Mme Lefebvre and also Karl's attempt at murder, show identical mechanisms. These murders have the emotional value of partial suicide, because these murderers discover in another person the hated, forbidden part of their instinctual drives and they kill it.

Freud considers that every *suicide* presents simultaneously the *murder of another person;* it appears that we are also justified in considering that the reverse is also true, i.e., that many *neurotic murders* represent *disguised suicides*.

A POSSESSED AUTOMOBILIST

$\mathbb{T}$HE FOLLOWING MATERIAL SERVED AS THE basis of an expert testimony I gave before a German court. It was obtained in seven sessions from the defendant while he was being held over for trial.

Introductory Remarks

In order to understand the behavior of psychopathic personalities, the judge needs the help of an expert. In the behavior of criminals who are not mentally sick, the knowledge of unconscious motives is less important, because they have less influence upon conduct. Under the influence of intensive emotions, however, even in healthy individuals, unconscious motives can gain the upper hand. I see the task of the psychiatric expert in the courtroom as one of making a diagnosis and in addition explaining to the judge the psychology of the offender. It is an especially painful task to pass judgment about conduct which one does not understand. I believe that there is hardly an occupation so calculated to call forth conflicts of conscience as the one of deciding the destiny of a fellow-man. Modern court procedure relieves the judge from the full burden of this responsibility by the appointment of more judges or a jury, by assigning one person for the defense and another for the prosecution and also by consulting medical experts.

In the Berlin Institute of Psychoanalysis, in coöperation with Hugo Staub, we started a psychoanalytic course for lawyers. To our great surprise, some of the most distinguished legal authorities—a number of leading judges—registered for this course. They explained their interest by the fact that in cases of neurotic or impulsive characters, the superficial psychology at their disposal did not help them to understand the behavior of the defendants. This is where they thought psychoanalysis could make a contribution.

The pathology of such criminals is a diffuse character disturbance rather than a circumscribed illness with well-defined symptoms. The technical terminology has changed in the course of time from "moral insanity" to "psychopathic personality" and more recently to: hysteric epileptic, schizoid or cyclothymic characters. The diagnosis "moral insanity," now in discredit, gave place to a more scientific-sounding terminology, without, however, deepening the understanding of motivations.

The importance of unconscious motives in the behavior of such offenders manifests itself in the irrationality of their conduct. In normal people the conscious Ego adjusts instinctive demands to external reality. From among mutually antagonistic impulses it selects those which represent the dominating interests of the personality and are in conformity with the social code. The conscious Ego has less influence on the mode of behavior of the neurotic character, hence his irrationality and failure to adjust to reality.

The fact that in neurotic characters the influence of the conscious personality on behavior is relatively slight, explains also the stereotyped nature of their conduct. The unconscious instinctive demands, released from the control of the conscious mind, are blindly enforced without regard either for earlier experience or for the external situation. This gives a predestined character to the life history of these persons.

The Delinquent

Fred, a twenty-one-year-old waiter, had been sentenced three times for the same kind of delinquency. Two court psychiatrists who previously examined him confessed frankly their inability to explain the apparently quite senseless acts of this otherwise intelligent boy, and diagnosed him as a "psychopathic personality with reduced accountability." In spite of this the court gave a prison sentence in each instance. After my testimony and Staub's defense, the prosecuting attorney recommended an acquittal. The judge discharged the defendant and advised him to undergo psychoanalysis.

Fred was somewhat above normal intelligence, had a rather practical orientation to life, and his general knowledge was greater than one would ordinarily expect from his education and environment. He possessed a quick perceptive faculty and had a somewhat sensitive, introverted and shut-in character. He brooded a good deal over himself and his delinquencies and showed signs of introspective traits often present in psychoneurotics.

Four times in the last two years he committed delinquencies which attracted attention only because of their striking similarity. Apparently quite aimlessly or at least without any rational motive, he would take long trips in taxicabs, at the end of which he would be unable to pay the fare and would disappear on some pretext, but would always leave the taxi driver enough facts and clues to lead to his arrest.

He was efficient in his work as a domestic servant or waiter and behaved himself creditably, but frequently changed his position, often without visible reasons.

He described his delinquent episodes in great detail. He took the taxi rides always in a state of excitement. This came about usually in connection with his mother. He committed his first delinquent act in 1927 in an excited mood after meeting his mother. At that time he was working as a domestic servant in a suburb of Dresden, after running away from his parents' home. For a while he worked there, "in hiding from his mother," until one day she learned where he was living and visited him. He reacted to her visit with a drinking bout, using money entrusted to his care. He was sentenced to six weeks in prison. His mother became desperate and threatened to kill both herself and her son. After his release he worked as a waiter and as a page boy and lived away from home because he felt that his stepsisters and his stepfather would not have him in the house.

His second delinquency he committed in 1928. He took a taxi ride for which he did not pay. He drove to a neighboring city to find work because his stepfather urged him to leave the house. He was unable to find a job and took a taxi back to his home town. He described his emotional state before the taxi ride as a great longing for his mother, mixed with considerable fear of her. Arriving, he could not pay for the trip and disappeared, but left his papers with the taxi driver, because he "preferred to be punished rather than to wander about under cover." He was sentenced to three months in prison, where he felt at peace, becoming disheartened only when he thought of his mother.

His third delinquent act was also committed after he saw his mother. At that time he was working as a waiter and not living with his family. One morning, when he knew that his stepfather would not be there, he visited his mother. The same afternoon he felt very excited and, without any reason, rode to a neighboring city. He could not pay for the ride and was once more arrested and sentenced. On another occasion he visited his mother in the forenoon. They had had a petty argument, and his mother had reproached him for his drinking. He felt excited all day and finally ordered a taxi and went to see his uncle, who owned a cafe in his home town. There he drank six grogs with the taxi driver and rode on to another city. During the trip he noticed that he did not have enough money to pay the taxi fare. He asked the driver to take him to the police station, where he gave himself up. The policeman allowed him to go on his promise to pay the next day. The unpaid balance seemed to have been small this time, and he was able to pay it the following day.

All of these accounts he gave from memory and was unable to remember most of the details. He remembered more about his last escapade.

In the spring of 1929 he had bought a bicycle on the installment plan, and had made one payment. Despite this, the stepfather ordered him, at the instigation of the stepsisters, to return the bicycle even though his stepbrother had been allowed to buy one on installments. Everyone advised him to yield to the wish of the stepfather—his mother, who wished to avoid a quarrel, as well as his fiancée, who was a frequent visitor at his parents' house. The stepfather took the bicycle away from him. Fred went into a rage, but he could not "vent his fury on his stepfather; he could only repress it, as usual." Furious, he ran away from the house without taking leave of his fiancée, with whom he had also quarrelled. He sent a note to his mother, asking her to send his fiancée to the hotel where he was working as a waiter so that he could talk with her. Both his mother and his fiancée appeared in the evening at the prearranged place in a garden restaurant. At the sight of his mother he became very excited and "trembled all over." Someone called his attention to the fact that his fiancée was waiting outside the restaurant. He sent his mother away, talked a little while with his fiancée, and, getting more and more excited, leapt into a taxi. He thought that his mother was following him in another car. He rode in a taxi at first, then the next day by bus back to his home town and from there by train to another city. Immediately after his arrival he took a ride to a village in the neighborhood. As to his choice of this place, he gave a vague and contradictory explanation. He wanted to visit his step-brother's former fiancée, who lived in this village. He changed this and said that he wanted to visit the stepbrother himself, who was serving in the army there. On arriving in the village he learned that his stepbrother was not there and rode back to the city, drank a glass of beer with the taxi driver in a restaurant at the railroad station, went out on some pretext, but intentionally left his papers lying on the table. Then he took another cab back to the same village, then on to another neighboring village, where the family of his step-brother's former fiancée lived. He made a flying visit to them, talked for a few minutes about the affairs of his stepbrother, asked the address of his stepbrother's former fiancée and then rode on to still another place. He could give no reason for choosing his last destination. There the senseless driving about came to an end after he had invited the driver into a hotel for a drink and was unable to pay, because, as he pretended, he had lost his pocket book.

I have no reason to assume that any of these accounts of Fred are not true or that they were conscious falsifications. I had a number of interviews with him and succeeded in establishing a confidential relationship. All of the rides were quite without defined purpose and were aimless to an extreme degree. He rushed off on the impulse of the moment. His choice of the different destinations of the taxi rides cannot be explained from conscious motivation. The unconscious motivation can be reconstructed only with a degree of probability. His acts were not committed in a true twilight condition but in an emotionally tense state. They were impulsive and unconsciously motivated. The impulse for the acts appears in his consciousness without connection—or only loosely—with the rest of his conscious mental processes. Therefore these acts appear senseless, even to him. Their meaning can be reconstructed only when the unconscious motives underlying his behavior are known.

This behavior is equivalent to a psychoneurotic symptom (symptomatic acts). It is a response to repressed impulses alien to the conscious Ego and can be understood only in the light of his previous life history.

Reconstruction of the Unconscious Motives Underlying Fred's Delinquent Behavior

Fred was an illegitimate child and spent the first six years of his life with relatives. After his mother married he was taken into the family. The stepfather brought to the newly established home nine children, some older and some younger than Fred. Fred had almost no memory of the first six years of his life. He knew only that at the age of eight he was in a sanatorium under treatment for tuberculosis. He was an average pupil and was almost never on intimate terms with his school comrades. His earliest interests were botany and chemistry. At the age of thirteen or fourteen, he wished to become a druggist and was placed as an apprentice in a drugstore. He remembers that his chief was very severe. In order to experiment at home he stole chemicals. This was discovered. On this account and also apparently because his stepfather wished him to earn money, he abandoned this occupation. At this time his mother was in a much excited state, suffered from fainting spells, threatened suicide, and was determined that Fred should die with her. In addition to this, his mother was frequently sick, and he nursed her with the greatest solicitude. His mother mentioned this care in her more recent letters written to him in the prison. As our interviews progressed, he became increasingly frank and conveyed to me the home atmosphere with considerable vividness. His mother suffered a great deal from reproaches on the part of the stepchildren that she pampered her own child, and even that she had married in order to provide a home for him. Fred and his mother had indeed an extraordinary attachment to each other, the mother being at least as strongly attached to him as he was to her. She lived in continuous inner conflict. To refute the reproaches of her stepchildren and husband, she tried to compensate for her excessive devotion and love for Fred by favoring the other children overtly and being severe with her own child. Fred felt that he was quite different from his stepbrothers and sisters. The stepbrothers were robust, practical, and efficient; he was frail and sensitive. He liked to ride on street cars. Because the stepchildren had to walk when they did errands, his mother gave him his carfare secretly. When this was discovered, his mother openly censured him. Similar everyday occurrences made Fred's situation in the family very precarious. A secret, tender love, burdened with conflicts and guilt on both sides, bound mother and son to each other. It brought the mother into conflict with the family, and the boy into an ambiguous situation which puzzled and bewildered him. Stepfather and stepchildren brought more and more pressure to bear on the boy to leave home, and this explains Fred's repeated disappearances from home. The first time—at the age of fifteen—he tried to become a sailor, but he was picked up at the station by a police officer, who telephoned his father, and was taken home. A short time after this he ran away. He could not tolerate the harsh way his mother treated him.

The last runaway episode occurred before his first delinquency. At this time, again he went to a neighboring city seeking work; he remained there, it seems, eight days. As he found no work, he returned to his home town and secured a job in a slaughter house. A friend told his mother where he was living, and she came to visit him. On the same day he committed his first delinquency; he embezzled two hundred marks.

All this gives us a picture of how disorganized his life was after he reached his fourteenth year. He had innumerable jobs as a factory worker, waiter, bellboy, servant, etc. Once he made an effort to become a coachman in a noble family, but did not carry out his intention and returned to his work as a waiter. He lived at home off and on, continuously moving in and out. When he was away from home he felt a great longing for his mother, but hardly had he visited her when he was impelled to leave her again. Her fits of desperation upset him, especially when she expressed suicidal intentions and also threatened to kill him. Once she made an attempt at suicide by taking gas. On another occasion she dragged him to the river so that they might drown together. Frantic with fear, he succeeded in tearing himself away from her.

His mother's letters, which he showed me in the prison, plainly corroborated these stories. They revealed unequivocally the involved emotional relationship between mother and son. Some of these letters were written in a tender tone, in which she emphasized their common destiny: mother and son belonged to each other; her husband and stepchildren were described as aliens. In other letters she appeared as the dutiful wife, accusing her son of delinquent trends and instability and reproaching him for besmirching the stepfather's name. This conflict culminated in her wish that both should die together, offering a death pact as the only way out for lovers whose wish to belong to each other cannot be realized in life.

Fred's sexual life had been quite undeveloped. During his puberty he had but little interest in girls. In his masturbation phantasies the picture of his mother often appeared as his wife. Full of guilt and anxiety, he pushed these phantasies aside.

In the years that followed, Fred could not free himself from these feelings. He repressed the sensual part of his attachment to mother and continued to long for his mother in an excessive manner. Vaguely he was aware of the fact that here was the source of his delinquency. After he established a confidential relationship to me and for the first time in his life was able to unburden himself, I asked him to explain to me in what way he connected his delinquency with his mother. His stereotype answer was: it is in some way connected. When he got into a taxi, he felt that he was fleeing from his mother. He was preoccupied constantly with his mother's suicidal phantasies and with her threat to kill him. The following is a verbatim account of his emotional state.

"I am in constant fear of my mother. I only need to think about her to get into such a state of excitement that I do not know what I am doing. Terrible pictures pop into my head and my only thought is to run away somewhere. I feel that someone is following me."

It is in such an emotional state that he gets into a taxi tortured by the phantasy that someone, probably his mother, is pursuing him. He wants to run away, the farther the better. Seated in the taxi he feels that the distance between him and his pursuer is becoming now shorter, now longer. When he comes to his senses, he feels "as if he were awakening from a severe fainting spell." He feels very tired afterwards, "quite weak, as if he would collapse." His anxiety while riding in the taxi has a pleasurable connotation without having a frankly sexual character.

This symptomatic behavior—we will thus designate the impulsive taxi rides—represents a flight from an internal danger—his own feelings—which are treated by his conscious Ego as an external danger. It is a flight from his repressed incestuous love for his mother which is perceived as an external threat, as someone who pursues him. He gets into the taxi to flee from this danger, but one cannot escape from one's own self. The auto ride represents both the forbidden wish and his fear of it, a simultaneous expression of longing and the flight from it. The feeling that "mother is pursuing me" is not only an expression of his anxiety, but also of his wish for mother. The feeling that the distance between him and his pursuer is becoming sometimes greater and sometimes less corresponds to the interplay of two opposing forces: longing and flight.

Because of this strong attachment to his mother, Fred's relations to women were unsatisfactory. At the age of seventeen he had his first sexual experience, with a barmaid. Following this, he had platonic friendships with two older women who served him as mother-surrogates. For a long time after the first sexual act he did not have sexual relations. When he was eighteen he was on intimate terms with a girl for a brief period, but they did not have sexual intercourse. He sensed her jealousy, her wish to keep him bound to her. "She was even jealous of my good friends!" he exclaimed.

Early in this year he met his present fiancée, with whom he had rather regular sexual relations. However, he knew that his feelings toward his fiancée "were not quite right." He spoke often in the same breath of mother and fiancée, the fiancée always taking the second place. The mother tried to cover up her jealousy of the fiancée by a great show of affection for her. Yet she complained whenever her son stayed out late spending an evening with his girl friend.

Just before his last taxi ride he had a disagreement with his fiancée and wrote a letter to his mother begging her to send his fiancée to him. The unconscious meaning of this letter was: "Let me alone, set me free, leave me to my fiancée." Therefore he wrote the letter to his mother instead of directly to his fiancée. At the same time this letter represents also a secret wooing of his mother. The mother responded and went to meet her son. When Fred saw her, he became terribly excited. He trembled all over, as a lover does when his sweetheart appears. He sent his mother away and also his fiancée, and avoided choosing between the two. What he could not send away was his repressed wish for his mother stirred up by her appearance. He jumped in a taxi in a desperate attempt to flee his unconscious desire.

In a letter written to her son, the mother's jealousy of the fiancée comes clearly to expression. In a moral, conventional tone she praised the fiancée and implored her son to mend his ways for her sake. Her real desire is revealed in a striking slip of the pen. She wrote: "Do not be so solicitous about Gertrude, but rather see to it that you get well. When you can work again, she should be your sole concern. Go off with her and stay with *me*. Then you will not be tempted to do such stupid things." (My italics.)

Fred's completely senseless trip to the family of the deserted fiancée of the stepbrother can be understood in the light of the following reconstruction. The taxi ride means a flight from the mother. The stepbrother's fiancée is a surrogate for the stepfather's wife, that is, for his own mother. However the unfaithful stepbrother had deserted his fiancée. Fred fled from the forbidden love-object, from the mother, to the surrogate, the stepbrother's fiancée, who was a legitimate love-object because she had been forsaken by the unfaithful stepbrother. From this unconscious association of ideas these trips, before inexplicable, become meaningful. It clears up the visit to the family of stepbrother's fiancée, which appeared so senseless and unmotivated. During that visit he talked about the disgraceful desertion of the stepbrother as if he wished to justify his own sinful desires for his mother, by criticizing his stepbrother's desertion.

Now it is also clear why he played himself into the hands of the police after the taxi rides. The pursuit in the taxi expresses not only flight from the mother, but also his longing for her. This is revealed by the pleasurable connotation of the ride. Then he needs and seeks punishment for his guilt.

Additional Remarks About the Unconscious Meaning of Fred's Taxi Rides

Riding in conveyances played an unusual role in Fred's memory material. One of his earliest memories is a train ride he took when eight years old with his stepfather, his mother and the other children to a summer holiday resort. At the station he suddenly vanished with the excuse of having forgotten something at home, and thus planned to miss the train. He did not remember his motive, however, for wanting to miss the train.

On school excursions to a strange city, he often secretly left the other excursionists and rode around the city alone on the street cars. At the age of fourteen he wished to become a chauffeur, but after seeing an auto collision on the street he abandoned the idea. During his taxi rides he often thought of this event and feared lest he, too, might have an accident. He suggested to me that his senseless taxi rides might be explained by a suicidal motif. At one time he wished to become a coachman in a noble family. In childhood, he often had the inclination to buy an adult's ticket when riding on street cars. As a passenger, he wished to be equal to adults. There is ample indication that he displaced his infantile sexual wishes with his predilection to ride in conveyances. Once his mother secretly gave him the carfare, which they concealed from the other members of the family.

Especially revealing is Fred's statement that he had had the happiest time of his life when he served as a waiter on a dining car. In this occupation he could satisfy in a way acceptable to his conscious ego, his symbolically determined fondness for riding. Yet he gave up this position because he was afraid that his stepbrother would divulge to the dining-car company his past criminal record. Riding was associated with incest; this gave rise to the fear of the stepbrother from whom he had actually stolen the mother's love.

A bicycle, too, contributed to his last delinquent act. He had bought himself a bicycle on the installment plan, in order "to be able to ride with my fiancée who also has a bicycle." Then his stepfather took it away from him. This threw him into a fit of rage.

Since his early childhood, riding was highly charged with emotion: it meant a forbidden pleasure mixed with guilt feelings. His running away from the summer excursion shows that even at that early age riding, a forbidden pleasure, was associated with anxiety and guilt feelings. In the rhythmic movements, as in riding or in a swing, many children experience a distinct sexual pleasure. Many a child has masturbated for the first time while swinging. Perhaps the roots of these feelings of pleasure go back to the earliest period of infancy, to the kinesthetic pleasure which the child feels when rocked in the mother's arms or in the cradle. Fred actually remembered that in childhood, swinging had given him a pronounced sexual pleasure. He readily recognized the similarity of this pleasure to the sensation experienced when riding in taxis. Fred had associated his first incestuously tinged sexual feelings with kinesthetic pleasure in rhythmic movements when riding, and riding retained the unconscious meaning of forbidden sexual wishes.

A dream which he had in prison gives further confirmation of the foregoing interpretation.

He dreamt that he came home late. He wished to go out with his mother and fiancée, but it was too late for that. Then suddenly he was in a taxi, his mother was riding with him, sitting at his side.

In the dream the repressed incest wish is represented symbolically. Burdened with guilt, he is punished by imprisonment which expiates his guilt. In his dream he is driving with mother in a taxi, something which he could never actually indulge in.

Fred is a psychopathic personality, a neurotic impulsive character. He is abnormally fixated on his mother at an age when ordinarily a normal person has already transcended his infantile incest ties. His delinquent acts take the place of symptoms of neurotically ill persons. They signify his efforts to free himself from an intolerable unconscious conflict, from a tension caused by the incestuous longing for his mother which cannot be borne by the conscious Ego. The apparently quite senseless and aimless taxi rides have an unconscious meaning. They signify simultaneously the anxious flight from the incest longing and the symbolic satisfaction of the same wish. His delinquencies serve no criminal purpose, such as fraud or injury. They are the results of a disturbance of his emotional life.

He was a recidivist; to punish him would not keep him from further neurotic behavior. On the contrary, through punishment, the inhibiting influence of his conscience is weakened, and this favors the repetition of his delinquent acts. Exemption from punishment, however, would be equally ineffective without psychotherapy. The solution of his problem would be to place him in an institution where, at least for the first part of his psychoanalytic treatment, he would be detained under supervision.

A DOUBLE MURDER COMMITTED BY A

NINETEEN-YEAR-OLD BOY[1]

IN THE COURSE OF A QUARREL, MARK, WHO was nineteen years old, shot his brother William, about two years younger than he, and his friend, Ferdinand, approximately the same age.

Mark was sentenced to a long term of imprisonment. In this sentence great weight was placed upon the fact that some months before the murder he had bought a revolver in the criminal quarter where he loafed about freely and that he had practiced target shooting.

Mark made two confessions but later he withdrew the second one. According to the first statement he was with his brother William and his friend Ferdinand in his parents' apartment. His brother reproached him for the disorderly condition in which he left the bookshelf. A quarrel arose, then a fight, in the course of which in a senseless rage he shot at his brother and then at Ferdinand who intervened. According to the second statement, he had shot first at his friend Ferdinand and only then at his brother who rushed in at that moment. In this second statement he explained that his

---

[1] The statement reproduced here was the basis of the expert testimony of the author which he delivered before the jury at the trial. The testimony was drafted on the strength of a psychoanalytic exploration which the author made in two weeks preceding the trial, while the defendant was in custody. The insight thus gained was then supplemented by the searching cross-examination of the nurse who was at service in Mark's family for fifteen years and knew him from his earliest childhood.

The Christian names—Mark, William, and Ferdinand, used in this report, are fictitious; the surnames have been omitted.

excitement had been caused by the slanderous remarks which Ferdinand is said to have made about Mark's former girl friend. The court accepted the first statement which he also repeated at the trial and which was substantiated by the investigation.

The psychological problem that the criminal act of this nineteen-year-old boy imposes on us consists fundamentally in how this weak, somewhat introverted, not especially aggressive young man with a constant feeling of inferiority committed such a surprising deed, a deed of which no one who knew him believed him capable. The psychological enigma only increases when one bears in mind that the immediate motive of the criminal act was relatively insignificant and can in no way account for it. An insignificant quarrel with the brother in the presence of a mutual friend ended with two fatal shots. He himself gave two different explanations of the crime, the second of which he later retracted. The substance of the first explanation consists of the description of his irritation with his younger brother, who was physically stronger than he and who in the last two years had repeatedly been very brutal to him, often thrashing him and ridiculing him. He remembered quite painfully an incident three-quarters of a year before the crime, when his mother wished to punish him corporally. This punishment he warded off but was then thrashed by his brother in the presence of relatives. The next day his brother came to his room, locked the door, threw him on the bed and struck him again. In one of his discussions with me he stated that on this occasion he became conscious for the first time of the full meaning of his powerlessness against his brother, his resistance was broken and a deep despair came over him. He thought that from this time on there was a change in his state of mind. He finally had to recognize his younger brother William as the stronger. He began to give way to this feeling of being the "underdog." He saw frequently in phantasy how the brother sat on him and struck him. When he got into a controversy with anyone, this tormenting picture appeared and paralyzed his power of resistance. His feelings towards women were also influenced by this phantasied picture. In the last two years, a weak sexual interest had often appeared when he was in the company of young women. Up to this point his sexual life had consisted of an automatically performed masturbation mostly without phantasy. He related how once in attempting a sexual advance to a young woman twenty-two years old he was paralyzed and unable to make further advances to her, by the almost compulsive appearance of the picture of being thrashed by his brother. The same thing recurred when he once ventured to speak to a prostitute. In the last year before the crime the feeling of impotence in the presence of his brother William was the center of his mental life and appears to have inhibited all his activity, his psychosexual maturing, and to have prevented the development of masculine self-reliance.

In the first confession he attempted to explain the murder by this complex of emotions caused by the brother. The role of the friend, Ferdinand, in this account, consisted mainly of having gradually alienated the brother from him. These two had formed an intimate friendship, from which he was excluded. In this first statement he can give no real explanation of why he had shot Ferdinand. It seems also, according to this statement, almost as if Ferdinand had been the fortuitous sacrifice of an unleashed rage which had taken Mark's conscious Ego completely by surprise. On the other hand, according to the second explanation, which to be sure he retracted, Ferdinand is the principal object of his aggression. He bases this hostile feeling toward Ferdinand upon a story, the main character of which is Rita, a friend of his sister. This young woman was the first one he ventured to kiss, but he was not in love with her, and he did not take it any too much amiss in his friend Ferdinand when he first heard that his friend was interested in the girl and had made sexual advances to her. But when he heard from Rita that Ferdinand had treated her brutally and noticed that his brother and Ferdinand spoke cynically and aggressively about her and other young women, he was torn in his emotional attitude. It is true that the friend meant more to him than the girl, but he was indignant at the way his brother and Ferdinand treated her. Then it happened that in a controversy over this girl his brother struck him in the face for the first time in his life. In one of his conversations with me he said he thought that after being thrashed by the brother, he took the side of the young girl, because he could put himself in the place of the weaker person. His brother tyrannized over him, the weaker person, just as Ferdinand did over Rita. Mark and Rita were fellow sufferers. This statement by Mark is important, because it furnishes the first key to the understanding of his pathological character. It was not the jealousy of a masculine-feeling person, but the identification of a weak-feeling man with a woman, the rebellion of weakness against brutal strength. Especially characteristic of this identification is the phantasied picture that appeared to him when his brother and Ferdinand spoke roughly about Rita. There arose in his mind the picture which he had seen in a film of the way Rasputin had mistreated a prostitute. He had a strong feeling of revolt against his brother whom he in his phantasy associated with Rasputin.

I have the impression that his two confessions are not in absolute contradiction, at least so far as the psychological motive of the crime is concerned. On the contrary, both statements supplement and confirm each other psychologically. His conduct, in accordance with the teaching of the psychology of the unconscious, was overdetermined and was caused by several motives. He was entirely unconscious of the really deep motives. The two statements correspond to different determinants of the crime and originated primarily out of the subsequent need of explaining it to himself. Up to the present time the real motives have been partially if not entirely concealed from himself.

The two confessions constitute a convincing example of how in such emotional behavior the person who commits the crime does not know the true motives and subsequently must somehow explain the act to others and, above all, to himself. The different statements then correspond to the different motives which conditioned the act. In the main, had the feelings directed against Ferdinand been operative in him, the crime could perhaps have occurred as he presented it in the second statement. So the second version contained a part of the psychological, or better, subjective truth and only the sum of the motivations contained in both statements presents the full explanation, and then only if we bear in mind the existing unconscious components back of the conscious motives. I shall attempt to indicate the unconscious factors so far as I was successful in grasping them in a comparatively short period of study. Only through the knowledge of these unconscious motives can the pathological and contradictory elements in Mark's character be understood.

The first picture of him is not at all an uncommon one. He belongs to that group of young people who show the signs of a protracted puberty. The typical characteristics of these developing years are present in them for a longer time and are more strongly marked than the average, normal youth. Their egos are less effectively pitted against the pressure of their awakening sexual drives. They suffer from this insecurity and ineffectiveness and try to conceal it from others and from themselves through clumsy, feigned gestures of manliness. With Mark, the feeling of inferiority of the immature man and the inner conflict against it are the center of the picture. This feeling of inferiority was greatly accentuated because the younger brother was better developed physically and freer, more amiable and therefore more popular. In the last two years, his whole life hinged on this tormenting comparison with his brother in a desperate struggle against his own frustration and feeling of weakness. The purchase of the revolver and the loafing about the criminal quarter are clumsy efforts to feign symbolically an inner feeling of security and manliness. Another method of covering up the feeling of inferiority was the display of indifference and apathy. The court psychiatrist who examined him first, characterized very properly this indifference and apathy as a mask covering an inner vulnerability and helplessness. This psychiatrist also observed that the child seeking for love and support hides behind this mask. It is, however, a mask not only for the outer world but also for himself. This feminine, or to be more accurate, childish longing to be loved, this yearning for help and support are the very feelings which in the main cause this sense of inferiority. Out of these, the split in his personality comes directly to expression. He has, as we see, manly aspirations and ideals. It pains him to be weaker, less active and aggressive than his brother; yet with another part of his personality he wishes to remain a child and to be dependent. He does not permit himself to admit these infantile, femininely colored wishes, for they do great injury to his self-reliance. He tries, therefore, to repress every such passive emotion that is reminiscent of weakness and to submerge it through the false expression of manliness. Those about him are often aware of this spasmodic, unfounded haughtiness and appraise it as conceit. This is characteristically illustrated in the report of the school principal who criticized him for an unwarranted superiority. This unwarranted superiority is only a weak effort to conceal from himself and others his boundless feeling of inadequacy. His deepest longing, which he does not wish to admit even to himself, is to be able to lean on a stronger person. One receives this impression unquestionably on a somewhat longer association with him. At first he appears indifferent, but one notices more and more how he begins to cling, how he wishes to prove his indifference at the beginning of every conversation until the need for dependence is gradually betrayed.

The origin of this strong infantile claim to dependence is easily understood from his previous history. Mark himself and most of the witnesses stated that his mother had taken none too great an interest in her children. The training of the children was left to the servants. The nurse who had been in the service of the family for fifteen years and knew Mark from his earliest childhood, stated, when questioned, that the mother had had no very great love for the children. Mark, who unquestionably had been a frail child with a weak constitution, suffered the most from this undernourishment in love. He soon turned to the father, as children often do who experience disappointment in the mother. The normal constellation of the instincts of the little fellow—love for the mother, jealousy of the father—did not seem to have manifested themselves very clearly in him. He soon showed the attitude typical for the girl in the family; the aversion to the mother and a passive attachment to the father. One sees this emotional attitude very clearly, when for example, he relates that as a child he had been very much pained that his father always sided with his mother whenever a difference of opinion arose between the boy and his mother. Consequently he felt that his father loved his mother more than him. The next conversation with me following this account, he began by saying he wished to qualify this statement somewhat. He begged me not to believe that he had felt his mother to be in any way a rival. This denial showed only too clearly how he did not wish to admit this feminine feeling.

This constellation of instincts is without conflict for the little child, but not for the young boy in adolescence, when the masculine claims awaken under the pressure of the biological development. This discrepancy between instinct-life and personality is often observed in unintegrated neurotic people. The increasing sexual impulses, the environment, the example of the brother, his mother's contempt for him which he instinctively felt, demanded that he become a man, but his passive attachment to the father, his whole unsatisfied infantile longing to be dependent opposed this intense masculine drive. He struggled desperately and ineffectually against this infantilism. The relentless course of biological development demanded that he become an adult and a man, but at heart he remained a child longing for love and help.

The history of his infancy and the first five years of his life give us further information about this development. Naturally in so short a time the reawakening of infantile memories was not possible. So I am dependent on the statement of the nurse, and this material can be used only with the greatest caution.

This much seems to be established. During his first fourteen or eighteen months Mark had a wet nurse, while the second son, in the first four months was nursed by his mother. Mark was from the beginning very delicate. At his weaning, food difficulties common in children arose. Apparently he rebelled against being weaned and often vomited. He was not quite two years old when the wet nurse was dismissed. On being questioned, the nurse who was entrusted with the care of his brother William said that at this time she first noticed that Mark masturbated. And then began a quite senseless struggle against this common and harmless infant masturbation. According to the statement of the nurse, the parents in the beginning paid little attention to this behavior. It appears that the nurse soon succeeded in applying her own medical theories in accordance with which the weakness of the lad was traced back to infantile masturbation. A doctor was consulted and apparently on his advice the boy, who was then three years old, was watched in the night. Alternately one of the servants watched at his bed to prevent him from masturbating. His hands were tied but this was of no avail. The nurse observed that he continued to masturbate by rubbing his legs together. With much naïveté, indeed with a certain pride, the nurse told me that the only means that helped, for a time at least, was her threat that if Mark continued to masturbate the gypsies would cut off his penis. We have no reason to doubt these statements of the nurse. This very common threat of castration (which the psychoanalyst so often meets in the memory material of the neurotically sick person) and the disastrous results of this threat had harmfully influenced the instinctual development of the boy. In the end the threat was not successful in restricting his masturbation, but certainly through it the first expression of the sexual impulse became inseparably associated with fear and thereby inhibited for his whole life. We now understand Mark's obsessional ideas at the age of eighteen, as for instance when he wished for the first time to make advances to women, there appeared before him the image of his brother sitting on him and striking him. These obsessional ideas were only the revival of his infantile phantasied terror with which his first sexual stimulations were inseparably connected by the threat of the nurse. We also understand why his masturbation ensued later, always quite mechanically and without psychic content. The psychic content of the sexual stimulation was repressed in consequence of the senseless intimidation of the first sexual excitement. The development of puberty followed with the impulse-tendencies crippled in his earliest childhood. Thus arose the lack of security, of self-reliance, of manly bearing, in short of all psychic evidences and concomitants of the masculine sexual instincts. Only the ambition to become a man was there—a hollow one, not maintained by any masculine drive. This explains the behavior which the school principal described as unwarranted superiority.

Surely it will not do to ascribe the failure in Mark's development only to his unhygienic training or to the insufficient warmth of motherly feeling. Certainly he came into the world with a weak instinct equipment. He bore the difficulty in weaning poorly—which is the first demand for adjustment and the first step from the dependency of infancy towards independence. Then through the senseless watching of the harmless masturbation in infancy he was driven to a strongly defiant masturbation. The nurse relates how the child in a rage wished to drive the watchers from the room. Here are to be found the first sources of his later seclusiveness, his difficulty in human relations, perhaps even his dislike of his mother. In his first experiences with women they played the role of disturbers of his efforts at pleasure. So he became suspicious of people and seclusive. In response to this, those about him gave him less love and interest. And so his longing for love and for a close relationship increased and was never satisfied. The love and dependence which the child is entitled to he had never received. Ever afterwards this longing for love remained alive, later to a degree that was no longer appropriate. Therefore, he had to repress this excessive need for passive dependence, this deepest source of his feeling of inferiority, in order to conceal it from himself. This lack of satisfaction in the childish need for dependence may have received a new reinforcement through the birth of a younger sister when he was about six years old. The little sister took away from him the rest of the parental interest. The incomplete psychoanalytic exploration cannot give a closer confirmation of this universal experience.

After we have understood from this early history the split in Mark's character, the struggle between masculine demands and the passive infantile need for dependence, his criminal act will be more comprehensible to us. His brother was the one who most of all, through his superiority, had intensified this conflict. It was the brother who continually goaded on the masculine ideal formation and stirred up in Mark the struggle against his weakness and passivity. Numberless times he reiterated that he was daily reminded by the brother of his own weakness, and ever and again struggled against it. An important crisis seems to set in after the scene when his brother thrashed him in the presence of the family and struck him again the next day, only to show his superiority. Because he felt his helplessness in the struggle quite clearly, he had to accept the passive submission. That the picture of the brother striking him should have appeared to him again and again indicated that a portion of his personality was accepting the passive submission. There are also other signs that indicate this repressed passive dependence on the brother. He himself said that sometimes he thought of his brother with mixed feelings and at other times even admired him. But most clearly this pressure of the feminine dependence on his brother, rejected by him and yet ever present with him, came to expression in his relationship to Ferdinand, his friend.

It sounds almost fanciful when he describes again and

again how Ferdinand hid behind the stronger brother and his brother defended and protected him. He had obviously felt envious about Ferdinand's place, perhaps had even transferred to Ferdinand his own frustrated wish for a relationship with the brother. He, the weaker one, would gladly have been protected by his stronger brother, had this wish not injured his pride, and his feeling of inferiority. He had longed in his inmost soul to be dependent on his brother, but had to repress thoroughly this longing from his consciousness, for his self-esteem could not have endured it. He envied Ferdinand as the one who was permitted to do what he must deny himself, namely, to have a protecting friend in William.

Further evidence of this feminine passive feeling, rigorously opposed, to be sure, by the conscious part of his person, is the previously mentioned conduct in the presence of Rita. As we have already seen, he had identified himself to a great degree with this young girl. He was indignant at the brutality of his brother and friend toward her and other girls. This brutality awakened in him the indignation of the weak person. When he defended Rita against his brother and Ferdinand, he was also defending himself.

With this our picture of Mark is finished. This infantile, femininely colored wish for dependency caused a strong feeling of inferiority against which he struggled with masculine instinct-components that had already been weakened in childhood and therefore were inadequate. The masculine claim was greater than the real strength of the masculine instinct. In order to overcome this discrepancy between ambition and ability he used the revolver. The tension became more and more intolerable as the repressed need for dependence grew stronger. It is easy to understand that such a need for dependence becomes very strong when self-confidence is completely lost. The failure in his first professional efforts, the superiority of the brother standing out more and more, strengthened in him the need for dependence, the feminine side of the instinct life, but even more strongly the flight from it. And so the murder of the brother and the friend was the desperate proof of his superiority, the denial of his own weakness, but still more than that, the denial of the wish to be submissive. Illustrative of how far back into his youth this passive feminine submission goes is one of his first childhood memories. He was standing on the railroad track and saw the locomotive rushing toward him. He remained standing there and felt himself being crushed by the locomotive, and at the very last moment jumped out of the way. It is unessential whether this is an actual event or a phantasied one; this memory picture is a sign of how strongly he was fixated to the situation of being overpowered by an overwhelming force. Against this situation, which was accepted by a part of his personality, he defended himself all of his life with the other part of his personality.

If the active aggressive impulses are inhibited in a boy, one frequently sees the passive feminine characteristics more strongly developed. In Mark this was the case and it is undoubtedly true that the intimidation of the first masculine sexual emotions in infancy contributed substantially to this. He was, however, not forced, as is often the case, into an inversion of the instincts, but there arose a deep conflict between the passive-feminine tendencies artificially strengthened by his upbringing and the masculine impulse. Recently he had fallen more and more under the influence of this tormenting inner conflict between both sides of his Ego. All of his thoughts circled around the comparison with his brother and his brother's friendship for Ferdinand. The masculine demands and the denied, but none the less powerful, longing for dependence on a stronger person came to expression in this tormenting train of thoughts. His criminal behavior was an explosion-like release of this instinct-conflict. In his brother he had killed the stronger person whom he envied because of his own masculine ambitions; in the friend, he killed the person whose place with his brother he envied because of his own passive-feminine feelings. The act was the desperate effort to resolve the inner insoluble conflict between the two opposing inner instinct-demands of his personality by an action. After this conflict had been gradually pushed into the focus of his mental life, claiming all his interest, the danger of an explosive discharge grew. At the moment of the act his whole conscious Ego was overwhelmed by the emotions that had constituted the foundation of the conflict, which has been described. All other emotional content, such as positive feelings to brother and friend, all moral inhibitions became meaningless in comparison with this great quantity of emotion that was involved in his instinctual conflict. The act manifests the simultaneous release of both opposing tendencies of his personality. In the degree to which the inner conflict had increased in importance in the more recent period, his remaining emotional life was impoverished and the explosive discharge had to follow eventually as the result of a dynamic necessity. After the act there came first of all a certain peace. The relief from tension explains his calmness and apparent indifference in the prison. The unbearable inner tension was so great that the act was immediately followed by a sense of relief and only later did the remorse appear. As evidence of the correctness of this view we have the fact that while he was held for trial, for the first time in his life, he had dreams with active sexual content. The first effect of this act was the freeing of the tied-up masculine claims.

It is almost superfluous to add that the act was in no way the result of conscious premeditation, but the explosive release of an unconscious conflict which had been present in him since his earliest childhood, but whose true content was not known to him. This conflict increased intolerably in puberty when he had to face the necessity of becoming more independent, to stop being a child and to become a man.

How little he was conscious of the true motives of the act is best shown by his confession, in which he wished to make his act intelligible not only to those questioning him, but to himself. Because the immediate occasion of the act had had only the minor significance of a spark which set off the explosion, he had to seek the motive from the past. But all the motivations which he produced as explanation—the brother always tyrannizing over him, Ferdinand hiding behind his brother—cannot explain this uninhibited act, if one does not understand the inner conflict which gave these insignificant external events such a prodigious subjective meaning.

In closing, there still has to be emphasized that only this interpretation of the personality of Mark can clarify for us the most obscure point of his testimony, namely, why he gives so confused an account of the motives, as well as the external course of the shooting of his friend Ferdinand. We understand that least of all can he admit as the truth that the motive of this act was the femininely colored jealousy of his friend on account of his friendship with William. This motive hurt his self-esteem much more than the jealousy of the brother which had its origin in the masculine demands. Therefore he had to repress this motive most forcefully because it would be quite impossible for him to admit that deep in his soul he admired the brother who tyrannized over him and wished to be loved and protected by him as Ferdinand was. Therefore he could give no adequate explanation of his shooting of Ferdinand and so he forgot all the details of this part of his act.

The special difficulty in making intelligible to the jury the split in Mark's instinct-life lay in the fact that the concealed childish need for dependence came to light very little on superficial observation. This was his secret that he hid behind the mask of indifference. Those about him saw only the other side: his boasting, his desire to show off, his fondness for firearms, his senseless target shooting and finally the criminal act. But all of this served only the denial of the inner weakness, the great submissiveness which threatened to destroy all his self-esteem.

Character disturbances of this kind, in which the emotional life is pathological, though the power of judgment is unimpaired, have not yet been taken into consideration by the Criminal Code of any country. Therefore this young man, despite the serious disturbance in his instinctive life, had to be convicted.

Epilogue

About six months after his imprisonment Mark developed, in jail, a paranoid type of schizophrenia.

GENERAL CONSIDERATIONS OF THE SOCIAL

PSYCHOLOGY OF PUNISHMENT

As WE NOW COME TO THE CONCLUSION of our work, and as we find that we have nothing more substantial to add to our attempt at gaining a deeper understanding of crime, may we express the hope that the better understanding of the phenomenon of crime and the deeper psychoanalytical insight into the inner life of the criminal will help to develop a more rational attitude toward various offenders of the law. More rational and more appropriate measures against the criminal are needed. We did not intend to discuss these measures; we wanted to and did limit ourselves to the consideration of the psychology of the criminal; it is this psychology, we believe, which will have to serve as a foundation for the science of criminological diagnosis and the penal justice of the future.

If, however, one would ask what practical consequences might be drawn from our study right now, one would find the answer somewhat disappointing. We believe that we succeeded in proving that a great number of offenders of the law, who are still generally considered criminals, should be treated differently than they are at present; the *neurotic criminal* we could designate as a neurotic without symptoms, who acts out his illness in real life; this acting out is unconsciously and at times even consciously condemned by the neurotic criminal himself, but he cannot help doing what he does; we believe that the neurotic criminal belongs to the group of sick people. By leading the reader to this conclusion we only enlarged the group of those sick people, who in the days gone by were also delivered into the hands of justice as people possessed by the devil. This is nothing new, of course. For modern forensic psychiatry also tries to obtain a different mode of treatment for these who are possessed by their own instinctual drives, and thus consider them apart from the normal criminals; what we actually did in this respect is merely this: using the microscope of deeper psychology we were able to define the pathological criminal in greater detail (more exactly), to uncover the nature of his illness and to describe some of the specific psychic processes which underlie a given individual criminal act. For *this type* of individuals we may propose something new and definite, namely, we recommend *the abolition of all forms of punishment* and suggest that he be turned over to a special agency for psychoanalytically minded reëducation, or to a psychoanalyst for *treatment.* The practical significance of this conclusion should not be underestimated; the number of neurotic criminals is very great; yet this fact does not remove our feeling of disappointment, for the recommendations in question do not involve any *fundamental* reconstruction of the criminal law as it exists today; they merely take away a number of individuals from the jurisdiction of the criminal law, in order to put them in the more competent hands of the educator or the doctor; the foundation of the present-day criminal law seems to be left by us untouched.

For the *rest* of the criminals, i.e., for those whom we described as *normal criminals,* we must admit that only fear of painful consequences, in other words, the mainstay of all the penal codes of today, may prevent their committing anti-social acts, or may at least reduce the number of the latter. If the criminal law of today set for itself the task of following this rational principle of protecting society with business-like perfection and without emotion, then our own task would end right here, for punishment (pain) would then be based on solid scientific considerations; it would be carefully weighed and measured and applied only against the normal criminals, the number of which we believe will be found to be very small.[1]

We must bear in mind, however, that this rational principle of intimidation and of prevention is actually followed by modern criminal justice much less than it appears; more dominant is the emotional conception of *atonement* and *retaliation*. The severity and the type of punishment, as prescribed by modern law, is dictated first of all by the emotional drive to retaliate. Our psychoanalytical insight into the nature of criminality, particularly the knowledge of how deeply rooted the connection of guilt and atonement is in every individual, compels us to take a definite stand in regard to this irrational principle of our criminal justice.

We shall, therefore, leave the subject which occupied us till now; we shall turn from the investigation of the psychology of the offender to the consideration of the psycho-sociological aspects of punishment.

At the very first step which we take in the field of social psychology, we are brought face to face with a problem which we were able to leave out of consideration, when dealing with the individual psychology of the criminal. As we studied the deeper psychology of the criminal we hoped to derive a viewpoint which would be more in harmony with the general sense of justice. We failed, however, to take into consideration the fact that the general sense of justice of the masses is not entirely built on a rational foundation. The people demand atonement; the psychological understanding of the offender, generally speaking, does not remove this demand; this demand may only change in conformity with the newly acquired understanding, but it will persist. When, for instance, we succeeded in proving that a given individual's crime was prompted primarily by an unconscious sense of guilt and by an obscure need for punishment,

---

[1] See a qualification of this statement in the Preface to the Revised Edition.

society's demand for expiation will have a different form
than the one in the case of an open, conscious enemy of
society; yet, even then the purely objective rational reaction
will be influenced and disturbed by deep emotional factors.
Thus our search for a system of justice which would be free
from affective prejudice, leads us directly to the problem
of investigating the affects which are characteristic of social
human beings, who demand the punishment of the transgressor.

Any criminal case which stands out because of its especial
cruelty or scope easily shows how deeply rooted within us is
the demand for retaliation and imposed expiation. Everybody demanded the head of the mass murderer Haarmann;
they would not listen if told that it was apparently a case of
mental illness, and that his conscious inhibitory reactions
were pathologically disturbed. In cases like Haarmann's,
strict isolation and an attempt to treat and cure the defendant, an attempt which would probably be of little avail,
would undoubtedly have served sufficiently the purpose of
rational protection of the public weal. Capital punishment
in such cases, as always, is but the expression of an impulsive
demand for retaliation, which insists that blood be paid with
blood.

We may be very exact and go very deeply into the study
of the personality of the criminal; we may use psychoanalysis
to discover the psychogenesis of a given crime, yet the treatment of the criminal in the light of, and with the consideration of, his unconscious motivations will be met with a
number of great resistances, unless this treatment remains
at the same time in accordance with the general affective
demand for atonement and reparation. Scientific insight will
sooner be thrown overboard than the gratification of an emotional drive. A better understanding of the criminal may in
a number of cases change the nature of the general sense of
justice, but it will not remove the emotional demand that
crime must be expiated; the criminal, it is true, will no
longer be punished for an act which was misunderstood, but

he will be punished for what he actually meant by his crime, for people cannot give up the idea of punishment entirely. It is clear, therefore, that a system of justice, devoid of affective prejudice, can be realized only then, when we succeed in explaining analytically the demand for expiation of one's crime and thus uncover its unconscious roots; this will not suffice, however; it will be necessary to bring the content of the demand into the *consciousness* of the popular masses, and only then will the general sense of justice change sufficiently to be in harmony with rational measures to be undertaken against the criminal, and will give up its demand for the gratification of irrational emotions.

We pointed out in the beginning that in a case of miscarriage of justice, the individual feels that the remnants of his personal freedom are endangered, that his common sense of justice is injured, and this leads to rebellion and subsequent regressive breaking through of the repressed instinctual impulses. We shall now supplement this contention with the statement that a totally different set of circumstances also offends the common sense of justice; thus, when a criminal escapes his supposedly well-deserved punishment, we feel aroused. In the case of miscarriage of justice, we feel that we ourselves might some day fall victims to the same type of injustice; in the case of escape from justice, however, every member of the community feels that he was wronged, for a man who violated the law escaped punishment; he was forgiven, as it were, for a transgression which is forbidden the righteous member of the community. We deal in both cases with the struggle for the individual freedom of one's instinctual drives; it is a protest against the restriction of these drives. It is as if the individual member of the community said to himself: "If other people are punished unjustly, then *my* personal freedom is also in danger, or if *another* escapes the punishment he deserves, why should *I* continue to conform?"

These simple psychological considerations lead to the understanding of one of the fundamental motives which prompts the public demand for the expiation of offenses. To put it in psychoanalytical language, the failure to punish an offender means to us a threat to our own repressive trends.

Reik[1] and, recently, Wittels[2] have pointed out how important a role the institution of punishment plays in the regressive drives of man. This psychological function of the institution of punishment will become particularly clear if we recall that the Superego is highly dependent on the outside authorities; as has been said before, Anna Freud, in her studies of children, proved this point in convincing fashion, but we had already mentioned the fact that such a dependence of the Superego on the powers that be is characteristic not only of children; in most men it persists to some extent throughout their lives.

We can state now that the power of the Superego over our instinctive life is undermined, not only when some one is punished unjustly and too severely, but also when the offender escapes punishment and thus fails to pay for his offense. Unwarranted acquittal means simply that the court permits the defendant to do things which we prohibit to ourselves. Under such circumstances, the righteous member of the community finds himself facing the following dilemma: he must either give up his own inhibitions and give in to his own anti-social tendencies, or he must demand that the offender be punished without fail. "What I do not allow myself must not be allowed others; if others are not called upon to pay for their violations of the law, then I shall not abide by my self-imposed restrictions."

We may say, then, that what creates the public demand for atonement is one's anxiety lest his own Superego be overturned and that one's own impulses, which have been curbed with so much difficulty, might break through to expression. This anxiety is quite justified, because before our Superego was set up, our unbridled impulses kept us always in a state of painful conflict with the outside world. Was not the

---

[1] Reik, *op. cit.*

[2] Wittels, "Richter und Rache," *Almanach* 1929, Int. PsA. Verlg.

Superego set up for the purpose of ridding ourselves of or escaping from such painful situations? Moreover, the original pressure of our instinctual drives remains so strong that man's Superego, if it is to preserve its power of repression, always needs the support of outside authorities. Hence, in the case of every violation of the law, our Ego makes an appeal for the atonement of the transgression; it does this in order to enforce the opposition of the Superego against the pressure of its instincts. The example of a criminal has a stimulating effect on our own repressed impulses, and increases the pressure coming from them. That is why our Ego needs the constant reinforcement of our Superego; it can obtain this reinforcement only from those in authority, who are the prototype of our Superego. If the Ego can show that the secular authorities agree with the Superego, then it is able to keep the instinctual impulses in check; if, however, these secular authorities happen to disavow the Superego by setting a guilty man free, then the individual feels that no support is given him to counteract a pending breaking through of his own antisocial tendencies. The demand that every crime should be expiated represents, then, a defense reaction on the part of the Ego against one's own instinctual drives; the Ego puts itself at the service of the inner repressing forces, in order to retain the state of equilibrium, which must always exist between the repressed and the repressing forces of the personality. The demand that the lawbreaker be punished is thus a demonstration against one's own inner drives, a demonstration which tends to keep these drives amenable to control: "I forbid the lawbreaker what I forbid myself."

As Wittels especially emphasized, the greater the pressure coming from repressed impulses, the more aware becomes the Ego that it needs the institution of punishment as an intimidating example, acting against one's own primitive world of repressed instinctual drives. In other words, the louder man calls for the punishment of the lawbreaker, the less he has to fight against his own repressed impulses. It is, as a matter of fact, a definite sign that the given individual failed to assimilate his own anti-social tendencies, if he becomes too zealous in his demands for the punishment of transgressions of the law. These psychological considerations explain, perhaps, the fact that *the underworld and its official prosecutors show not infrequently a sort of a subterranean affinity.* The unconscious, impulsive part of every man's psyche, particularly that of the too zealous prosecutor of crime, takes the side of the violator of the law. This unconscious sympathetic understanding of the criminal is prevented from appearing in our consciousness by the repressive agencies; it becomes overcompensated and expresses itself in the form of a protest against the criminal. If and when, however, the criminal is duly punished, our demand for atonement is thoroughly satisfied and we feel that we have proved to ourselves that we are good and loyal to society; under such circumstances, we can afford, as we do, to express sympathy with and kindliness toward the very same criminal. What happened is this: through the gratification of our demand for expiation of the crime, we won a victory over the evil within ourselves; we may well be grateful to the criminal, for *he* paid for what *we* unconsciously wished to do. That is why our forefathers preferred a penitent sinner to a hundred righteous men, for the repenting sinner is much more helpful to us in our struggle against our own repressed impulses.

Reik states that the reason why the court and public opinion value the confession made by the criminal so much is that the criminal thus condemns his own deed; this eases the unconscious sense of guilt of the judges and they are able to pronounce the man guilty with greater ease of conscience. We should like to point out another deeper factor which, from the standpoint of psychological economics, is not less important. The refractory criminal, even if he is condemned, represents a danger to our own repressions, for the instinctual impulses of each one of us demand gratification and tend toward a spiteful rejection of society and of the demands of our Superego; the defiant criminal is thus a constant ally and seducer of our own repressed instinctual demands. The mere existence of a spiteful, hardened law-breaker is a living proof that such a rejection *is* possible; that is why we punish such lawbreakers with particular severity; it is an act of self-defense; on the other hand, the repentant sinner who confesses his transgression, disavows his own in-stinctual impulses; he promises to reform; hence, he is a faithful and powerful ally of our Superego; the Superego of the lawbreaker, by winning its victory, increases the prestige of the Superego of those who witness the confession; this being the case, the judge can afford to impose a smaller penalty, for the latter is not needed as a support of our own endangered repressions; the defendant himself reinforced our repressions by the very virtue of his confession, and thus he reduced the importance of the penalty as a mode of atone-ment; even our repressed impulses are unable to identify themselves with the forbidden deed, for the defendant him-self arose against his own deed. The repentant criminal is no longer a threat to the accepted order of society, nor is he the seducer or stimulator of the repressed impulses of his fellow men; moreover, he has a definite right to expect leniency, since he is a living and instructive example of the victory of the Superego over the instinctual drives of man.

These psychological processes explain the remarkable custom of a Chinese ceremony of capital punishment, which was told us by an eye-witness, a British officer.

Lots are drawn by several accomplices who were con-demned to decapitation; the one thus chosen is given the sword with which he must try to decapitate the others by a single blow; if he succeeds in carrying this out successfully he is set free, but if he fails, he must lie down among the doomed, and the next in the row of survivors becomes the executioner. The one who accomplishes this cruel task well is pardoned. In other words, the one who, through becoming an executioner, shows definitely that he served the punish-ing community and thus disavowed his solidarity with his accomplices, should be pardoned, for he rendered a great service to the cause of repression of anti-social tendencies.

If we accept the common sense of justice as the indicator

of the equilibrium between the restriction and freedom of instinctual drives, we shall then understand that the principle of expiation is the function of the common sense of justice, by means of which the restrictions of these drives are reinforced at the very moment when they threaten to break through to expression. We must recognize, then, that the principle of expiation which underlies every punishment acts chiefly not against the offender, but against our own forbidden impulses. The characteristic equilibrating role of the common sense of justice is most clearly demonstrated by the following fact: in cases of too severe sentences, i.e., when the instinctual drives are taxed with undue severity, we take sides with the offender as a representative of our instinctual demands; however, common sense turns against the offender who is undeservedly acquitted, since then our own impulses threaten to gain the upper hand over us.

In addition to the principle of expiation, which comes to expression in our modern philosophy of law as the right principle of punishment for crime, punishment has still another affective root, and this is *revenge*. The latter is an older principle than the one of atonement; it is an instinctive demand which is active in every living being and is independent of social agencies, like the Superego, which was created later. Every animal strikes back with hate at the one who attacks it.

When man's instinctual drives strike the resistances of reality, an inner tension, a state of discomfort (pain) ensues, which is caused by these resistances, but when a painful and damaging circumstance arises from without, man takes over the role of reality and insists on injuring the assailant. This interchange of roles lies at the bottom of revenge; Freud formulated this process in the following way: What one suffers passively, one strives to live out actively. The little boy coming home from the dentist urges his little sister to play dentist with him, *he* taking the role of the dentist; in this case he avenges himself on an innocent victim for the pain he suffered at the hands of another; it is quite natural, however, that in most cases the revengeful feelings are directed directly against those who caused us to suffer. Any deeper study and analysis of this primary process is beyond the scope of this book.[1]

Since every lawbreaker threatens the rights and interests of others, it is natural that his deeds release in everybody the desire for revenge; revenge in its crude form disappeared with the establishment of the talion principle, which formed the backbone of the primitive penal system of primitive races. While the demand that a transgression be expiated serves as a protection against our identification with the violator of the law, the impulse of revenge serves as a self-defense against our enemies. The demand that a crime be atoned for is a reaction against the pressure of our own impulses coming from within, while revenge is a reaction against the assailant from without; we thus can distinguish two fundamental sources for the origin of the institution of punishment; the inner demand that a violation of the law be atoned for and the tendencies of revenge; we shall designate the latter as the impulse to *retaliation* as differing from the impulse to expiation. Even today one can find the affect of revenge expressed in our laws, but it appears in a modified and softened form. It still comes clearly to expression in the retaliatory nature of the punishment imposed, especially in the primitive hardness and in the irrational nature of our mode of punishment, the purpose of which is to cause suffering.

In our modern philosophy of law and in our own psychology, both the expiatory and retaliatory trends are blended together and they are at times hardly distinguishable from one another; we must bear in mind, however, that the differences of one type of trend from the other is but a qualitative one; both represent a reaction of the Ego against an inimical attack, but each represents an affect going in a

---

[1] Gerland, *Die Enstehung der Strafe* (Jena: Rektorsrede, 1925), considers this a primary instinctive reaction. He considers the talion principle a general mode of getting rid of tension by means of "projection."

different direction. In the face of any criminal act committed by another, our Ego has to fight on two fronts at once; it finds itself facing an outer as well as an inner enemy; it considers every criminal as its own enemy, who threatens it directly; at the same time, it must face the inner enemy, the repressed impulses, which are awakened by the example of the criminal and which threaten to rise to expression. The necessary reactive reinforcement of our own repressions comes to expression through the principle of expiation, while the retaliatory trend serves as a revenge for the attack coming from without. In other words, both voices, that of expiation and that of retaliation, are identical psychological processes, but they differ in the accentuation of direction; each is directed to a different audience, as it were. The voice of expiation is addressed more directly to our own instinctual drives; that of retaliation is directed against the offender himself.

From the standpoint of the psycho-economics of our life, the institution has yet another meaning:[1] it presents a socially acceptable outlet for our own aggressions, the asocial nature of which prevents them, as a rule, from being lived out freely; normally they remain repressed. Hence, the institution of punishments represents a compensation, as it were, for the restrictions one puts on one's own sadism, and the identification of the righteous member of the community, with the latter's punishing functions, helps him to live out his own aggressions in an acceptable fashion; this living out of one's aggressions diminishes the amount of aggressive hostility one has to repress; it therefore makes the work of repression much easier. That is why court trials, especially those of capital crimes, frequently have the character of a public performance and serve as an outlet for our aggressions, even as gladiator battles of ancient Rome or bull fights of some of the modern Latin races serve the same purpose.

---

[1] Wittels particularly emphasizes this point.

The three unconscious, affective sources of the institution of punishment, which were described above, present serious obstacles to the development of a purely rational criminal law, which would function without the principles of *expiation* and *retaliation* and which would not permit the popular masses to utilize it for the purpose of a disguised living out of their own aggressive hostile impulses. Such justice, i.e., one purified of its affective admixtures, will become possible only when the Ego will have acquired sufficient power to keep our instinctual life always and securely under control; then it will not be necessary to demand or impose any expiation in order to reinforce the Ego; moreover, the goal will not be achieved until, in addition, various forms of sublimations will be acquired, in order to diminish the hostile aggressiveness of the masses of people. We must make clear that we consider human society still very distant from the realization of this ideal state. The present-day individual is more and more called upon to give up the outlets of his aggressions; thus, in addition to the cultivation of national solidarity, the *pacifist* trends of our time call upon a new solidarity, which tends to abolish the living out of one's aggressions by means of war; also our modern economic development offers fewer and fewer opportunities for the living out of aggressions. The modern economic growth abolished at first the free competition among manual labor and gradually ensured the spirit of collective thinking among the laboring classes; the number of free and independent small contractors has become considerably reduced under the pressure of the tendencies to consolidation which modern capitalism shows with increasing definiteness; in other words, various classes of those who have been economically individualistic fall into solidarity, which is forced by our economic development. The individualistic battle of all against all is losing ground; the aggressions no more find their sublimated expression in the free economic struggle.

Many statesmen and sociologists frequently overlook completely the fact that our modern capitalism, through its great tendencies to consolidation, carries in its wake a rapid enhancement of the principle of collectivism. Many fight capitalism, for they see in it an individualistic form of economic structure; they confuse our latter-day capitalism with the earlier capitalism, which was based on planless series of individual enterprises. Thus our civilization drives the individual more and more into the frame of communal life, his individualism becomes more and more absorbed in the collectivistic trends; his hostility and aggressions, which threaten the solidarity of such a complex social organism, are all immobilized and refused an outlet; such a civilization can hardly be willing to sacrifice the last refuge which its sadism finds in a form so well acceptable to the Ego, as in the institutions of criminal justice. Politics and sport are not sufficient outlets for all our sadistic impulses, which are held in check by circumstances of civilization.

The history of criminal law is filled with attempts and strivings to replace the irrational and impulsive bases of punishment by rational thinking; in the field of *theory* of criminal law, the talion principle appears to have been overcome and abandoned long ago; instead, measures of intimidation and of educational correction, i.e., purely rational principles appear to have taken its place. But the *practical* introduction of these principles hardly goes beyond a weak compromise with our affective unconscious forces.

The various methods of the quantitative determination of the penalty and the practical application of the latter are the clearest examples of how strong the irrational trends which dominate our modern criminal law; as a matter of fact, rational considerations are hardly taken cognizance of. Why, for instance, should one pickpocket be sent to prison for two years, while another thief to five years. Why send one to prison and another to forced labor? On what basis is the equation "eight months forced labor equals one year's imprisonment" arrived at? Is it impossible to find an answer that would be based on rational principles of purposefulness? The determination of the type of sentence and its execution are nothing but playgrounds for the gratification of our affects, of which we are unaware. It is the presence of these unconscious affects in modern society which leads us to believe that the practical application of our psychoanalytic knowledge to the reconstruction of the criminal law will meet with strong resistances. Only when the community, in its dealings with the criminal, will become ready to give up the gratification of those affects which demand *expiation, retaliation* and *compensation for the socially inhibited sadism,* only then will our sense of justice find itself in harmony with a purely rational and scientifically sound treatment of the lawbreaker. In order to bring about such treatment, it is necessary to fulfill one preliminary condition: it is necessary to have a clear psychological understanding of the criminal; we hope that these pages will serve as a beginning in this direction.

PSYCHIATRIC CONTRIBUTIONS TO CRIME PREVENTION

THE PREVIOUS CHAPTER, WHICH WAS THE last one in the original publication, dealt with the emotional needs of the public when confronted with a violator of the law. This chapter was written thirteen years after the first publication of this book, and in it some practical conclusions are discussed which were only briefly hinted at in the original text. We ended our book by pointing out that crime is one of those problems the scientific study of which offers particular difficulty. This is not primarily due to the complexity of the problem itself, but to the investigator's attitude toward crime. Scientific study requires an objective, unemotional attitude. Under influence of emotions the intellect becomes clouded and cannot follow its own laws. It is much easier to adopt such an unemotional attitude in physics or in chemistry than in those fields which deal with human nature or social phenomena. Moreover, crime is a problem of great practical and immediate importance. Our interest— and with justification—is not so much to understand this particular type of human behavior as to rid society of this evil. Long theoretical discussions about crime are apt to make us impatient. Hearing complicated theoretical discourses about crime, we feel, "Well, that is all well and good but what I want to know is what is the safest and quickest way to protect the law-abiding portion of society from the offenders against the law." Unfortunately this impatience is not a very helpful attitude. If we want to change something in the world we must understand the nature of the very phenomenon which we want to control. If we want to cure society of crime we must understand its nature. And in order to achieve this, we must study crime with the same detached, objective and scientific attitude as we do the phenomena belonging to the field of physics, chemistry or medicine.

I cannot stress this point emphatically enough. I am convinced that our failure in controlling crime is primarily due to our inability to study it in a calm intellectual way because it necessarily arouses in everyone horror, condemnation and the wish to retaliate.

Our first natural reaction is to protect ourselves and society from the offender against the law. Law and order give us a feeling of security. Their maintenance is not a theoretical issue, but probably one of the strongest desires. The criminal not only endangers our personal safety, but undermines our confidence in society's ability to maintain law and order in general. The most natural reaction is fear and a revengeful, retaliatory spirit toward the criminal who endangers one of our most important values, order and security. This explains why the policy of a firm hand and a retaliatory spirit in handling criminals finds understanding and approval.

Intimidation by punishment and, if necessary, incarceration for life or even capital punishment, may seem the shortest and safest devices. And this explains also that when a psychiatrist or a sociologist undertakes a painstaking study of criminal personalities and social conditions, it is usually considered an esoteric, anemic procedure. One goes even so far as to say that the psychiatric study of a criminal personality is a kind of coddling of the criminal; why waste so much time and give so much attention to these worthless individuals?

It may appear that in our first publication we were attacking straw puppets, that this attitude is antiquated and today the public and the authorities have an open-minded attitude toward the scientific study of crime. Yet my personal experience in the last ten years in this field has taught me the opposite. Of course we live in an enlightened era and if somebody has such a peculiar hobby as to waste his time studying the personality of a few bad boys, why not permit him to do so? But the majority of those who deal practically with crime, i.e., legislators, judges, wardens, officers—not to speak of the general public—secretly still look upon the psychiatrist or psychologist who studies the human side of the problem of crime, with a benevolent but supercilious if not a contemptuous attitude, with the feeling that they alone know how to handle these boys. I do not question that practically they know much better than the psychiatrists how to handle these boys. Yet nothing is more dangerous than to assume a too practical or a so-called "common-sense" attitude if we want really to master any natural phenomenon. According to common sense the earth is still a big flat dish, the sun moves around the earth, the earth is the center of the universe, and man the crown of creation. Common sense cannot explain electric waves and for common sense it sounds incredible that every man is a potential criminal at his birth and might become one if not subjected to proper education and training.

The extermination of crime by catching and imprisoning a few clumsy criminals who cannot get away with it then seems similar to an attempt to empty the ocean with a drinking glass. We recognize that the way to crime prevention leads through the study of human nature and of methods by which the originally nonsocial human nature can be made to accept social order.

I must admit that we are only at the very beginning of our understanding of that highly complex interaction between human personality and social organization which leads to criminal behavior. In practical life we cannot wait until science can answer the most urgent problems. We have to take action and deal with these problems even though imperfectly. Our penal system certainly is not based on scientific principles, but at present even if we had all the freedom to do so we would be unable to provide a scientifically founded penal system. Increasing knowledge of the psychological and social aspects of criminality can therefore be translated only gradually into practice by minor but continuous improvements of our present institutions and procedure. We will have to continue to concentrate upon improving our methods of crime detection, improving the constructive aspects of our jails, improving the parole system, etc. We must realize, however, that by all these measures the evil of crime cannot be radically combatted. We must progress to the roots of crime and this can come only from an unemotional, objective study of the mind and of social life.

It was stated before that at birth the child is not adjusted to the requirements of collective life in the least; he is not an antisocial, but a nonsocial being, because the social aspect is quite outside of the scope of his mere vegetative existence. Everything which interferes with the immediate satisfaction of his wishes provokes in him violent reactions which fortunately he cannot release otherwise than by crying and harmless, disorganized muscular contractions. This truth was anticipated by Diderot in his statement that the very small child would be the most destructive criminal if only he had the physical power to carry out his aggressions. But he is merely a little helpless being, biologically and psychologically entirely absorbed in the process of growth, in the satisfaction of his needs, fully governed by the simple principles of securing pleasure and avoiding pain without consideration for anybody else except himself.

Only gradually does the child learn to accept certain rules of behavior. At first it is fear of retaliation, of punishment, that forces him to renounce certain gratifications and the expression of his hostile impulses. Gradually this fear from without changes into a fear of something within himself—a part of his personality gradually assumes the attitude of the adults, and this portion of the personality begins now to demand from the child the same type of behavior that the adults demand. Instead of getting punished and risking the love of the adults whose support the child so direly needs, he begins to forbid himself those things which his parents condemn. This internalized code of socially accepted rules we call the conscience.

The further study of this complex process of internalization of external rules has shown that fear of retaliation alone cannot bring about a reliable form of self-control. The positive attachment of the child to his parents is indispensable for a thorough assimilation of this inner advocate of the social demands. Education that is based only on intimidation will necessarily result in a pathological form of conscience. If the child renounces his nonsocial tendencies only on account of fear he will assume the same fearful and hateful attitude toward the incorporated image of the parents, against his own conscience. The conscience will remain a foreign body in the personality, toward which the child will employ the same tricks and compromises as he did against his severe preceptors. Education based only on punishment and intimidation leads to a peculiar caricature of morality. The child learns that a certain amount of punishment is considered as an atonement for a forbidden act. Now he will assume the same technique in dealing with his own conscience—he will inflict on himself punishment which allays his sense of guilt, appeases his conscience. He treats his own conscience like some foreign agency. He has learned that with a certain amount of punishment he can pay for his misdeeds and therefore he will voluntarily endure sufferings or even provoke punishments in order to get rid of his guilty conscience. The danger which lies in such an attitude is obvious. Suffering becomes not only atonement, but provides an emotional justification for discarding the restrictions requested by the conscience. This explains the paradoxical fact that punishment often has not a deterrent effect on the delinquent, but just the opposite. His conscience is relieved by the punishment, he feels that he has amply paid for his misdeeds, and if the punishment was severe he feels even that he is now justified in feeling inimical to society.

Only if the social portion of the personality becomes deeply assimilated as an organic portion of the personality, its second nature, can we speak of real social adjustment. Only if the social self becomes one with the rest of the personality can this paradoxical intra-psychic abuse of suffering and punishment which undermines the influence of the conscience be avoided. And we know today that such a deep organic assimilation of the social requirements by the personality takes place solely if the child learns not only to fear, but also to love, those who demand from him the first restrictions and modifications of his original instincts. In other words education cannot rely entirely upon fear, but must be based also upon love. Education which is based on punishment alone and depends only on fear does not deserve the word education; it is nothing but drill.

The description of what I called pathological conscience, based on a neurotic abuse of suffering by which punishment is used for absolution as justification for further crime, makes one think of our present-day penal system. This primitive, neurotic concept of justice and some of the ideas underlying our present penal system are unpleasantly similar. Society takes an attitude toward the criminal analogous to the neurotic conscience's attitude toward one's own nonsocial tendencies. Also, society assumes the principle that through punishment the criminal pays for his misdeeds. This can best be seen in the proportioning of punishment according to the severity of the crime. A smaller crime can be atoned for by a smaller amount of punishment; a bigger crime by a bigger amount of punishment. Of course this emotional attitude, which to be sure is deeply rooted and almost universal, cannot stand the test of logical scrutiny.

It is obvious that the suffering imposed upon a person by punishment, no matter how severe, does not represent an exchange value for a criminally extinguished life or misappropriated property. By suffering the criminal does not make good for the damage done. This is so obvious that since the second part of the last century most criminologists—the first of them was Friederich Liszt—discarded the idea that the aim of punishment is retaliation and put all emphasis upon the deterring effect of punishment. This concept is based on the psychological principle that the suffering involved in punishment deters an individual from repeating such acts again which caused him suffering in the past. We saw, however, how the neurotic person abuses suffering so that in the end it has not a deterrent but a stimulating effect for the commitment of new crimes. By receiving punishment he gains absolution from his own conscience. The more severe the punishment, the more he will feel that society has put itself into the wrong, that he does not owe anything to society and need not respect its laws. The internal policemen we called conscience is eliminated by severe punishment. There remains only the fear of the external policeman who enforces the law. That explains why hard punishment creates tougher and tougher criminals. All internal inhibitions are eliminated through hard and continued punishment, even those remnants of a conscience which every human being possesses. If such an individual refrains from lawless behavior he will do it only out of fear of severe punishment. But many of these individuals have not much to lose; having a criminal record they are severely handicapped, feel desperate, and are inclined to take risks again.

Here we arrive at a seemingly unsolvable dilemma. We see that punishment has a double effect; its intimidating influence is amply counterbalanced with its demoralizing influence. In other words there are about as many offenders whom punishment will drive toward even more brazen criminality as individuals who through punishment will be deterred from it. This fact is demonstrated by the startlingly high rate of recidivism. This dilemma therefore seems unsolvable apparently because punishment—incarceration in particular—is the only weapon which we have in our fight against crime. And now this weapon turns out to be ineffective and in many cases even a contributing factor to criminal behavior.

Yet there is a solution, a solution which many progressive men in the field of modern criminology are beginning to recognize with increasing clarity. We saw that punishment in its primitive form as retaliation is based on a primitive emotional reaction, that of revenge, which has no constructive aspect whatsoever. We saw, furthermore, that we may discard its retaliation aspect and retain punishment merely as an intimidating factor to curb the violation of law. It turned out, however, that even this deterring effect is only partially successful because punishment has also a stimulating influence upon criminal behavior. It increases the fear of the external police but decreases the inhibiting influence of the internal controlling factor of human personality, that of conscience.

Is there no other way of treating the criminal besides taking revenge on him or intimidating him?

At the present day all the primitive forms of punishment —with the exception of capital punishment—as beating, public exposure, etc., have been abandoned in favor of incarceration. That seems to be in contradiction to the statement that in the development of our penal ideology the revenge aspect of punishment has been more and more abandoned in favor of its intimidating effect. Incarceration obviously is not the best measure either for revenge or intimidation. It is well known that both whipping and public exposure have upon most individuals a greater deterrent effect than has imprisonment in a more or less humane penal institution.

I was surprised to find during my psychoanalytic studies of inmates in a Boston prison how often the criminal without consciously admitting it, dreads the day of freedom which means for him renewed unemployment and insecurity. One of my criminal patients, whom I analyzed in the prison, the day before his release wistfully exclaimed, "Farewell, good old shadow soup," referring to the thin soup served daily for breakfast.

It is obvious that incarceration must contain still another penal principle distinct from both retaliation or intimidation. If we still believed in retaliation and intimidation as the prime factors in dealing with criminals our present trend to improve prison conditions would be fully inconsistent. This trend could then be rightly defamed as stupid sentimentalism. Yet there is a principle in incarceration different from both retaliation or intimidation which justifies the trend to make the treatment of prisoners more and more humane.

Incarceration, at least for a while, rids society of the criminal. Life imprisonment does it permanently. From this point of view incarceration would seem to be an indication of our helplessness in the fight against criminality. We take recourse to this most expensive way of handling criminals because we realize that retaliation has no constructive value whatsoever and also that the deterring effect of punishment is of questionable value. It seems that tacitly we even recognize that nothing is obtained by increasing the suffering of imprisonment, because by maltreatment we only make the inmates more depraved after their release. And for those who remain in prisons for life or for the major part of their life, the increase of suffering in prison is entirely pointless.

At first, incarceration appears as a kind of social surgery. We get rid of the diseased portion of society by the radical procedure of elimination. Yet this simile does not hold. In surgery we do not care any more for the portion which we have extirpated; we simply throw it away. Unlike in surgery, for the social members which we have cut off from society by incarceration, we pay high taxes to keep them in costly prisons. Through constantly improving the hygienic conditions in the prisons we even rapidly increase these costs. Are we doing all this for merely sentimental reasons? It is obvious that by improving our prisons we are detracting from both the retaliatory and the intimidating effects of imprisonment. What is then the justification for improving prison conditions?

The answer to this question contains the solution of the dilemma which appears so utterly unsolvable. The answer is that the primary value of incarceration—a value which at present is far from being fully utilized—is neither revenge nor intimidation nor merely temporary segregation of dangerous individuals, but rather those constructive possibilities which incarceration offers. The answer is that we are beginning to recognize the only constructive factor which our present penal system offers; we are in the process of discovering the possibility of rehabilitation during the period of incarceration. It is clear that the only justification for all the expenses involved in the improvement of prison conditions is that by incarceration we hope not only surgically to eliminate a portion of the population like a diseased organ, but we try to save at least a part of them for society.

This argument is irrefutable, and yet if we investigate our prisons as they actually are, we must confess that we are far from having drawn practical conclusions from this insight. Our prisons are far from being primarily educational or therapeutic institutions. Their intimidating and retaliatory aspects are still in the fore. Of course institutions cannot change as fast as scientific insight progresses. We have to reckon with the inertia present in every social development. I see one of the most important contributions of psychiatry to the prevention of crime in transforming our prisons into institutions in which the offender against the law has the opportunity for reform and rehabilitation. Psychiatry in the last forty years has developed systematic procedures by which personality traits can be methodically influenced and changed. The application of these methods to the rehabilitation of the criminal personality is perhaps one of the most important social functions of psychiatry.

I may add a few words about the question of how far our present penal procedure, without far-reaching and Utopian reforms, can afford opportunity for the realization of certain therapeutic possibilities leading to the rehabilitation of the prison inmates. It is obvious that the period of imprisonment affords excellent opportunities for certain therapeutic measures. Almost all our prisons maintain psychiatric service as a part of their general medical service. Without far-reaching reforms this existing psychiatric service could be intensified and modified, thus making it more effective. This can be accomplished because the management of the criminal during imprisonment is a behavior problem and as such coincides with the psychotherapeutic problems of psychiatry which are the same—behavior problems. The treatment of the prisoner during imprisonment is aimed toward bringing about certain personality changes in him. For example, the occupation of the prisoners and their instruction much resemble the occupational therapy of modern psychiatric hospitals.

This intimate relationship between penal procedures and psychiatry is evinced also by historical facts. The treatment of the mentally disturbed only very recently has differentiated itself from treatment of criminals, having consisted also in confinement (not long ago in chains) if necessary, solitary confinement and other procedures of a punishment type. Between modern prisons and modern psychiatric hospitals similarities are still present to a certain degree. This similarity goes in both ways. The mental hospitals still retain some of their past prison-like character, while at the same time modern prisons are gradually assuming hospital-like features.

In spite of the fact that the problems of the management of the criminal during imprisonment are problems overlapping upon the field of psychiatry, psychotherapeutic measures on a large scale would require extremely profound reforms of penal institutions, reforms which would be tantamount to a transformation of the present penal institutions into behavior clinics. As a first step we must be satisfied by introducing a change in our attitude toward the treatment of prisoners. At present the psychotherapeutic needs of the inmates can be best served by the management of the inmates' life during imprisonment in a manner that is conducive to increasing the chances of their rehabilitation.

From the point of view of rehabilitation the attitude of the prison officials, or what one could call the spirit or the atmosphere of the prison, perhaps is of greater importance than anything else. The introduction of such a constructive psychotherapeutic view in the place of the retaliatory attitude is the greatest contribution which the psychiatrist can make at present to the management of prisons.

Therefore, the most constructive use of the psychiatrist in the prison system would consist in advising and informing the prison officials concerning every incident which involves personality difficulties of the prisoners. Apart from giving advice concerning occasional incidents, the function of the psychiatrist should include giving systematic instruction to guards in the main facts of human behavior. Present experience shows that the guards' attitudes toward the emotionally unbalanced prisoners are far from being satisfactory or favorable for reconstructive changes in personality during the time of imprisonment.

Since guards at present are given systematic instruction in practically less important fields such as target practice, an elementary course in human behavior easily could be included in the present system.

As has been mentioned before, under the present conditions, it would be premature to think of individual treatment on a large scale, although unquestionably many prison inmates would profit from individual psychotherapy, especially psychoanalysis.

In order to achieve such an extension of psychiatric service in our present penal system, first a clear demonstration of the efficiency of psychotherapy in the rehabilitation of criminals would be important. Consequently the next step should be the establishment of experimental psychotherapeutic units in selected prisons. Such a plan seems to me timely and practically possible, because imprisonment is explicitly considered as a measure to influence the personality of the prisoners in a constructive way leading to their rehabilitation. The occupation and teaching of prisoners in different crafts is based on the clear recognition of this rehabilitative purpose of imprisonment. Those prisoners whose criminal behavior is a symptom of a major or minor mental disturbance constitute an even more explicit psychotherapeutic problem. Isolated experiences, for example may work in collaboration with Dr. William Healy,[1] has shown the possibility of reforming criminal behavior through psychotherapeutic measures. In such experimental units in which systematic psychotherapeutic work would be carried out on selected cases, the practical significance of psychotherapy for the rehabilitation of criminals could be well demonstrated. It is needless to emphasize that a positive result would be of a tremendous practical significance. The period of imprisonment could be used for accomplishing changes in personalities which would decrease the probability of recidivism. Apart from its economic importance this would be the first really effective step in the problem of crime prevention. In this way the excellent opportunity which prisons offer for such an experimental study would be utilized without especially great financial expenditures or any radical reforms.

I am fully aware that these measures do not nearly exhaust the psychiatric-therapeutic aspects of criminality. The major issue lies in the field of crime prevention. The individual criminal is the product of a complicated interplay of hereditary factors, personality features acquired during the early period of life, and general cultural influences. Almost all of these factors are beyond our control. The attempt to reform the final product of all these influences—the adolescent or adult criminal—does not promise a radical effect upon the crime situation. There is no question that with the continuous improvements of the psychiatric service many individuals could be helped in the direction of rehabilitation, but the core of the problem itself cannot be approached by any

---

[1] Frank Alexander and William Healy, *Roots of Crime* (New York: Alfred A. Knopf, 1935).

therapeutic measures. As in the field of medicine, prevention is the ultimate goal, and not therapy. The study of individuals during the therapeutic procedure constitutes, however, the road which will lead to the knowledge upon which future preventive measures can be based. In the whole field of medicine, prevention requires a much more precise knowledge than therapy. A diseased organ can be eliminated by surgery even if the pathological processes leading to the final disease are not known. To prevent the pathological process from developing requires a thorough knowledge of the whole natural history of the disease. In the field of criminology this can only be acquired through an integration of biological, psychological and sociological knowledge. The study of individual criminal careers, eliciting step by step how these individuals became offenders against the law, is the only way to achieve such knowledge.

In conclusion, psychiatry has two great contributions to make toward solving the problems of criminology. First, it could be utilized effectively for the rehabilitation of the already criminal individual by introducing into penal institutions the modern methods of reforming human personality. This is the therapeutic contribution of psychiatry. Its second, more important contribution lies, however, in the study of those psychopathological processes which lead to criminal behavior. Such a knowledge alone could serve as a scientific basis for crime prevention on a large scale. The period of incarceration in penal institutions offers a unique opportunity for psychiatry to accomplish both these objectives. These goals, however, can only be approached if the treatment of the criminals will be purified from all the emotional remnants of the past. Both the public and those who deal professionally with criminals must be freed from those age-old emotional reactions toward the criminal which interfere with an intelligent, scientifically founded penal procedure. We must finally understand that punishment as retaliation is not conducive to ridding society of crime; that punishment as intimidation by infliction of suffering is of questionable value; and that rehabilitation of the criminal, no matter how difficult it may seem, is the most economical and the only effective method. Above all, we must realize that one cannot apply successfully all three penological principles at the same time—retaliation, intimidation, and reconstruction—as it is done at present in our institutions. We cannot at the same time take revenge on the criminal, intimidate him, and try to reform him, because these different principles require different attitudes which are mutually exclusive because they interfere with each other. One cannot make the prisoner hate his authorities, fear them, and at the same time expect the prisoner to trust them and accept from them advice and guidance.

We must clearly make up our minds what penal principle we want to accept, and then we must treat the criminals accordingly from the time they are detected and arrested by the police until they are released from the prison. On the basis of psychiatric diagnosis, we will have to classify the prisoners into two large groups: those who seem to us unimprovable and resistant to any psychotherapeutic approach, and a more promising improvable group. Toward the latter we have to assume not a retaliatory but a purely therapeutic attitude. The unimprovable group must remain segregated from the rest of society so long as they appear as potential dangers.

Psychiatry, however, will have no chance to contribute anything of real consequence to crime prevention so long as we have not freed our fundamental attitude toward the problem of criminality from those more primitive emotional reactions which have pervaded our whole penal system in the past.

BOOKS PUBLISHED BY

The Free Press

Joseph Eaton and Albert J. Mayer,
Man's Capacity to Reproduce 2.00
Joseph Eaton and Robert J.
Weil, M.D., *Culture and Mental
Disorders* 4.00
Abraham Edel, *Ethical Judgment:
The Use of Science in Ethics* 5.00
Paul Edwards, *The Logic of Moral
Discourse* 4.00
S. N. Eisenstadt, *The Absorption of
Immigrants* 6.00
S. N. Eisenstadt, *From Generation
to Generation: Age Groups and
Social Structure* 6.00
Heinz Eulau, Samuel Eldersveld
and Morris Janowitz, eds.,
*Political Behavior: A Reader in
Theory and Research* 7.50
E. E. Evans-Pritchard,
Social Anthropology 3.00
E. E. Evans-Pritchard and others,
*The Institutions of Primitive
Society* 3.00
E. K. Francis, *In Search of Utopia* 6.50
E. Franklin Frazier,
Black Bourgeoisie 4.00
Georges Friedmann, *Industrial
Society: The Emergence of the
Human Problems of Automation* 6.00
Lawrence Fuchs, *The Political
Behavior of American Jews* 4.00
Harlan W. Gilmore, *Transportation
and the Growth of Cities* 3.00
D. V. Glass, ed., *Social Mobility
in Britain* OP
Max Gluckman, *Custom and
Conflict in Africa* 3.50
Max Gluckman, *The Judicial
Process Among the Barotse of
Northern Rhodesia* 6.75
Herbert Goldhamer and Andrew
Marshall, *Psychosis and
Civilization: Two Studies in the
Frequency of Mental Disease* 4.00
Walter Goldschmidt, *As You Sow* 3.50
Joseph Goldstein, *The Government
of a British Trade Union* 5.00
William J. Goode, *After Divorce* 6.00
William J. Goode, *Religion Among
the Primitives* 5.00
Alvin Gouldner, *Patterns of
Industrial Bureaucracy* 4.50
Charles M. Hardin, *The Politics of
Agriculture: Soil Conservation
and the Struggle for Power in
Rural America* 4.00
Charles Hartshorne, *Reality as
Social Process* 4.00
Paul K. Hatt and Albert J. Reiss,
Jr., eds., *Reader in Urban
Sociology*, revised ed. 6.50

Amos Hawley, *The Changing Shape
of Metropolitan America* 4.00
Frederick A. von Hayek,
The Counter-Revolution of Science 4.00
Andrew F. Henry and James
Short, Jr., *Suicide and Homicide* 4.00
Roger Hilsman, *Strategic
Intelligence and National
Decisions* 4.00
George Homans and David
Schneider, *Marriage, Authority
and Final Causes* 2.00
Everett C. Hughes and Helen M.
Hughes, *Where Peoples Meet:
Racial and Ethnic Frontiers* 3.50
W. H. Hutt, *The Theory of
Collective Bargaining* 3.00
Herbert Hyman, *Survey Design and
Analysis* 7.50
Morris Janowitz, *The Community
Press in an Urban Setting* 3.50
Elihu Katz and Paul Lazarsfeld,
*Personal Influence: The Part
Played by People in the Flow of
of Mass Communications* 6.00
Patricia Kendall, *Conflict and Mood:
Factors Affecting the Stability of
Response* 3.50
William Kroger, M.D. and
S. Charles Freed, M.D.,
Psychosomatic Gynecology 8.00
Harold D. Lasswell, *Political
Writngs of Harold D. Lasswell:
Psychopathology and Politics;
Politics—Who Gets What, When,
How; Democratic Character,*
3 vols. bound in one 5.00
Harold D. Lasswell, Charles E.
Merriam and T. V. Smith,
A Study of Power, 3 vols. bound
in one 6.00
Paul Lazarsfeld and Morris
Rosenberg, eds., *The Language
of Social Research: A Reader in
the Methodology of the Social
Sciences* 7.50
Paul Lazarsfeld, ed., *Mathematical
Thinking in the Social Sciences* 10.00
Nathan Leites, *A Study of
Bolshevism* 6.50
Nathan Leites and Elsa Bernaut,
*Ritual of Liquidation:
Communists on Trial* 6.50
Seymour M. Lipset, Martin Trow
and James Coleman, *Union
Democracy: The Internal Politics
of the International Typographical
Union* 7.50
Charles Loomis and others,
*Turrialba: Social Systems and
the Introduction of Change* 3.00

Bronislaw Malinowski, *Magic, Science and Religion* — OP

Henri De Man, *Joy in Work* — OP

Maurice Mandelbaum, *Phenomenology of Moral Experience* — 5.00

Karl Marx and Frederick Engels, *The Russian Menace to Europe* — 3.75

Marcel Mauss, *The Gift: Forms and Functions of Exchange in Archaic Societies* — 3.00

Carl Menger, *Principles of Economics* — 5.00

Robert K. Merton, *Social Theory and Social Structure,* revised and enlarged ed. — 6.00

Robert K. Merton and others, eds., *Reader in Bureaucracy* — 5.00

Robert K. Merton and Paul Lazarsfeld, eds., *Studies in the Scope and Method of "The American Soldier"* — 4.00

Robert K. Merton, Marjorie Fiske and Patricia Kendall, *The Focused Interview* — 3.00

Martin Meyerson and Edward Banfield, *Politics, Planning and the Public Interest* — 5.00

Robert Michels, *Political Parties* — OP

S. F. Nadel, *Foundations of Social Anthropology* — 5.00

S. F. Nadel, *Nupe Religion* — 6.00

S. F. Nadel, *The Theory of Social Structure* — 6.00

Ernest Nagel, *Logic Without Metaphysics* — 6.00

Ernest Nagel, *Sovereign Reason* — 5.00

Franz Neumann, *The Democratic and the Authoritarian State* — 6.00

James Olds, *The Growth and Structure of Motives* — 5.00

Robert Owen, *A New View of Society* — OP

Robert E. Park, *Human Communities: The City and Human Ecology* — 5.00

Robert E. Park, *Race and Culture* — 5.00

Robert E. Park, *Society: Collective Behavior, News and Opinion, Sociology and Modern Society* — 5.00

Talcott Parsons, *Essays in Sociological Theory,* revised ed. — 6.00

Talcott Parsons, *The Social System* — 6.00

Talcott Parsons, *The Structure of Social Action* — OP

Talcott Parsons and Robert F. Bales, *Family, Socialization and Interaction Process* — 6.00

Talcott Parsons, Robert F. Bales and Edward Shils, *Working Papers in the Theory of Action* — 3.75

Talcott Parsons and Neil J. Smelser, *Economy and Society* — 6.00

Wilhelm Pauck, *The Heritage of the Reformation* — OP

Herbert Phillipson, *The Object Relations Technique* (Book and Test Cards) — 10.00

Jean Piaget, *The Moral Judgment of the Child* — 4.50

Henry Quastler, ed., *Information Theory in Psychology* — 6.00

A. R. Radcliffe-Brown, *The Andaman Islanders* — 5.00

A. R. Radcliffe-Brown, *Structure and Function in Primitive Society* — 5.00

The RAND Corporation, *A Million Random Digits with 100,000 Normal Deviates* — 10.00

Fritz Redl and David Wineman, *Children Who Hate: The Disorganization and Breakdown of Behavior Controls* — 3.50

Fritz Redl and David Wineman, *Controls From Within: Techniques for the Treatment of the Aggressive Child* — 4.50

Audrey Richards, *Hunger and Work in a Savage Tribe* — 3.50

David Riesman, *Individualism Reconsidered* — 6.00

Natalie Rogoff, *Recent Trends in Occupational Mobility* — 4.00

Peter Rossi, *Why Families Move* — 4.00

Bertrand Russell, *The Scientific Outlook* — 3.50

Edward A. Shils, *The Present State of American Sociology* — OP

Edward A. Shils, *The Torment of Secrecy: The Background and Consequences of American Security Policies* — 3.50

Georg Simmel, *Conflict* and *The Web of Group-Affiliations* — 3.50

Georg Simmel, *The Sociology of Georg Simmel* — 6.00

Marshall Sklare, *Conservative Judaism: An American Religious Movement* — 4.50

James S. Slotkin, *The Peyote Religion* — 4.00

Werner Sombart, *The Jews and Modern Capitalism* — 4.50

Georges Sorel, *Reflections on Violence* — 4.00

Joseph Spengler and Otis Dudley Duncan, eds., *Population Theory and Policy: Selected Readings* — 7.50

Joseph Spengler and Otis Dudley Duncan, eds., *Demographic Analysis: Selected Readings* — 9.50

9,56